FACING THE WORLD

ORTHODOX CHRISTIAN ESSAYS ON GLOBAL CONCERNS

FACİNG THE WORLD

ORTHODOX CHRISTIAN ESSAYS ON GLOBAL CONCERNS

ARCHBISHOP ANASTASIOS (YANNOULATOS)

Archbishop of Tirana, Durrës and All Albania
Professor Emeritus, University of Athens
Corresponding Member of the Academy of Athens

Translation by
PAVLOS GOTTFRIED

ST VLADIMIR'S SEMINARY PRESS
CRESTWOOD, NEW YORK 10707
2003

The publication of this book has been underwritten by
Anne and Sabry Mackoul.

Library of Congress Cataloging-in-Publication Data

Anastasios, Archbishop of Tirana and all Albania, 1929–
  [Pankosmioteta kai Orthodoxia. English]
  Facing the world : Orthodox Christian essays on global concerns / Archbishop
Anastasios (Yannoulatos) ; translation by Pavlos Gottfried.
    p. cm.
  Includes bibliographical references (p.).
  ISBN 0-88141-246-5
   1. Globalization—Religious aspects—Orthodox Eastern Church.   2. Orthodox
Eastern Church—Doctrines.   I. Title.

BX323.A5713 2003
261—dc21

                                      2003041379

ST VLADIMIR'S SEMINARY PRESS
575 Scarsdale Road, Crestwood, NY 10707
1-800-204-2665

ISBN 0-88141-246-5

To my excellent "fellow workers in the Lord,"
who in their struggle remain faithful
to Orthodoxy's universal perspective

Table of Contents

List of Abbreviations

ANF   Alexander Roberts and James Donaldson, eds., *The Ante-Nicene Fathers: Translations of the Fathers down to* A.D. *325*. Peabody, MA: Hendrickson Publishers, 1994

Bul.   *Bulletin*, Pontificium Consilium pro Dialogo inter Religiones. Vatican.

EEE   *Ekpaideutike Ellenike Enkyklopaideia* (Greek Educational Encyclopedia). Athens: Ekdotike of Athens.

ThEE   *Threskeutike kai Ethike Enkyklopaideia* (Religious and Ethical Encyclopedia). Athens: A. Martinos Publishers, 1962-68.

IEE   *Istoria tou Ellenikou Ethnous* (History of the Greek Nation). Athens: Ekdotike of Athens, 1970-78.

IRM   *International Review of Mission*. Geneva.

MEE   *Megale Ellenike Enkyklopaideia* (Great Greek Encyclopedia), 2d edition, updated. Athens: Phoinix.

NPF   Philip Schaff, ed., *The Nicene and Post-Nicene Fathers of the Christian Church*, 1st series, 14 vols., and Philip Schaff and Henry Wace, eds., *The Nicene and Post-Nicene Fathers of the Christian Church*, 2d series, 14 vols. Peabody, MA: Hendrickson Publishers, 1994.

PG   J.P. Migne, ed., *Patrologiae cursus completus, Series Graeca*. Paris, 1857-1866.

PL   J.P. Migne, ed., *Patrologiae cursus completus, Series Latina*. Paris, 1844-1864.

WCC   World Council of Churches, Geneva.

Introduction

There has been a steadily increasing amount of discussion in recent times concerning globalization, a word that carries with it a variety of implications, mostly economic but also cultural. Many see globalization as an unmistakable sign of progress, others as an unquestionable threat. In any case, regardless of the euphoria or alarm with which it is greeted, the process of globalization is currently in progress. The fact remains that the accelerated development of economic, scientific, political, and social links between all the peoples of the world has turned our planet into a megalopolis with a large number of slums.

It cannot be denied that under modern conditions not only the achievements of our era but also its problems have become global. Social discrimination within countries, the proliferation of new and fabricated needs, religious tension, terrorism, drug addiction, economic crisis and collapse, and the plundering of the environment are all phenomena whose effects can be felt worldwide.

This global development has long been an issue of primary concern in theological circles throughout the world. Twenty-six years ago, for example, in 1974, an interfaith conference on this very question was held in Colombo, Sri Lanka, with the title "Toward World Community: Resources and Responsibilities for Living Together." In 1979, the desire of international organizations such as UNESCO to support the affirmation of human rights by religious communities around the world resulted in a gathering of experts in Bangkok to discuss "The Position of Human Rights in Religious and Political Traditions Around the World." With regard to international Christian circles specifically, issues of global concern have been a focal point for numerous discussions: "Culture and Gospel" (Riano, Italy, 1984); "Islamic-Christian Dialogue" (Vienna, 1986); and "A Theological Approach to Understanding Other Religions" (Brookline,

11

1987). Each of the first five essays published in the present volume
was written to address one of these topics. The essays were written
in order to offer a theological view of each issue, based on Orthodox
spiritual experience and tradition.

In 1982, at a festive gathering at the University of Athens, I had
the opportunity to address "The Dynamic of Universal and Continuous Change" as this subject emerges in the thought and lives of the
three ecumenical teachers of the universal Orthodox Church. Their
writings, which in their time defined the Orthodox position on the
problems of human life, have maintained their value for the entire
world. Lastly, at a scholarly gathering held at the same university in
1998, I was able to take a more direct look at the question of "Globalization and Religious Experience."

These seven essays on issues in theology and the study of religion
were all originally published in scholarly journals or dedicatory volumes and were therefore not easily accessible to the Greek public.
For this reason it was decided, upon the kind urging of Akritas Publishers, to collect them in a single volume under the general title
"Universality and Orthodoxy."

These essays were all written for different audiences; it is natural,
therefore, that the basic theological truths on which they are all
based should be repeated in each essay. In the present edition an
attempt has been made to limit such repetitions as much as possible;
in several cases, however, repetitions were preserved, so that the
structure and autonomy of each essay would remain intact. Taken as
a whole, the essays form—if I may borrow a phrase from musical terminology—a series of variations on a theme. The reader should also
bear in mind that each subject is handled in a way that was felt to be
most suitable for the particular audience addressed. The specific circumstances in which each essay was first presented are described in
the introductory notes that precede each chapter; for example, the
first essay was written with the understanding of an interfaith symposium in mind.

Bibliographic references have been limited to the year in which
each essay was first published. Any additional bibliographic information that was felt to be absolutely necessary has been appended in

the footnotes. Heartfelt thanks are in order at this point for the invaluable contributions of those who worked with me in producing the present volume in its final form, and especially to Ms Argyro Kontoyiorgi.

～ • ～

My personal study of humanity's religious traditions, as well as my direct knowledge of different cultures on all the continents, has strengthened my conviction that the ecumenical vision of our church is the best response to the new global conditions that are now in the process of formation. Moreover, Orthodox teaching and worship broaden our field of vision and open our hearts to encompass the entire world. In Orthodox tradition and thought everything is understood in a universal context: from the creation of the world, with which the Old Testament begins, to the New Testament's final vision of a new heaven and a new earth. The human enterprise as a whole and the salvation of the entire world remain the fundamental themes of holy scripture.

The fact that universality constitutes a basic component of Orthodoxy is often overlooked by various Orthodox theological and ecclesiastical circles. Preoccupation with regional matters and immediate problems usually pushes this concern for universal issues to the sidelines. Universality, however, is not unrelated to, nor does it exclude, regional concerns; on the contrary, it embraces them and enables us to see them in their true dimensions.

The basic theses of these essays were widely adopted after their first publication, even though at that time they were by no means self-evident. Ecclesiastical and social ministry in various countries has strengthened my conviction that the issues dealt with in the following pages have maintained their relevance, not only as theological questions but also as part of the broader search for an Orthodox response to modern problems of global concern.

✝ ANASTASIOS
Archbishop of Tirana, Durres, and All of Albania
Tirana, Pentecost 2000

~ 1 ~

Toward a Global Community

RESOURCES AND RESPONSIBILITIES*

The trend toward global community is clearly a historical process that is still unfolding; it is taking place independent of our desires or objections and is driven by completely secular forces.

Directly or indirectly, religions have played a very significant role in this process, whether for the purpose of encouraging it or inhibiting it. Therefore, before discussing the obligation that religions have in the creation of a global community and their future contribution toward it, it would be wise to acknowledge the responsibility that

*This chapter was first presented at the International Interfaith Conference held in Colombo, Sri Lanka, from April 17 to 27, 1974. This multilateral dialogue on the topic "Toward World Community: Resources and Responsibilities for Living Together" was organized by an international group of scholars from different religions and took place under the auspices of "Dialogue with People of Living Faiths and Ideologies," a program of the World Council of Churches. The fifty specialists who participated in the conference hailed from twenty countries and belonged to the world's five major religions: Christianity, Hinduism, Buddhism, Judaism, and Islam. Professor K. Sivaraman, of the University of Benares, India, and McMaster University, Ontario, presented the Hindu point of view; Professor L.G. Hewage of Colombo, Sri Lanka, presented the Buddhist view; the Jewish approach was elaborated by Professor Shemaryahu Talmon of Jerusalem; Dr Mushir-ul-Haq of Aligarh, India, articulated the Islamic point of view; and with the following chapter the author of the present volume offered the Christian approach. These presentations, together with the minutes of the conference, were published in English in "Toward World Community," *Ecumenical Review* 26 (Geneva, 1974): 619-36, with synopses in French (652-53), German (661-62), and Spanish (668-69). They were reprinted in expanded form in S.G. Samartha, ed., *Toward World Community: The Colombo Papers* (Geneva, 1975). The present chapter was published in Greek with footnotes and a few additions under the title "Toward World Community: Resources and Responsibilities" (*Pros pankosmion kinotita—Dynatotites kai evthynai*) in the scholarly yearbook of the Theological School of the University of Athens, volume 20 (1975).

religions bear for some of world history's blackest pages and to understand the new context in which religions must now function.[1]

THE CONTEXT OF THE PROBLEM

It must be admitted that while in the past religions as intellectual and social institutions helped to unite the world, they could also be divisive forces. They helped to transcend old boundaries, but at the same time created new "closed" communities that, although widespread, remained entrenched behind mighty and impenetrable walls. The history of the so-called Christian nations, of the Israelite community, of the Islamic *umma*, and of various other religious groups demonstrates a competitiveness that has taken many forms and has

---

[1]From the eighteenth century to the Second World War, western Europe fostered the expectation that the domination of the entire world by western Christianity and its concomitant culture would lead to the creation of a world community. The colonial policies of the western European powers exploited such aspirations. History also documents the efforts of Islam to impose unity and uniformity on the world through military and political power: for example, the Arab dynasties from the seventh to the thirteenth century and later, down to the beginning of the twentieth century, with the Mongolian and Ottoman empires. In our own era, aspirations for a world community based on the imposition of one religious faith are no longer encouraged. The existence of religious diversity in the world is taken for granted, and it does not seem likely that this diversity will decline due to the domination of one religion or another, or due to the disappearance of religion in general. We can say with some certainty that different religious beliefs will continue to coexist for a long time, and this is taken as the starting point for our line of reasoning.

For the world domination of Christianity up to the middle of the twentieth century, see K. Latourette, *A History of the Expansion of Christianity*, vols. 1-7 (New York and London, 1938-1945), especially vol. 7, *Advance through Storm*, 483-505, for a summary of the conclusions reached. Some of this distinguished historian's predictions were disproven by events after only a few decades: for example, the statement that "the course" of Islam "appears to be downwards" (7:493). During the second half of the twentieth century Islam has had exceptional successes in Africa and Indonesia, contributed toward the formation of Pakistan, and today exhibits particular vitality. See W. Cantwell Smith, *Islam in Modern History* (Princeton, 1957 and 1966); P. Rondot, *L'Islam et les musulmans d'aujourd'hui, de Dakar à Djakarta* (Paris, 1960); and N. Ahmad, T. Grin, J.-C. Froelich, *L'Afrique islamique (Islamisches Afrika, Africa Islamica)* in *Le monde religieux*, 29e volume de la nouvelle série (Lezay, Deux-Sèvres, 1966), especially J.-C. Froelich, "Essai sur l'islamisation de l'Afrique noire," 171-299. Scholarly research in the field of religion has shown that no religion has yet been able to overpower the others and completely domi-

employed various, often violent methods. When these have operated in conjunction with racial, social, and political interests, religious conflicts have taken extremely cruel forms.[2]

Furthermore, it must be admitted that while in the past religions have often served the cause of freedom, they have also suppressed human freedoms. Various studies have pointed to many instances in history when religion became a vehicle for objectives that are alien to it—whether political, military, economic, or otherwise. Even world religions based on humility, sacrifice, and peace have often appeared as socio-religious formations that became lured by the temptations of worldly power and caused damage to the idea of world unity. This happened because they lost touch with and deviated from their deeper spiritual message.

Coping with the Secularization of Modern Life

In the past, religion determined all facets of human life, and the range of concerns that fell within its province was therefore complex: religion was interwoven with philosophy, medicine, law, politics, art, and recreation. In our own era, however, each of these various aspects of life has acquired an existence and character of its own. Therefore, the first thing that is necessary is for religion to find

nate the world. See H. von Glasenapp, *Die fünf Weltreligionen* (Düsseldorf and Köln, 1963), 364. For a summary overview of the vitality of different religions in our era see G.F. Vicedom, *Die Mission der Weltreligionen* (München, 1959). See also *Vitalité actuelle des religions non-chrétiennes* (Paris, 1957), which includes articles by Swami Abhishikteswarananda, A. Zigmund-Cerbu, M.-J. Stiassny, V. Monteil, P. Humbertclaude, P. O'Reilly, B. Holas, C. Pidoux, and M.-M. Dufeil.

[2]Many religious groups, acting in self-defense, protest that they are being oppressed; however, when they find themselves in a position of power, they often demonstrate pitiless cruelty toward members of other religions. See P.H. Ashby, *The Conflict of Religions* (New York, 1955); A. Hartmann, *Toleranz und christliche Glaube* (Freiburg, 1955); J.W. Hauer, *Toleranz und Intoleranz in den nichtchristlichen Religionen* (Stuttgart, 1961); J. Lecler, *Geschichte der Religionsfreiheit im Zeitalter der Reformation* (Stuttgart, 1965); and O. Rieg, "Toleranz und Religionsfreiheit in der Geschichte der Kirche" in H. Köster, ed., *Über die Religionsfreiheit und die nichtchristlichen Religionen* (Limburg, 1969), 11-37. Noteworthy and concise articles on religious persecution can also be found in J. Hastings, ed., *The Encyclopaedia for Religion and Ethics* 9 (London), 742-69, "Persecution": Modern (W.T. Whitley), Indian (A.S. Geden), and esp. 765-69, Muhammadan (T.W. Arnold); for anti-Semitic persecution see volume 1, 593-99, "Antisemitism" (H.I. Strack).

its proper place among the new forces that unify humanity, without feeling either inferior or superior to them.

Many secular features of modern life[3]—such as the rapid development of science and technology, international law, and international organizations whose programs are worldwide in scope—have been characterized as the secularized products of religion, and more specifically as the secularized products of Christian civilization.[4] Some of these features are more directly linked to Christian civilization, while others have a less immediate association. Certain social forces, such as the socialist movement, have often taken the form of protests or even uprisings against religion; nevertheless, at bottom, they do not cease to remind one of rebellious children, who still preserve much of what they learned from the parents and relatives that nurtured them. Many movements have put forward slogans and ideas that were originally religious—most of them explicitly Christian ideas, such as equality, justice, individual freedom, and brotherhood—while certain professional spokespeople for religion have either not represented these ideas properly or have even betrayed them.

[3]In international terminology such features of modern life are usually referred to as "secular," as are the powerful trends and conditions that they create: secularization and secularism in English; sécularisation and sécularisme in French; Säkularisierung, Säkularismus, and Säkularität in German. These terms imply being wholly absorbed in the life and the interests of the present world and time (saeculum means the present era) with no regard for values and hopes associated with the transcendental or with any anticipation of "the age to come." "The forces of secularization have no serious interest in persecuting religion. Secularization simply bypasses and undercuts religion and goes on to other things." H. Cox, *The Secular City: A Celebration of Its Liberties and an Invitation to Its Discipline* (New York, 1966), 2.

Also pointed to as secular factors that promote worldwide rapprochement are athletics, art, and international trade, which has developed a network of large, multinational companies throughout the world. On this extremely timely subject and the problems that secularization poses for the religious person, see F. Delekat, *Über den Begriff der Säkularisation* (Heidelberg, 1958); M. Jarrett-Kerr, *The Secular Promise* (London, 1964); S.H. Miller, *Säkularität-Atheismus-Glaube* (Neukirche, 1965); C. von Ouwerkerk, "Säkularität und christliche Ethik, Typen und Symptome," *Concilium* 3 (1967): 397-416; A. Dondeyne, "Monde sécularisé et foi en Dieu," *Eglise Vivante* 22 (1970): 5-28; and J. Morel, ed., *Glaube and Säkularisierung* (Insbruck, Wien, and München, 1972).

[4]The phrase "secularized products of Christian civilization" comes from A.Th. Van Leeuwen, *Christianity in World History: The Meeting of the Faiths of East and West* (London, 1965), 333.

We should not view such secular or "extra-religious" forces as rivals, but as collaborators in the struggle to realize our universal spiritual goals of world understanding and rapprochement. Our aim should not be to dominate or to create a religious common front against other intellectual forces in the modern world, nor should we adopt a hostile, crusader-like attitude. We should attempt, rather, to make a substantial contribution toward coping with the new conditions that exist.

In taking this positive approach, however, religion must maintain its essential role as critic. Its contribution must not be limited merely to attempting to bring about greater understanding, proposing minor alterations, or interpreting only the outward appearance of things. In many instances religion should simply refuse to interpret. Religion has an obligation to express itself frankly, with prophetic insight and clarity, regarding our need to change our orientation, to repent, and to hold up the stop signs that will turn us from the wrong path we have taken. Religion is called upon to heighten our sense of what life is all about and to provide us with the strength we need to transform the perceptible world, by keeping our gaze firmly fixed upon the transcendental.

The Dangers and Bizarre Distortions of Modern Civilization

It is common knowledge that the secular forces that have been crucial in bringing people around the world closer together have at the same time created new and powerful inducements for people to become more isolated and divided. They have also created menacing problems, such as gigantic and nightmarishly impersonal cities and callous economic alliances. Many wonder in anguish whether we are being led toward global community or are being homogenized into a characterless and impersonal global mass. They point to the following dangers and distortions in modern culture:

⁓ We have a contradictory sense both of power and of extreme helplessness. Anxiety and insanity are the hallmarks of our age. We often boast about the power we have acquired through modern technology and science. At the same time, however, we live as individuals, with an increased sense of our own powerlessness, recognizing that we are at the mercy of a variety of anonymous forces—that we are mere "numbers," and it makes no real difference whether we exist or not.

⮑ We are assured that freedom generally prevails, yet simultaneously witness a lack of individual freedom. There is incessant talk of freedom, but millions of people are completely unable to escape the chains of hunger, oppression, illiteracy, and misfortune.

⮑ We have been incorporated into "the family of man," but have a sense of tragic isolation. We are surrounded by crowds of people—on the streets, on television, in our imaginations—but are relentlessly plagued by loneliness, which neither our wealth nor our technological comforts are able to overcome.

⮑ For decades now, individuals, nations, and organizations have been extolling peace; however, many are beginning to wonder whether talk of peace by the strong simply means ensuring more favorable conditions to oppress the weak.

⮑ Bringing people closer together results not only in unity, but very often creates tragic conflicts of interest. In addition to the military conflicts that ensue, there are intense battles of a different nature, on an international scale, between economic blocs and corporations.

All these issues simply indicate the complexity of the new relationships that are being created as we proceed toward global community. Gone is that first inspiring glow of optimism that believed that secular forces, based on logic and technology, would be able to satisfy all of humanity's needs.

Humanity's spiritual relationships have proven to be complicated problems that are difficult to investigate, creating unbearable headaches for electronic brains. Religion's old injunction here is particularly timely: cleanse your heart, so that the human mind can be used properly. In this global crisis, religions are called upon to reach down into their deepest reserves of inspiration and intuition, that they might offer both effective spiritual resistance as well as positive guidance.

From "Global Community" to a "Communion of Love"

It was noted above that secular forces are accelerating our current course toward global community. Does this global community represent an ideal? Or is it merely a new ordeal, a new threat? Billions of people live together, but what does this mean? People in mental hospitals also share a common life. Their sense of unity, however, is created mainly by their location, their proximity, and their insanity. In the history of the modern world's development, the central role has usually been played by common interests and technocratic organization, not God's charismatic gifts or the inspiration of love. We are in danger of ending up with a form of symbiotic coexistence that is both superficial and tragic. The current trend toward unification does not spring "from within," from spiritual maturity and a loving desire to learn about other people; on the contrary, it has been imposed "from without," by purely material factors, as a form of behavior. People who are brought together through this kind of unification remain strangers or are only united because of their common economic or political interests. It reminds one of the crushing crowds in the trains at rush hour or, even more, of the suffocating embrace of two wrestlers—not the embrace of familial love that characterizes a union of persons. The slogan "toward a global community" is not an adequate ideal.

A global community cannot be an end in itself, and religion should not allow itself to be drawn into the logic and the messianism of secular forces. Neither is it the obligation of religion to lament this process by which people are being brought closer together, nor to make vain attempts to impede it. Rather, religion's duty is to reveal the crucial issue, to point out the danger of creating a formless social hodgepodge, and at the same time to offer alternatives for achieving unity of a different quality and kind. Taking Christian principles as our starting point, it is our belief that the real problem is how we can advance from being merely a community to becoming a communion of love—or, to use the Greek word, a *koinonia* (pronounced *kee-no-NEE-a*), a "communion, society, communication, interconnection" of love—with our fellow human beings, with the entire universe, and with the Supreme Reality. What religion can offer here is

something radically different in quality and significance from anything promised by secular forces in our society, and it is indispensable. The backbone of the discussion that follows is this: let us make
our goal a *koinonia* of love—meaning an organic social whole made
up of people who are complete personalities and whose relationships
are based on love—not merely a form of coexistence shared by isolated individuals.

Toward a *Koinonia* of Love:
The Christian Vision, The Christian Struggle

The conditions created by our global, technological culture have
given rise to a terrible crisis in people's sense of their own legitimacy.
It is a crisis of identity. If religions are to respond in any meaningful
way to this crisis, they will have to answer the question "what is a
human being?" in a way that goes beyond a mechanistic, biological
description. Christianity's decisive contribution to this critical issue
has been its discovery of the human being as person and of the person's need to be in a *koinonia* of love.

In the street, in the workplace, and in the family, we observe with
dismay the ever-increasing prevalence of the social "mask" and the
disappearance of genuine faces, of the real person. People act out
their mindless roles, functioning like parts in a machine; they are not
persons. One very often has the sense of being at a strange masked
ball, where the identity of all the participants is hidden. At this particular masquerade, however, whenever someone's mask is pulled
away, another mask appears in its place. In this kind of crisis, where
one's very authenticity is called into question, mere coexistence can
never become a *koinonia*.

In the Christian view, although human beings were created "in
God's image," they degenerated into an "ugly mask" (as St Gregory
of Nyssa expresses it) when they abused their own nature by rejecting a *koinonia* of love with God.[5] In order to understand this

---

[5]St Gregory of Nyssa: "Hence the misery that encompasses us often causes the
Divine gift to be forgotten, and spreads the passions of the flesh, like some ugly mask,
over the beauty of the image" (*The Making of Man* 18, PG 44:193C [trans. NPF, 2d ser.,

Christian conception of humanity, history, and society, it will be necessary to give a systematic account of the fundamentals of the Christian faith. Only then can it be adequately shown what Christians, drawing on the quintessence of their religious beliefs, see as the spiritual basis for and source of human unity and how these inspire the Christian vision of and struggle for global community.

At this point, two issues require clarification:

⌐ The Christian world, like all large religious groups, contains a wide variety of standpoints, each with its own special emphasis, and it is not possible in this essay to express the full consensus of Christian views. The theological outline that follows primarily represents the views of an Orthodox theologian who is trying to maintain an open perspective, one that encompasses the concerns of all humanity.

⌐ It is not my intention here to adopt doctrinally neutral forms of expression or to use language that, from a religious point of view, is flat and colorless. Such language is not genuine and does not reflect the views of any existing religious group. Certain Christian tenets, such as those concerning the Holy Trinity, the cross, and the Resurrection, are clearly obstacles for people of other religions. For faithful Christians, however, they provide the hidden strength needed to overcome self-centeredness in the arduous struggle for a *koinonia* of love. At this stage in our efforts at mutual understanding, we all need to explain our deepest religious ideas as clearly as possible, not search for some artificial common denominator. The problem is not how each one of us, as individuals, can verbally transcend the closed boundaries of our own religious thinking in order to make contact with others; rather, the problem is how we can open the doors and the windows of our religious systems from within, in order to facilitate true *koinonia* between all human beings.

vol. 5]); and ". . . the filth of sin debased the beauty in the image" (*On the Beatitudes*, PG 44:1197BC). Cf. K. Skouteres, *The Consequences of the Fall and the Waters of Rebirth: From the Anthropology of St Gregory of Nyssa* (in Greek) (Athens, 1973), 51-61.

The Supreme Koinonia *of the Trinitarian God:*
The Starting Point for a Koinonia *on Earth*

The starting point for Christians is their certainty that there exists a supreme *koinonia*. This is the highest expression of communion. This is the reality that truly exists: God. The unapproachable and infinite trinitarian God is primarily understood as perfect communion: an infinite and perfect unity; the existence of a unified essence in which persons share a unity in three and a trinity in one. This ultimately entails transcending numerical categories. It is a departure from the confusion inherent both in multiplicity as well as in the isolation of oneness. It is neither static nor simply dynamic, but transcends both through a *koinonia* of love.[6] Although this certainty is a "cross" for human modes of thinking, it nevertheless remains a key element in Christian thought and is therefore crucial with respect to the issue of moving "toward a global community."

"In God's Image": The Basis for the Unity
Inherent in Our Nature as Human Beings

The trinitarian God created and sustains "the world and everything in it" (Acts 17:24). He remains "the Lord of heaven and earth" as well as the Father of all humanity: "One God and Father of us all, who is above all and through all and in all" (Eph 4:5). Humanity exhibits great variety and diversity, but its true nature is rooted in unity, not only because God "made from one [blood] every nation of men" (Acts 17:26) but primarily because he "made him in the image of God" (Gen 5:1).[7] This means that sharing in a "*koinonia* of love" is

[6]"In the Holy Trinity the union is neither static, nor merely functional: it is hypostatic; that is, each of the Persons retains His unique characteristics in a union without confusion, and the union communicates these characteristics to men in order to establish communion through the Holy Spirit in the grace of the Son and the love of the Father." N.A. Nissiotis, "The Importance of the Doctrine of the Trinity for Church Life and Theology," in A.J. Philippou, ed., *The Orthodox Ethos* (Oxford, 1964), 43.

[7]For a scriptural analysis of this crucial point, see P. Bratsiotes, "Genesis 1:26 in Orthodox Theology" (in Greek), *Orthodoxia* 27 (1952): 359-72, also published in German in *Evangelische Theologie* 11 (1951-52): 289-97. Cf. P. Bratsiotes, *Man in the New Testament* (in Greek) (Athens, 1955); N. Bratsiotes, *The Anthropology of the Old Testament* (in Greek), vol. 1, *Man as a Divine Creation* (Athens, 1967); and I. Karavidopoulos, "The

intrinsic to human nature, since humanity was created on the model of the Holy Trinity. By their very nature, human beings are in harmony with all of creation and with the source of love, God. All human beings thus bear the image of God, regardless of their race, color, language, or education; that is, they all possess intellect, free will, and love.[8] The fact that all human existence shares in this divine image makes human nature an indivisible unity.

Life in a community—more precisely, a *koinonia*—is therefore the natural condition for human beings. Unfortunately, however, at the beginning of history humanity became fragmented, thus departing from its essential nature. This happened when human beings became attached to their own individual egos and chose to control their future destiny, thus calling into question their *koinonia* with God, which had been the basis for their unity and *koinonia* with each other and with nature.

Following this rupture in its relationship with God, humanity's tragic proclivity led to ever-greater separation between people and their fellow human beings—who were created in God's image—and ever-greater separation between people and nature, a process that

Image of God" and "In the Image" of God according to the Apostle Paul: The Christological Basis of Pauline Anthropology (in Greek) (Thessaloniki, 1964).

[8]St Gregory of Nyssa examines the issue in his characteristic way: "In saying that 'God created man' the text indicates, by the indefinite character of the term, all mankind. . . . Thus we are led by the employment of the general name of our nature to some such view as this—that in the Divine foreknowledge and power all humanity is included in the first creation. . . . So I think that the entire plenitude of humanity was included by the God of all, by His power of foreknowledge, as it were in one body, and that this is what the text teaches us which says, 'God created man, in the image of God created He him.' For the image is not in part of our nature, nor is the grace in any one of the things found in that nature, but this power extends equally to all the race. . . . The man that was manifested at the first creation of the world, and he that shall be after the consummation of all, are alike: they equally bear in themselves the Divine image. . . . Our whole nature, then, extending from the first to the last, is, so to say, one image of Him Who is; but the distinction of kind in male and female was added to His work last as I suppose, for the reason which follows. . . ." *On the Making of Man,* PG 44:185BD (trans. NPF, 2d ser., vol. 5). In emphasizing the unity of the human race, St Gregory also points to the distinction between essence (referring to all humanity) and existence (referring to individual human beings). For more on the views of St Gregory of Nyssa on this issue see I. Moutsoulas, *The Incarnation of the Word and the Deification of Man according to the Teachings of Gregory of Nyssa (in Greek)* (Athens, 1965); and K. Skouteres, *The Unity of Human Nature as a Factual Precondition for Salvation (From the Anthropology of St Gregory of Nyssa) (in Greek)* (Athens, 1969).

ultimately led to a fragmentation of the human self. The impetus
behind this process has always been viewed by Christian thought as
degeneration, as "sin," as alienation from the essence of human
nature. Moreover, since the "clay" or "stuff" that humanity is made
of is one, the entire human race degenerated together into a state of
infirmity. We see, therefore, that human nature, both in its splendor
and in its fall from grace, is homogeneous and that the plight of all
human beings vis-à-vis the judgment of God is shared in common,
"since all have sinned and fall short of the glory of God" (Rom 3:22-
23).[9] Ever since then, human history has been defined by two opposing tendencies: the path toward unity, which is an attribute of our
"divine image," and the path toward fragmentation, which is a consequence of the fall.

Under these conditions it was no longer possible to speak of
koinonia in the original sense. It was imperative, however, that at
least some ability to coexist and live with others should be maintained, until the original koinonia of love should be restored. People's
basic duty to respect justice and to help one another is continually
repeated throughout the Old Testament as a commandment of God
and reaches its supreme expression in a most moving fashion in the
pages of the New Testament.

The Incarnation of the Word of God: A New Force for Koinonia

If Christians are to make a substantial contribution toward the unity
of the human race, they must speak clearly about a single occurrence: an event that surpassed all others; an event that they believe
gave new depth and meaning to the relationship between God and
humanity; an event that is both the basic focal point for unity in the
universe and the crucial factor in restoring the divine koinonia of
love. This event, put succinctly, was when "the Word became flesh
and dwelt among us, full of grace and truth" (Jn 1:14). The incarnation of the Word of God is the critical impetus that was needed to

[9] The fact that all human beings are sinners and in need of forgiveness and reconciliation sheds light on a peculiar aspect of humanity's oneness. When we humbly comprehend our sinfulness—the tragedy of our human existence—we become aware of our
common nature. Cf. C.W. Forman, *A Faith for the Nations* (Philadelphia, 1967), 42-45.

move us toward a *koinonia* of every human person with all other human beings and with the entire natural world. By assuming human nature, Christ "emptied himself" (Phil 2:7) and became one with the "lump" (φύραμα) of humanity. "As has often been said, the body of Christ is the totality of the human nature into which he was mingled."[10] The coming of the Word of God brought with it an ontologically new force for the cleansing of the "divine image," for the restoration of love, and for the elevation of human nature in its oneness into the sphere of the divine.[11] Humanity, which had once been alienated from its own true nature, could now return to *koinonia* with the Holy Trinity through Christ.

[10] St Gregory of Nyssa, *Sermon on "When all things are subjected to him . . ."* (PG 44:1320B). Cf. idem, *On the Meeting of the Lord* (PG 46:1165AB): "He makes holy unto our God and Father not only the first born of humans, but now also the entire human race, through the first-fruit of our substance which is in him . . . providing as it were the leaven of holiness for the whole composite being of humanity." And in his *Refutation of Apollinarius* (PG 45:1152C), he adds: ". . . he was mingled with humanity and received in himself the whole of our nature, in order to deify what is human with himself, since the whole substance of our nature joined in being sanctified through those first-fruits." By the second century A.D. Irenaeus had already stressed the idea that the entire human race is "recapitulated" in Jesus Christ: "But when he became incarnate and was made man, he recapitulated in himself the long story of mankind, giving us salvation in a brief and comprehensive manner . . ." *Contra Haereses* 3.18.1 (PG 7:952B); cf. also ". . . he summed up in himself the whole generation of humans, including Adam himself," ibid., 23.3 (PG 7:958A). See also A. Theodorou, *The Teaching of Irenaeus on Recapitulation* (in Greek) (Athens, 1972; reprinted from the scholarly yearbook of the Theological School of the University of Athens, 18). This certainty pervades the thinking of many fathers of the Eastern Church. Cf. Cyril of Alexandria, *On the Gospel of John* (PG 74:432D): Christ "has made us stand in the sight of the Father, being himself the beginning of humanity . . ." And ibid. (PG 73:753): "For when he became man, he possessed in himself the whole of human nature, in order to restore the whole and transform it into its original state." Cf. John of Damascus, *On the Orthodox Faith* 46 (PG 94:985C): "He brought into being for himself flesh animated with a soul of reason and spiritual understanding, thereby taking on the first-fruits of human nature, since the Word himself became a hypostasis in the flesh."

[11] A much-beloved teaching from patristic theology is that human nature is deified in Christ and that this elevates the "lump" of human existence into the glory of communion with God. Cf. Georges Florovsky, *Creation and Redemption,* Collected Works, 3 (Belmont, Mass., 1976), 97. For additional patristic views see A. Theodoros, *The Teachings of the Greek Church Fathers through John Damascene on the Deification of Humanity* (in Greek) (Athens, 1956); G.I. Mantzarides, *The Teaching of Gregory Palamas on the Deification of Humanity* (in Greek) (Thessaloniki, 1963); D.G. Tsames, *The Perfection of Humanity according to Nikitas Stethatos* (in Greek) (Thessaloniki, 1971); and N.E. Metsopoulos, *The Glorification of Humanity in Jesus Christ* (in Greek) (Athens, 1972).

It is precisely because human nature constitutes a single, unified whole that the implications of the incarnation, the passion, and the resurrection of Christ are global in space and time. His coming redeems the world through the constant activity of the Holy Spirit. The human race acquires new power for understanding and approaching God, and this new power is also the source of unity among human beings.

A reconciliation of global proportions was achieved through Christ: "God was pleased to dwell, and through him to reconcile to himself all things" (Col 1:20).[12] When all the beings of creation have become reconciled with God, thus coming full circle, they can then be reconciled with one another. All Christians have a responsibility to remain keenly aware of the tragic schism experienced by all of humanity and to press on with their "ministry of reconciliation" (2 Cor 5:18-21), taking the entire world as their field of vision and their field of action. Under no circumstances are Christians permitted to close themselves off from others by making themselves autonomous in any way; nor are they permitted to construe redemption through Christ as their own exclusive salvation for their own little egos. The kingdom of God announced by Jesus is open to all.

The Church as Striving toward the Unity of All Human Beings

The event described above, which is the fundamental creed of every conscious Christian community, initiated a new trend in human history toward unity, toward a *koinonia* of a different quality and order. It is for this purpose that the Church is called together in Christ, through the Holy Spirit, into a *koinonia* of love, where all the things that divide people—race, language, sex, class, and cultural background—are abolished. The true Christian Church is therefore not conceived of as some novel, insular community or as some kind of corporate enterprise that seeks to expand so as to increase its own power; rather, the Church is a symbol, an indication of the desire for worldwide unity. The Church operates as a "sacred mystery," as the

---

[12]Cf. S. Agourides, *The New Testament Teaching on Reconciliation according to the Orthodox Tradition* (in Greek) (Athens, 1964).

vital core of the kingdom of God, which extends beyond the perceptible boundaries of our church communities. Everything the Church has and everything it does belongs to everyone; everything is done— it must be done—for the sake of the entire world.

We are not talking here about the kind of unity that is based on dragging everyone down to the same level and that ultimately leads to the creation of a characterless human hodgepodge. On the contrary, we are talking about the kind of unity that exists in a living organism, not the unity that exists in a piece of rock. The faithful Christian is a living cell in the body of the Church. Every person, as well as every assembly of persons, is called upon to realize his or her own unique self, to develop his or her inner powers in harmony with the whole and in love—love being the fundamental attribute of the "divine image." The universality of the Church does not mean exclusivity; it means all-inclusiveness.[13]

A Unifying Spirit

Among the most crucial concepts for understanding global unity from a theological viewpoint is the way that Orthodoxy sees the activity of the Holy Spirit. At the beginning of creation, the Spirit "was moving" over the void (Gen 1:2), so that the world could be fashioned. Throughout history the Spirit has continued to perform this same function, inspiring the prophets and in various ways guiding human beings out of the darkness of chaos and into the land of spiritual creation. The Spirit was directly involved in the incarnation of the Savior and in the birth of the Church. The Spirit—"who is present everywhere and fills all things," as we hear in the prayer with which Orthodox services usually begin—continues to do its work, sanctifying human beings and fulfilling and completing the salvation of the entire universe.

[13]With regard to the subject of the universality of the Church from an Orthodox point of view, there were some very interesting contributions and observations at the Second International Conference of Orthodox Theology (St Vladimir's Seminary, September 25-29, 1972) by J. Meyendorff, S.S. Verhovskoy, T. Hopko, R. Stephanopoulos, T. Istavridis, T. Dobzhansky, N. Chitescu, D. Sahas, L. Milin, J. Klinger, G. Mantzarides, and J. Boojamra, published in *St Vladimir's Theological Quarterly* 17:1-2 (1973): 1-186.

Some theologians prefer to see the Holy Spirit's activity as restricted to those institutional structures of the Church with which we are familiar. However, the most profound Christian awareness firmly senses that "the Spirit blows where it wills" (Jn 3:8)—that the Spirit is the active force of love, everywhere—and chants with delight, "The Holy Spirit has full command over all the seen and the unseen" (from the Sunday *Anavathmoi*, first plagal tone). It is a widespread conviction in the theology of the eastern Church that the Holy Spirit works to achieve the unity of all beings in ways that transcend human thought and imagination, ways that cannot therefore be contained within any theological system, as they defy description. The perfect building materials for harmonious coexistence— namely, "love, joy, peace, patience, kindness, goodness, faithfulness, gentleness, self-control"—are the "fruit of the Spirit" (Gal 5:22). I believe that these assurances from the apostle Paul justify the conclusion that wherever such qualities are present—and they are undeniably found in more than a few "non-Christian" environments—it is possible to discern signs that the Holy Spirit is at work.

Bearing the Imprint of the End: Eschatological Unity

History and Christian hope have been imprinted with a vision of ultimate unity. The work of calling people together in unity continues, through the Holy Spirit, until the end of time. The road that leads there, however, will take us through turbulent crises, both personal and global. The cross, with its relentless afflictions and tragic uncertainties, continues to dominate our lives in the form of suffering and misfortune and in the failures of our noble aspirations and struggles. The forces of evil and sin continue to mount their defense, to fight back, and to sow hatred and discord among people. Nevertheless, through constant self-criticism, through the spirit of repentance that infuses the gospel, and through the presence of God's grace we will not lose our orientation toward a *koinonia* of love.

Our final end is symbolically portrayed as a gathering of people in a new and different kind of city, a heavenly city, the "new Jerusalem," which arises in "a new heaven and a new earth" (Rev 21:1).

This city "on high" is a gift that has been offered to the entire human race, and the gathering of people that takes place there includes everyone.[14] This is not a mere public assembly but a *koinonia*—a communion of free persons in God—through which human beings will become transformed and thus be able to return to the very heart of history and of the world: the trinitarian God, who is "the alpha and omega" of existence, the beginning and end of the universe. The complete panorama of human history thus begins and ends with the same vision: a divine *koinonia* of love.

Active Participation

People do not merely view this whole process from the sidelines; they participate in it. Every human being bears personal responsibility for the world's future course, even though its momentum and direction have already been determined. Each person's responsibility is proportional to his or her individual abilities, but no one is exempt.[15] We could call it a kind of democracy of responsibility, an "international congress" of responsibility. This should not be understood merely in ethical or moral terms. It is not a moral imperative of the Kantian type, but a process in which Christians must participate in order to exist. The faithful Christian is an organic part of the process that was set into motion by the historical events described above. This participation is organic because each cell in a body, as a member of a larger organism, not only reaps the benefit of life but also contributes toward it.[16]

[14]This restoration "is universal, since it affects all human beings, as bearers of the divine image, and addresses the entire human being, as a unity of soul and body." D.G. Tsames, *The Dialectical Nature of the Teachings of Gregory the Theologian* (in Greek) (Thessaloniki, 1969), 44.

[15]Communion with God and active participation in the victory of "his righteousness" are mutually dependent. "God's ally is also God's communicant." A.P. Hastoupes, *The Difference between Jewish and Greek Views of Religious and Philosophical Issues* (in Greek) (Athens, 1968), 27.

[16]It is a contradiction for someone to be a Christian and at the same time to be indifferent to the world as a whole and its historical course. The individual person's relationship to the human race as a whole extends in time and space. The faithful Christian belongs to the past and to the future. This sense of responsibility for the whole is an essential motivation behind the impetus toward a global community because it marshals

Entering into the body of the Church and into communion with Christ means acquiring "the mind of Christ" (1 Cor 2:16); it means imitating the personal conditions under which Christ lived, and our living in Christ today. The Christian desire for a *koinonia* of love does not constitute escapism into some dream, full of all the delightful things we hope for. On the contrary, it expresses itself under the conditions of modern life and in the form of concrete service: giving of oneself on a daily and continuous basis to everyone, both near and far, regardless of their religious faith, their moral character, or the spiritual or cultural circumstances of their lives. It means taking Jesus—who "came not to be served but to serve, and to give his life as a ransom for many" (Mt 20:28)—as the unrivaled model for service to humanity. The principal vantage point from which Christians view their responsibility for global community, as well as their principal source of inspiration and strength, is LOVE, in all the depth and breadth that Christian theology and life give to it. Together with reason and freedom, love constitutes the basic element of humanity's "divine image." Through love, human beings are able to transcend the limits of the self and fully realize their "return" to union with true Being.

The attitudes of others do not restrict our freedom to love. Christ loved others regardless of their response—others who very often did not love him or were not worthy of his love (1 Jn 4:1)—for the simple reason that he was Love itself. For Christians, love means more than just a general disposition to be kind and to perform certain charitable deeds. Love emanates from God[17] and finds its supreme

---

all of our individual powers. Indifference toward the needs of other human beings is depicted in holy scripture as a mortal sin, as contempt for God himself. It is repeatedly inveighed against in the parables of Jesus (the foolish rich man, Lk 12:15-21; the rich man and Lazarus, Lk 16:19-31) and can exact severe penalties at the final judgment (Mt 25:31-46). Christianity compels us to respond to life with action and stresses the responsibility that each of us bears for the world's development. And, as Fr Georges Florovsky once remarked, "Anyone who takes an apathetic stance toward history can never become a good Christian."

[17]"Again, God is love, and the fount of love: for this the great John declares, that 'love is of God,' and 'God is love': the Fashioner of our nature has made this to be our feature too: for 'hereby,' He says, 'shall all men know that ye are my disciples, if ye love one another':—thus, if this be absent, the whole stamp of the likeness is transformed."

realization in the incarnation and crucifixion of Christ. When this is lived, it leads to a new relationship with all other beings. Love transforms human beings and, through the grace of the sacraments, leads them to deification (*theosis,* in Greek)—to use Orthodox terminology. It does this by including them, once and for all, within the Holy Trinity's blessed *koinonia* of love, which constitutes the end of the human journey and our final destination. "God is love, and he who abides in love abides in God, and God abides in him" (1 Jn 4:16).

Holy Communion: For the Sake of the Entire World

Living one's every breath "in Christ" does not become a reality all by itself; one must follow the procedure that has been mapped out in various ways by Christian tradition. The daily experience of communion with all other human beings and nature through God requires deep faith. In its practical expression this means a way of life marked by ascetic conscientiousness, self-restraint, contemplation of the great Christian truths, "quietness," constant reference to God, who is the center of the universe, and an unceasing dialogue of prayer with him.

Our worship of God reaches its highest expression in the spiritual gathering of the faithful, and especially in the sacred mystery of the divine eucharist, which is considered the "divine *koinonia* or communion" par excellence. This sacred mystery is the extension of

St Gregory of Nyssa, *On the Making of Man* 5, PG 44:137C (trans. NPF, 2d ser., vol. 5). In every human person—even one that is "the least of these" (Mt 25:45) and even one that has been corrupted through his or her own shortcomings, false religious beliefs, or errors—the faithful Christian discerns a brother for whose sake Christ died, one of God's collaborators destined to be a living temple of the Holy Spirit, an inheritor of eternal life, and a communicant in God's divine nature; in every human person the faithful Christian perceives the person of Christ. A prerequisite for communion with God is love for individual persons. The road to God proceeds through people: "If anyone says, 'I love God,' and hates his brother, he is a liar; for he who does not love his brother whom he has seen, cannot love God whom he has not seen" (1 Jn 4:20). Love has a universal character, because everyone—whether old or young, important or unknown, educated or illiterate, and regardless of race—has the ability to offer love in any given place and at any given time. Love transforms human relationships, both in the smallest human nucleus, the family and, more broadly, within humanity as a whole.

what took place at Christ's incarnation and crucifixion—the extension, that is, of the mystery of divine love intervening in time. Here, all the great truths mentioned above regarding *koinonia* become tangible realities for the faithful. God's love is experienced, charging human beings with new power, so that, by transferring "the fruit of the Spirit" (Gal 5:22) into everyday life, they can contribute to the continuation of Christ's work, which was to reconcile the entire human race with God and to reestablish its bond with him.

Christian worship is not a simple reenactment or commemoration but a continuous, dynamic process: *koinonia* with the life of the Holy Trinity for the sake of the entire world. When the faithful participate in worship, especially in holy communion, they become larger than themselves through the act of giving thanks, transcending their individual limitations. When they receive the "body of Christ" they become incorporated in him: they become "universal," united with all those whom Christ has included in his limitless love. "[The faithful Christian] extends himself in order to bring all of humanity into himself."[18] What is more, the faithful become reconciled with the world and enter a state of harmony with all of creation.

This experience allows us to gaze upon the nature of our existence, as well as our ultimate end; or rather, it is a foretaste of humanity's complete "communion" in God, an experience that serves to stir our souls, so that we can return afterward to our daily lives in the hope that love can become a reality and that progress can be made toward a *koinonia* of all human beings. This kind of worship has been the basic factor in the spiritual replenishment, endurance, and self-sacrifice of Christians at all times and in all places, even in the most atheistic environments.

---

[18]O. Clément, *Questions sur l'homme* (Paris, 1972), 56: "[The faithful Christian] is not separated from any existing being whatsoever—neither in time nor in space. He extends himself in order to bring all of humanity into himself." This certainty is to be found very widely in the writings of modern theologians. For example: "to be in communion with all men in the economy of the Mystery within which we are moving slowly towards the final consummation, when all things will be gathered up in Christ." G. Khodr, "Christianity in a Pluralistic World—the Economy of the Holy Spirit," in S.J. Samartha, ed., *Living Faiths and the Ecumenical Movement* (Geneva, 1971), 140.

The Vision and the Historical Reality

The foregoing analysis of basic Christian views regarding a universal *koinonia* of love might be open to the criticism that it describes a closed system—a dream or ideal, constructed out of doctrines or "dogma." I must point out in response that, in the Orthodox Eastern Church at least, life and doctrine are inseparably linked. Our doctrines are not arbitrary ideas based on nebulous theories and useful mainly in theological disputes; on the contrary, they determine our lives, safeguard our experience of life, and give direction to and reveal life's meaning. They are like mathematical equations or theorems that express, in condensed form, basic laws of the universe, and they have tremendous importance for comprehending the universe and solving many of its practical problems.

Of course, as world history demonstrates, life abounds in deviations from the gospel. Nevertheless, the fact that Christian precepts such as those in the Sermon on the Mount have often been violated does not prevent them from providing us with the unsullied source of inspiration we need for our common life together. Nor is the issue at hand whether Christians have or have not conscientiously upheld those precepts. Rather, we are concerned here both with the spiritual resources that are available to us for living together in harmony and also with our responsibility to do so; these flow from our deepest reserves of faith, which in turn are safeguarded within holy scripture and holy tradition. Moreover, the relentless self-criticism that is taking place in Christian circles today concerning the disparity between precept and practice demonstrates Christianity's ability to preserve a sensitive conscience among its followers and to renew itself by relying on its own powers.

Furthermore, in addition to the well-known "history of Christianity," which delineates the transgressions of bishops, theologians, kings, and nations, of supposedly Christian governments and of every established order in general, there is also the unwritten history of simple folk, who have lived and continue to live quiet lives, faithful to their Christian principles, even though world history has shown little concern for them. Many details about life in the past have also been preserved in the recorded lives of the saints, revealing another, largely unknown, history of Christianity, one that is a truer "history of the Church" than all the scandals and irregularities of ecclesiastical leaders. Indeed, the saints of the Church still remain the most authoritative representatives of Christianity, for they have made the best use of the inexhaustible spiritual resources and strength to be found in the Word and the Grace of God.

SOME CRUCIAL ISSUES REGARDING GLOBAL COMMUNITY

My principle aim in the foregoing analysis has been to offer a cohesive view of Christianity as found in Orthodox tradition and to point out the potential, the power, and the responsibility that Christians have to further the world's progress toward a global community. At the same time, however, we must not ignore the fact that many concrete issues have arisen in connection with this matter, and these need to be addressed directly.

A Koinonia *of Love with Creation*

What has been the approach of Christian communities to the incursion of technology in our lives, to the rapid increase of population in our cities, and to the problem of humanity's relationship with nature? As far as I can tell, these issues have caught some Christian circles by surprise. In most cases, however, their initial uncertainty has been followed by sound analysis. Since human beings, as Christianity sees them, were created "in God's image," it follows that they were intended to be the masters of nature. It is desirable, therefore, that human beings should develop all their potential to the greatest degree possible, and this includes their relentless quest to uncover the truths and secrets of nature. At the same time, however, Christian thought points out that there is a danger that people may become intoxicated by their success and succumb, once again, to the very temptation with which the history of their fall began—namely, to the satanic illusion that their achievements enable them to usurp God's throne and become gods themselves (Gen 3:5).[19] Christian teaching continually points to our limitations as human beings and to the fact that the path toward *theosis,* which is the true *koinonia* of love, is to be found in God, not anywhere outside of him.

Human beings have a vital need to be in a *koinonia* of love, not only with the rest of humanity but also with the world of nature and the entire universe. If we continue to abuse nature rather than "use" it, there is a danger that the development of our technology will lead us to terrifying feats of self-destruction. Christianity delivered humanity from the fear inherent in magical beliefs and from the deification of nature; moreover, by cultivating an active rather than a passive attitude in human beings, Christianity also encouraged the development of science. In the end, however, modern humanity has lost any and all sense of the sacred and in fact has already arrived at the opposite extreme, gazing at nature with impious eyes that lack respect and are often filled with hostile cynicism rather than love. We have thus become increasingly alienated from nature; we behave like robbers of nature, shutting ourselves away in our man-made hide-outs. But nature, too, can retaliate.

Some reconciliation between humanity and nature is urgently needed. It is time we understood that nature is something sacred. It does not lie outside the sphere of the Holy Spirit's activity.[20] In Christ, holiness became united with humanness; as a result, holiness no longer evokes fear, but inspires respect and love—indeed, it invites us to share in *koinonia.* The various elements in Orthodox worship that represent nature are not used as mere decoration but play an *organic* part in the service. Bread, wine, fire, and incense are

[19]From among the many works that have been published on this subject, we refer to the following studies: H.R. Müller-Schwefe, *Technik als Bestimmung und Versuchung* (Göttingen, 1965); H. de Lubac, *Le drame de l'humanisme athée* (Paris, 1959); E. Mascall, "Die wissenschaftliche Weltanschauung und die christliche Botschaft," *Concilium* 3 (1967): 490-94; A. Rich, *Christliche Existenz in der industriellen Welt* (Zürich, 1957); and A.Th. Van Leeuwen, *Des Christen Zukunft im technokratischen Zeitalter* (Stuttgard and Berlin, 1969).

[20]"This transformation [of creation] through the Spirit of God has been noted at various times in the lives of the saints." N. Arseniew, *Die Verklärung der Welt und des Lebens* (Gütersloh, 1955), 201ff. For examples of harmonious coexistence between saints and wild beasts, see pp. 201-6.

integral components in a liturgy of loving communion. Rediscovering the dimensions of nature's sacredness and its original harmony with humanity's intrinsic nature constitutes an indispensable contribution toward achieving real global *koinonia*.

Social Justice and Inner Genuineness

Whenever the demands put forward by modern social and political movements most thoroughly articulate people's thirst for justice, equality, freedom, and human respect, I believe that they express the same message as Christianity. The history of thought reveals that belief in these ideals was nurtured in the deepest layers of the Christian conscience and by Christian thought and that these beliefs matured in the intellectual climate Christianity had created. Christian thinkers have always sought the most genuine expression and realization of these ideals. They point out that the purest human intentions become tainted and perverted by humanity's corrupt tendencies, by selfishness, and by a host of demonic forces that arise in personal relationships and relationships between groups, tragically leading us away from the right path. Hence, these thinkers insist on our need to purify ourselves inwardly and to be true in our motives and sincere and honest in our intentions.

When seen in the light of Christian thought, problems such as racism, inequality between classes, nations, or the sexes, and disregard for human rights all clearly constitute deviations from humanity's true nature, for they deny the basic principle that "there is neither Jew nor Greek, there is neither slave nor free, there is neither male nor female . . ." (Gal 3:28; cf. Rom 2:11). That is, they deny the principle that the human race is one and that the entire "lump" of human existence is redeemed in Christ. Ultimately, they impede God's basic plan for a *koinonia* of love.

Universality and Individuality

Equally unacceptable, however, is the misguided trend to drag everything down to the same level: a uniform—or rather, formless—"internationalism" that is currently in vogue and that has no regard for national heritage or individuality. It is true that some European Christian churches are guilty of having allied themselves in the past with the nationalist slogans and capitalist ideals of their own countries, but we must not repeat their mistake by rashly adopting the opposite position, in the form of an international steamroller. While the former denied that humanity shares one common nature, the latter denies that people and nations have individuality. It fails to distinguish between universality and individuality. Equality does not mean that everyone must be the same. When we speak of equality between the sexes, no one would think of suggesting that men should stop being men or that women should stop being women. Equality does not negate a person's genuine identity; on the contrary, genuineness is a basic requirement for equality. A work of art, in spite of its idiosyncrasies—indeed, often because of them—has universal value when it expresses profound and universal truths about life. Whenever we speak about universality we should also stress the importance of individuality. Christianity has never viewed the individual human being as a speck within the larger mass of humanity.[21] It has always maintained the distinction between a unified "essence" and separate hypostases, or "persons." This explains Christianity's insistence on the idea of a *koinonia* of free persons in love, based on the model of the Holy Trinity.

Global and Regional Perspectives

Just as individuality is not counterposed to universality when the two are brought into harmony through love, so too a global perspective need not negate the regional or local aspect of our lives, which after all is the basic condition of human existence. We do not have to travel continuously or participate in international meetings in

[21]The importance of the individual is often emphasized in holy scripture, as in the parables of the lost sheep and the lost coin (Lk 15:1-10) and in Jesus' concern to heal the specific individuals who approach him. The faithful Christian is seen as a living cell of the body of the Church, not as a grain of sand on the beach. The Christian concept of unity is organic. The central doctrine of the Holy Trinity reveals the harmonious coexistence of unity and personhood, the relationship between multiplicity and oneness. Cf. the bibliography in note 7 above, and N. Bratsiotes, *The Place of the Individual in the Old Testament* (in Greek) (Athens, 1962), chapter 1, "Introduction."

order to be living members of a global *koinonia* of love. By being true
to ourselves as real human persons, organically part of the place we
live, we are also being "global." The reverse is also true: in order to
be genuinely "of our region" we must share a spirit and a love that
are all-embracing. In the Orthodox tradition a local church can be
independent as well as "catholic"—in the word's original meaning of
"all-inclusive," "universal," or, as used here, "global"—and complete. This is so because localness epitomizes the all-inclusiveness of
salvation and of the Church, which is universal in space and time.

Being "global" does not necessitate uniformity. Being universal is
a way of functioning together, not a process of conglomeration. It
does not mean gradually abandoning the most highly developed
cultural forms in any particular place and time for the sake of a universal and colorless uniformity. Localness is not antithetical to universality; on the contrary, it constitutes the vital underpinning of
universality. Seeing things from a global perspective has nothing to
do with the kind of indifference that ignores local life out of an utter
lack of interest in it. The real criterion is the degree to which local
forms genuinely express our common nature as human beings. A
Christian ascetic can be more global in outlook than one of our modern, homeless trekkers, who travels in order to escape the conditions
of life in a particular place but feels like a stranger everywhere. When
ascetics are filled with love for the world they are truly "global," for
they have become organically integrated within global society. Furthermore, they implicitly elevate the common "lump" from which all
of humanity was created—through their continual transcendence of
the self, through their prayers, and by making their lives part of the
Love that truly exists.

This way of seeing things inspires profound respect for local traditions, because it reveals the way that the beauty of humanity's common nature expresses itself in a particular place. The equilibrium
described here between global and regional perspectives offers us a
different way to perceive things, a way that also enables us to look
upon the local religious traditions of other peoples with respect and
to discover the universal meaning that lies hidden behind their
particular forms of expression.

History and a Sense of the Tragic: Reawakening Hope

The unique characteristics of place are not the only things that share in a global *koinonia* of love; there are also the distinct features of time—the different eras of history and the things they have created. Time is a special dimension of universality. It makes no sense to disdain the past for the sake of the future or vice versa. Time has unity and universality. Every human person belongs both to the past and to the future. Christian thought places particular significance on time. The final place of each one of us in the *koinonia* of love "in the age to come" will be determined by our behavior in the present.

History is humanity's extraordinary evolution toward its ultimate *koinonia* in God. There are, of course, many different schools of thought on the proper way to understand history, and many different theories and interpretations exist.[22] The Christian vision is composed of a host of secret, "hidden" realities whose existence we become aware of through our faith. Nevertheless, the daily "realities" that take place before our eyes, in their various forms, do not always correspond to these hidden truths. History is not so easy to interpret. The contradictions described above often create conflict in the Christian soul and sometimes lead to discouragement. Things do not always go as we think they should, nor are we always what we should be or would like to be. This sense of the tragic that pervades history is vividly present in the Christian mind and is epitomized in the symbol of the cross.

The reality of evil, which manifests itself in the various dark forces that operate within human souls and social formations, continually corrupts our purest efforts and aspirations. Even the Church—the "mystery" and the "locus" of salvation—is, in her historical and social persona, a splintered reality. There is no room for excessive optimism regarding the future of the world. The new is not necessarily better in any significant way, nor is it necessarily worse. The Christian viewpoint reveals the element of uncertainty that

---

[22]For an interesting though often schematic comparison of Islamic, Hindu, Christian, and Marxist views on history, see W. Cantwell Smith (note 1 above), 21-25. See also O. Cullmann, *Christus und die Zeit, die urchristliche Zeit und Geschichtsauffassung* (Zürich, 1946), English trans. *Christ and Time*, 2d ed. (London, 1965).

exists in the historical process and the ambivalent nature of many of the forces that are shaping modern history. Christianity does not oversimplify things by characterizing everything as either wonderful or diabolical. Our doubt sometimes reaches such intensity that only Jesus' sharp words are able to convey it: "Nevertheless, when the Son of man comes, will he find faith on earth?" (Lk 18:8). This is precisely why Christians constantly keep uppermost in their minds the reality of the cross: the reality of the passion, of outward failure, which is a permanent fact of life and a focus of the Church's contemplation. Patient acceptance of the cross is a way to embrace all of humanity's pain and the reality of life around the globe.

But this tragic dimension of the cross, which casts a shadow over our lives, is ceaselessly illuminated by an unswerving eschatological hope, a hope that is filled with the mystical light and power of the Resurrection, and this lends strength to the creative struggle of the faithful. Our final and all-embracing victory—world unity, in the present case—does not belong to the present. It is coming, however. Our foretaste of this victory in the present fills us with peace and fortitude. The reality of Christ transcends history.

It is this perception that reawakens hope. We can look beyond the actual course of events and foresee the possibility of a change in direction. This provides us with the driving impetus we need to transcend even the most inflexible institutions and situations. It cultivates a realistic approach that is dynamic. It turns anticipation into a form of action. Finally, it does all of this through a faith in miracles. By orienting ourselves toward the "impossible," we can achieve the possible.

Secular political movements also project their own "utopian" images—pictures of an ideal future society—through which they attempt to awaken the secret forces in people's souls that long to transcend the tangible. Whenever people are deprived of hope or become entrenched in rationalistic and legalistic forms of thought, they lose this vital vision because its very nerve center becomes deadened.

Christianity's Approach toward Other Religious Systems of Thought

If we are to promote the development of a global community we must have a genuine understanding of the most profound pursuits and intellectual accomplishments of other cultures. This includes understanding their religious achievements.[23]

An analysis of Christian theories on how to understand other religions will not be undertaken here. I believe that a satisfactory solution to this problem has not yet been found. We are still looking. We can say, however, that it is precisely at the moment when we make an effort to understand others that we come to know them better. Furthermore, in the course of such efforts to approach others we mystically experience God's love. In this way we discover, all of a sudden, that we are already evolving toward a *koinonia* of love.

Becoming a Neighbor to Every Human Being

If Christianity has taken a dubious and sometimes hostile attitude toward other religions as self-contained systems of thought, it has nevertheless maintained an absolutely positive attitude toward people who live within the context of other religions and ideologies. People who have different beliefs never lose the basic attributes of their spiritual identity: they never cease to be "children of God," created "in God's image," and hence our brothers and sisters. God is the Father of us all. Consequently, a spontaneous and sincere openness to making contact with and serving all human beings, all peoples, without expecting anything whatsoever in return, is the criterion by which the true Christian is to be measured. The old conception of a "neighbor" that prevailed in the Old Testament was expanded to an unimaginable degree in the New Testament. In one of the places where Christ speaks about the limitless, spontaneous love that expresses itself in action, he presents the Samaritan, a heretic, as a model for the rest of us. In this parable Jesus not only demolishes the old religious concept of "neighbor," but turns the static question

[23]When this essay was first published it included a paragraph here that has been omitted in this version, since chapter 5 of the present volume, "A Theological Approach to Understanding Other Religions," deals with this subject in greater detail.

"who is my neighbor?" completely upside down, with a new, dynamic question: "Which of these three, do you think, proved neighbor to the man who fell among the robbers?" (Lk 10:36). Proving oneself to be a neighbor to any human being whatsoever, regardless of his race, religion, or language, and especially in his hour of need, is the obligation of every faithful Christian.

Offering spontaneous, brotherly love to all our "neighbors," for no other reason than the simple fact they are human beings, is acknowledged as Christianity's quintessential message. How do we respond, therefore, to the question, "Should we cooperate with individuals from other religious and ideological backgrounds?" When the purpose is to serve the entire human family by promoting justice, equality, freedom, respect for the human personality, peace, and the welfare of one's people and nation, our answer must clearly be "yes."

The Common Duty of All Religions

Although cooperation often proves difficult, we must not allow it to be thwarted by the fact that we have different conceptions about the meaning of history, the purpose of human beings, and humanity's ultimate hopes. We can very well walk a large part of the way together. Despite our different responses to major issues, such as pain, death, the meaning of existence, and the nature of human society, the fact remains that we grieve and die, laugh and weep, become discouraged and continue to hope—together. While we must not underestimate the seriousness of our differences, neither are we permitted to ignore the points where we agree or to take no interest in securing a place for religion in today's world—a place for the certainty that there are experiences and capabilities that are "unworldly," i.e., that lie beyond our everyday existence.[24] There are things that we, as bearers of this religious experience, can do.

[24]From the many studies that have pointed to the common spiritual values inherent in different religions, we note the following: W.C. Smith, *The Faith of Other Men* (New York, 1972); H. Dumoulin, *Christlicher Dialog mit Asien* (München, 1970); H.J. Singh, ed., *Inter-Religious Dialogue* (Bangalore, 1967); R.S. Misra, "Religion, Reality and Truth," *Bulletin,* Secretariatus pro non Christianis 8 (1973): 17-29; and P. Rossano, "The Theo-

Together we can present the "vertical" dimension of existence, living as we do at a time when the accomplishments of material culture, with its emphasis on objectifying the truth, threaten to confine the human race within the "horizontal" dimension of life, where there is no height or depth.

We can demonstrate that the solution to the problem of evil cannot be limited to improving society externally, but must confront the root of evil's existence, which lies deep in the abyss of human selfishness.

Material culture, by cultivating individualism, arrogance, and greed, has led us into a dead end. We can remind people that the way to achieve spiritual equilibrium is not to subordinate nature to the desires of the individual, but to subdue our own, individual desires—through renunciation, asceticism, and purification of the self. In short, we can present people with our basic faith in Something—or rather, in Someone—who exists beyond our earthly and visible reality. We can offer them the experience that has been garnered through centuries of seeking the divine and the holy.

"Bearing Witness" and "Martyrdom"

This feeling that faithful Christians have of being united with all of humanity—the spontaneous love they feel for the specific individuals they meet in the course of their lives—makes them want to tell every one of their "neighbors" about this supreme good they have discovered. God's gifts cannot be selfishly withheld. They must be made available to all. Every one of God's actions, whether it involves an entire people or only an individual, concerns humanity as a whole, just as an inoculation, although administered at one particular point on the body, is intended to benefit the entire body. Woe to the individual or the nation that tries to keep God's treasures exclusively for itself. They are to be judged as guilty as any embezzler who steals what belongs to others. In the end they will lose what they have been given.

logical Problem of the Religions," *Bulletin,* Secretariatus pro non Christianis 9 (1974): 164-73.

This does not mean, however, that Christians are permitted to
spread their spiritual message by coercion or, even worse, to use it
as a pretext for achieving other political or economic goals. Their
message cannot be imposed on others, but must be presented as
simple testimony about something we are certain of because we
have experienced it. In the early centuries, Christians commonly
spoke of "bearing witness" and of "martyrdom." The words used in
the original Greek texts are *martyria* (pronounced *mar-teer-EE-a*)
and *martyrio* (*mar-TEER-ee-o*), respectively, and they referred to
testimony offered by people who were certain of the truth of what
they said because they had personally witnessed it with their own
eyes or heard it with their own ears. Moreover, such testimony
was offered at the cost of one's life, as a personal sacrifice, through
"martyrdom."

It is regrettable that in many countries during the past few centuries the meaning of the word "mission" has been so misunder-
stood, due the attitude of conquest that missionary efforts have
taken on at various times.[25] The ideal of spreading the gospel in the
world was exploited to a large extent by the governments of great
powers in their desire to obtain colonies. The idea of Christian

[25]On the issue of the character of Christian missionary efforts since the Second
World War and their new orientation, see K.B. Bridston, *Shock and Renewal: The Christ-
ian Mission Enters a New Era* (New York, 1955); R.P. Beaver, *The Christian World Mission:
A Reconsideration* (Calcutta, 1957); S. Neill, *The Unfinished Task* (London, 1957); J.S.
Stewart, *Thine Is the Kingdom* (New York, 1957); L. Newbigin, *One Body, One Gospel, One
World: The Christian Mission Today* (London 1958); W. Freytag, "Changes in the Patterns
of Western Missions," *International Review of Missions* 47 (1958): 163-70; and Ch.W. Forman, "The World Mission: New Facts Shatter Old Patterns—The Challenge to Christian
Exclusiveness," *Religion in Life* (Nashville, CT, Summer 1958): 352-61. There is also
important material in the following three collections of essays: J. Hermelink, H.J. Mar-
gull, eds., *Basileia: Walter Freytag zum 60 Geburtstage* (Stuttgart, 1959); *History's Lessons
for Tomorrow's Mission: Milestones in the History of Missionary Thinking* (Geneva, 1960);
and G.H. Anderson, ed., *The Theology of the Christian Mission* (New York, 1961). See also
T. Ohm, *Machet zu Jüngern alle Völker* (Freiburg, 1962); J. Blauw, *The Missionary Nature
of the Church* (London, 1962); D.T. Niles, *Upon the Earth* (London, 1962); G.F. Vicedom,
Die christliche Mission in der Entscheidung, in the series Christus und die Welt 11 (Bad
Salzuflen, 1963); A. Yannoulatos, "The Purpose and Motive of Mission—From an Orthodox Point of View," *International Review of Missions* 54 (1965): 298-307; and M.M.
Thomas, "The Post-Colonial Crisis in Mission: A Comment," *Religion and Society* 18
(1971): 64-70.

mission has consequently been denigrated throughout Asia and Africa as a means of furthering the political ambitions and economic interests of the peoples of Western Europe and North America. With the exception of Russia, which endeavored to spread Christianity throughout its vast empire and even somewhat beyond its own borders, the Orthodox churches did not share in the visions and designs of western Christianity. Living as they did under the heel of states with other official religions—in Asia Minor, Egypt, and the Balkans—they found themselves once again under the same conditions as the early Church, with persecutions and martyrdoms. For this reason the Orthodox are unable to share the "guilt feelings" or pronouncements of regret on the part of certain Christians in the west for the colonial policies of Christianity in general—pronouncements that many representatives of other faiths often exploit. The Orthodox feel that socially and politically they are among those peoples that have been oppressed by other religions and creeds and do not belong to the side of the oppressors.

The colonial policies of the so-called "Christian" nations do not represent "the Christian position" but a political and national stance that used Christianity as a disguise and as a means to an end. We must not confuse Christian principles with specific groups of individuals who invoke Christianity at the same time that they reject it in practice. No one has ever repudiated "justice" because a few ex officio servants of justice, such as judges, have at times violated and betrayed her, nor has anyone ever considered repudiating motherhood because more than a few mothers have proved unfit. Sadly to say, the colonial-type "missionary crusade," in all its forms, is a rejection of Christ's spiritual *kenosis*. On the other hand, a passive Christianity, one that is indifferent to other peoples, would be every bit as much a rejection of Christ—insipid as well as impotent. Maintaining that all people have the right to share in the world's good things but at the same time excluding religion from these is a blatant contradiction. The deep spiritual anxiety from which humankind suffers cannot be ignored. Every single thing that the human race possesses must be made available to all, and all human beings must be absolutely free to make their own choices.

~ • ~

I have avoided using the kind of polite but vague language that would gloss over the things that make Christianity different because I believe that those participating in an international interfaith conference such as this can more easily become acquainted with and understand one another when the speakers formulate their positions as clearly as possible. This truthful approach is at bottom a loving approach, one that promotes a *koinonia* of love. The most important thing is not for Christians to keep silent about our most profound experiences, but for us to make a genuine and conscientious effort to be what we profess to be. People have often found us unlikable because what we say, what we believe, and what we do are different. We have a duty to live out conscientiously the mystery of our faith— at the heart of which lies the rediscovery of the one, universal and divine *koinonia*—so that we can offer, without seeking anything in return or any worldly reward, the kind of genuine love that reveals the life of the trinitarian God. The Christian Church must offer whatever it has and whatever it is with humility, sincerity, and deep respect for all others, not only in order to help humanity find global harmony but primarily to help orient humanity toward a higher plane of existence: toward a global *koinonia* of love.

~ 2 ~

Orthodoxy and Human Rights

ON THE UNIVERSAL DECLARATION OF HUMAN RIGHTS
AND THE GREEK ORTHODOX TRADITION*

A ny coherent consideration of the "Rights of Man" or "human rights" necessarily involves a broader notion of what man is. The question "what is a human being?" holds a central place in religious inquiry in general, and particularly in Christian thought. It is clear that religious conscience and faith play a decisive role, both directly and indirectly, in the formation of views on human rights and in people's willingness to accept these views. International declarations on human rights and the specific language employed to discuss this issue are of course recent phenomena. Nevertheless, church history and Orthodox theological thought have a valuable contribution to make regarding the substantive issues involved.

SOME GENERAL OBSERVATIONS ON
EXISTING HUMAN RIGHTS DECLARATIONS
Some Ambiguity in the Concept

An examination of the relevant declarations, international agreements, and other documents concerning human rights reveals a

*This chapter was first delivered at a conference of specialists organized by UNESCO in Bangkok on December 3-7, 1979, to discuss "The Position of Human Rights in Religious and Political Traditions around the World." The second and third sections of the paper were published under the title "Eastern Orthodoxy and Human Rights" in IRM 73 (1984): 454-66, a condensed version of which later appeared under the title "Human Rights in the Orthodox Church" in the anthology Conscience and Liberty, International Journal of Religious Freedom, 4th Year, 2:8 (1992): 75-79 , and in French as "Les droits de l'homme dans l'Eglise orthodoxe" in Conscience et liberté 46, 2me semestre (Berne, 1993): 70-77.

certain fluidity in the way the concept "human rights" is understood. The constant addition of new definitions has only increased this lack of clarity.

When the documents in question are arranged chronologically, three successive strata can be distinguished. The first contains the original founding documents that have served as the basis for all such declarations, from the oldest to the most recent; they express faith in individual freedom, in equality for all without exception, and in human dignity. The second stratum consists of documents that enumerate specific bourgeois political rights, placing emphasis on freedom of conscience, freedom of thought, freedom of speech, freedom of the press, the right of all citizens to run for public office, the inviolable right to private property, the right to safety of one's person, and the distinction between public office and popular sovereignty. Documents in the third group are the most recent and contain exhaustive definitions of economic, social, and political human rights.

The original concern of human rights declarations was to protect citizens from the arbitrary use of power by the state. In subsequent documents, however, this concern was extended to include the abuse of authority by other groups or individuals that possess power.

For the purposes of the present discussion, we will consider the Universal Declaration of Human Rights as our main document.[1] This declaration is the mature fruit of a long quest and a long history of social and political turmoil, starting with the American declarations of 1776 and the Declaration of the Rights of Man and of the Citizen by the French National Assembly in 1789. The scope and perspective of the Universal Declaration are clearly global, and it has served as the core for the further elaboration of human rights in subsequent documents.[2]

[1]Adopted by the United Nations General Assembly in resolution 217A (III) on December 10, 1948.

[2]See the International Covenant on Economic, Social, and Cultural Rights, which was adopted on December 16, 1966, and put into force on January 3, 1976; see also the International Covenant on Civil and Political Rights of the United Nations (1966) and the related Optional Protocol to the International Covenant on Civil and Political Rights, both of which were adopted on December 16, 1966, and put into force on March 23, 1976. Other global treaties have subsequently been entered into under the aegis of the

Orthodox thought is not always in full agreement with every-thing that has been characterized from time to time as "human rights." On the basic core concepts—freedom, equality, and human dignity—there is of course immediate agreement and absolute affir-mation. Most of the ideas expressed about human rights are accepted by Orthodox thinking as corollaries of its own views on humanity. There are a good number of issues, however, on which Orthodox thought prefers not to take a stand, allowing them to remain open questions, within the realm of purely human speculation.

When discussing what Orthodox thinking agrees with and what it has misgivings about, we must not forget that the perspective of human rights declarations and the perspective of religion start out from different premises. The declarations under discussion seek to regulate human life based on the view that people are political beings and are therefore subject to the power that belongs to Caesar; human rights declarations are concerned with the relationship that exists between the individual and the state. For the Orthodox Church, however, "Render therefore to Caesar the things that are Caesar's, and to God the things that are God's" (Mt 22:21) delineates a clear boundary, distinguishing the sphere of religion from the sphere of the state. Christian faith starts and ends with God. Orthodoxy has never established or adopted a sociopolitical system, as Islam, for instance, has attempted to do; it has never made natural institutions

United Nations. The most important of these are the Covenant against Discrimination in Education (1960) and the International Convention on the Elimination of All Forms of Racial Discrimination, which was adopted in 1965 and has been in force since 1969. For additional information on this subject, see Egon Schwelb, "Human Rights," *Encyclope-dia Britannica*, Macropaedia, Knowledge in Depth, 8:1183-89. In 1968, in celebration of the International Year for Human Rights and the Conference on Human Rights, the United Nations published a collection of all declarations, agreements, and recommenda-tions that it had adopted on this subject as of December 31, 1966. Revised editions were published in 1973 and 1978, on the twenty-fifth and thirtieth anniversaries of the origi-nal 1948 declaration. Documents of special importance with regard to Europe include the European Convention on Human Rights, entered into by the members of the Coun-cil of Europe in 1950, and the five supplementary protocols that followed it, along with the creation of two important bodies: the European Commission of Human Rights and the European Court of Human Rights. See also the Final Act adopted by the Conference on Security and Cooperation in Europe (Helsinki, 1975). For additional bibliography on this subject see note 23 below.

absolute. It has sought and continues to seek in every instance to place such institutions within the context of our life in Christ and in the Holy Spirit.

There is also another clear difference in the way declarations and religion seek to achieve their respective aims, as well as in the profundity of those aims. Declarations seek to impose their views through legal and political forms of coercion, whereas the Christian message addresses itself to people's way of thinking and to their conscience, using persuasion and faith. Declarations basically stress outward compliance, while the gospel insists on inner acceptance, on spiritual rebirth, and on transformation. Any attempt to consider human rights from an Orthodox point of view must therefore maintain a clear sense of the differences between these two perspectives.

The Question of Basic Premises

The official volume published for the thirtieth anniversary of the Universal Declaration of Human Rights states:

> The roots of this concern can be found in the humanistic traditions of the Renaissance; in the struggle for self-determination, independence and equality that has taken place and continues to take place in many parts of the world; in the philosophical ideas of people like the Englishman John Locke, the Frenchman Jean-Jacques Rousseau, the American Thomas Jefferson, the German Karl Marx, and the Russian Lenin; as well as in the influence of such events as the signing of the Magna Carta by King John of England in 1215, the adoption of Habeas Corpus by the English parliament in 1679, the issuing of the Declaration of Independence by representatives of the thirteen northern American colonies in 1776, the adoption of the Declaration of the Rights of Man and of the Citizen by the French National Assembly in 1789, and the publication of the Communist Manifesto in 1848.[3]

[3]Louis B. Sohn, *Human Rights, 1948-1978: Changing Perceptions: A Wingspread Conference on Human Rights Commemorating the 30th Anniversary of the Universal Declara-*

Several reservations regarding the full historical accuracy of the wording in the above paragraph might justifiably be expressed. First of all, it would be useful to remind ourselves that the celebrated Magna Carta was not so much a victory for the recognition of people's rights as it was a successful effort of the barons to secure their own rights in opposition to the power of the king. Furthermore, although it is generally believed that the articles in the Declaration of the Rights of Man and of the Citizen in the French Revolution of 1789 express universal truths, at bottom they reflect the interests of the bourgeois class that drafted them. This is precisely the reason why the right to hold private property was presented as inalienable; moreover, the various provisions of the declaration also sought to make it possible for members of the middle class to secure key positions in society. Such considerations, of course, do not mean that we should underestimate the importance that this basic document has had in the subsequent process of social change.

The roots from which the "tree" of human rights has sprung are clearly older and more complex than the documents that are usually mentioned. These roots are connected to religious beliefs and basic concepts found in the major religions. To be more specific, the western world indisputably owes a great deal to the gospel, and it was the spirit of inquiry inspired by Greek thought that enabled the seeds of the gospel to grow during the Renaissance. Even at those points that run counter to Christian principles, human rights documents presuppose the Christian legacy, which is not only a system of thought and a worldview that took shape through the contributions of the Christian and Greek spirit, but also a tradition of self-criticism and repentance.

With emphasis on the "sacred rights of people and citizens," the French Revolution formulated its principles "in the presence of the Supreme Being and in anticipation of his blessing and his grace." Subsequent declarations were more neutral and avoided reference to a superhuman principle. The concept of human autonomy began to emerge more clearly, and the entire structure became grounded on

tion of Human Rights, Convened by the Commission to Study the Organization of Peace in Cooperation with the Johnson Foundation (Racine, Wis.: Johnson Foundation, 1978).

natural law. Human rationality was posed as the foundation, and logic itself at times became deified. This is the point at which Christian thought first intervenes: Are human rights simply and merely an outcome of human rationality, or are they innate to the human personality?[4]

A questionable ideology lies hidden behind the well-known declarations on human rights. The predominant view is that people are autonomous beings capable of developing on their own, primarily by using their intellect and their inner abilities. This theoretical basis for human rights is really quite simplistic, as it is based on a conception of humanity that is indifferent to the parameters of the human mystery. This is a point to which it will presently be necessary to return in greater detail. For the moment, however, we limit ourselves to the observation that the tragic events of our era demonstrate the naiveté of this attempt to base the entire edifice of human rights on logic pure and simple. The deification of human rationality arose as a substitute for faith in God. It did not take long, however, for doubt in logic itself to succeed this denial of the living God. The tyranny of the Absurd began its ascent soon thereafter.

Simplistic Overoptimism

When we read between the lines of human rights declarations, a rather glib overoptimism can be found regarding human nature. In contrast, recent decades have contributed to a deeper awareness of human savagery, an awareness that often leads to despair. Humanity's tragic aspect and contradictory nature are becoming increasingly more apparent as a result of historical events. Daily life around us and within us points to the power wielded by transgression—or,

---

[4]No systematic doctrine regarding natural law was ever developed in Orthodox theology; natural law is viewed neither in a positive light, as it is in Roman Catholic theology, nor negatively, as it is by the majority of Protestants. In general, Orthodoxy accepts the existence of natural moral law (consistent with Rom 2:14), but avoids any attempt to make natural institutions, including natural law, absolute or autonomous, seeking instead to place them within the wider context of Christian doctrine on humanity and its salvation. See D.I. Evrygenes, "Human Rights, Written Law, and Natural Law" (in Greek), *Armenopoulos* (1967): 3-11; and N. Georgopoulou-Nikolakakou, *Natural Law: A Historical-Critical View of the Problem* (in Greek) (Athens, 1976).

to use Christian terminology, what we call sin. All people take every opportunity to speak about human rights, and almost all, when they can, violate them. Recognizing human rights in theory is not enough. What we lack is not knowledge, but the will. This is why there is greater discouragement today rather than enthusiasm regarding declarations on human rights. We have reached the point where the strong have an implicit "right" to violate the rights of the weak.

The great danger of human rights violations in our modern, polymorphous society does not come only from the state, from which the various declarations attempt to protect the individual; it also comes from the various non-state forms that power takes, trampling on human rights in a variety of ways. As Christianity sees it, there is an inherent conflict in human existence; Christianity still takes as its basic point of view the tragedy of human sin and the possibility that it can be overcome.

A Onesidedness That Must Be Brought into Balance

It is understandable that our original human rights declarations should place exclusive emphasis on rights, without coupling or correlating these to human obligations; these documents were written during times of revolution against state power and sought to protect citizens from the arbitrary use of that power. In the more sober climate of today's global perspective, however, this onesidedness will have to be redressed. The separation of rights from their corresponding obligations threatens to destroy human rights themselves, because equilibrium has been lost. Accepting responsibility for one's actions is as fundamental to human existence and human dignity as being able to claim one's rights. A onesided emphasis on rights can result in unhealthy individualism and also makes it easier for those rights to be abused. It is precisely in order to defend rights that responsibility and duty must also be stressed.

It is also clear that individual rights must be brought into harmony with social rights. It is not correct to pose the issue merely as one of "my rights" or "your rights" exclusively, but to make common reference to both. The proper relationship between these two is defined in the gospel with the words, "You shall love your neighbor as yourself" (Mk 12:31); for the ultimate goal is finding a way to transcend "you" and "I" so that we can rise to a "communion of persons" (*koinonia prosopon* in Greek).

On this point Christians share a central Indian experience, beautifully expressed by Mahatma Gandhi in his reply to J. Huxley, Director General of UNESCO, in 1947:

> I learnt from my illiterate but wise mother that all rights to be deserved and preserved came from duty well done. Thus the very right to live accrues to us only when we do the duty of citizenship of the world.[5]

Responsibility remains a basic component of human dignity.

The Vagueness and Ambiguity of Fundamental Terms

The preamble to the Universal Declaration speaks of "faith in fundamental human rights, in the dignity and worth of the human person." Article 29 alludes to "the free and full development" of the "personality" and calls for "meeting the just requirements of morality, public order, and the general welfare in a democratic society." Within the formal legal framework of the declaration, such phrases are unquestionable opportunities to broaden the purview of the concept of the human personality. It is clear, however, that such fundamental terms as "morality," "democratic society," and "personality" remain philosophically vague and ambiguous.

It is understandable, of course, that the authors of such a document, which hopes to gain general acceptance from people and societies with different religious views, would be compelled to avoid any explicit references to questions regarding humanity's origin, nature, and destiny. Nevertheless, although the expediency of this approach is justifiable, it does not change the fact that in the end the Universal Declaration is anthropologically vague.

---

[5]*Human Rights* (in Greek), an anthology of texts by K. Tsatsos, M. Gandhi, J. Maritain, et al. (Athens: Euthyni, 1977), 29.

In general, Orthodox thought considers the current discussion on human rights to be extremely important, but ultimately sees it as the prelude to a discussion of humanity's much more intrinsic "rights." After all the searching and all the effort to arrive at a definition of human rights, the underlying questions still remain: "Where do human rights begin, where do they end, and what is their ultimate purpose?" Declarations remain confined to descriptive legal definitions of human rights; at the same time, however, they reflect hope and express a moral judgment.

In an era such as ours, in which there is a great diversity of ideological views, it will clearly be impossible to reach philosophical and religious agreement on these immense issues. Let us simply note here that to the Orthodox way of thinking, which is the subject at hand, the formulations that have been put into writing in existing declarations constitute a starting point, but do not safeguard human dignity from becoming enslaved to human egotism, which is the cruelest of all the powers that must be abolished; nor do they safeguard human dignity from the complex factors that operate in our modern technological society's multiform and impersonal structures. This should stand as a warning of the utmost significance, lest we deceive ourselves into believing that the acceptance of human rights declarations is enough to safeguard human dignity.

～ • ～

It is obvious that the pluralistic society in which we live today must seek a common basis for agreement. We need to remain vividly aware, however, that at the very moment when compromises are reached for the purpose of achieving consensus, something of the universal and ultimate truth about the human mystery is lost. Therefore, while remaining faithful and dedicated to human rights, we must also remain open to another realm, the one that concerns those more profound and essential human rights that no legal declaration can encompass. This is precisely the point at which the timeliness of religion continues to be found.

An Outline of Orthodox Thought on the Human Condition and Its Relationship to Fundamental Human Rights

In order to clarify the conception of humanity on which Orthodox thought is based, let me briefly describe some basic features of Orthodox Christian anthropology, i.e., the Orthodox understanding of humanity's origin, nature, and purpose. In doing so, however, it is not my intention to attempt to impose these views on the texts of international documents. My purpose, rather, is simply to offer a carefully considered outline of fundamental Christian beliefs that inevitably influence our attitudes toward and our ideas about human rights.

A Summary of Orthodox Anthropology [6]

The cornerstone of Christian anthropology remains the belief that God made Adam "in the image of God" (Gen 5:1). Every subsequent biblical view of humanity is built upon this foundation. The New Testament also stresses that the human race is a divine creation (Mt 19:4, Acts 17:28) made in God's image (Col 3:10) and in his likeness (Jas 3:9). God is revealed not only as a Supreme Being but as a *personal* God: an existence whose essence is unity; a sharing between persons; a unity in three and a trinity in one; a perfect *koinonia agapes* (communion of love). "Likeness" to God is offered to human beings as a possibility, not as an accomplished fact. It is ultimately achieved through the action of the Holy Spirit.

The entire human race is descended from the first human pair that God created; all human beings, regardless of their race, color, language, or education, are therefore endowed with the dignity of this divine origin. While western thinking has stressed the mind, the intellect, and the will as the most salient features of this divine image,

[6]As explained in the prologue to the present volume, a number of fundamental theological truths reappear, usually expressed in different ways, throughout the book's various essays, all of which were originally addressed to different audiences. These theological truths recur because they constitute the theoretical underpinning of the Orthodox point of view. In order not to disturb the structure and autonomy of each essay, I have chosen to leave them all in their original form.

eastern theology has placed greater emphasis on freedom and love, taking as its point of reference the love and communion—in freedom and harmony—between the persons of the Holy Trinity.

God is not simply our creator, however; he is also the Father of all humankind. This view is repeatedly emphasized in the New Testament (Mt 6:9, 23:9 and Rom 1:7 are some examples) and is directly related to the conviction that all people, without exception, are God's children and are therefore brothers and sisters. The belief that all human beings share a common origin in God's creative energy is vividly underscored by the apostle Paul on the Areopagus in Athens: "The God who made the world and everything in it . . . made from one [blood] every nation of men" (Acts 17:24, 26). All humanity is thus one great, undivided and unified whole, the core of whose existence is the living trinitarian God: "One God and father of us all, who is above all and through all and in all" (Eph 4:6).

It is not only their common origin that binds human beings together into a single family; they are also bound together by their common mission in life. The purpose of their existence is to realize their God-given potential and approach the state of being "in his likeness." Their purpose is to raise themselves from a condition of mere biological coexistence to a state of true communion between persons, in harmony with all creatures and all of creation, through the selfless love that is found in the Holy Trinity, which is the supreme *koinonia agapes* and the model for our lives.

Furthermore, in addition to this common origin and purpose, there is another essential feature that makes humanity homogeneous: all human beings have participated in the same unfortunate misadventure, and all share in the same guilt. At the outset of human history, human beings chose not to orient themselves toward the trinitarian God; that is, they chose not to pursue their own "deification," which is the purpose of their existence and which is realized by sharing in the communion of love that exists among the three divine persons of the Holy Trinity. Instead, human beings became attached to their own individual egos, rejected God's love, and sought to achieve "deification" based on their own criteria and on the promptings of the "devil" ("and you will be like God," Gen 3:5).

This misadventure of the human race is linked to the fact that human beings were endowed with freedom as an essential attribute. They were even free to reject unselfish love, which they did, only to become imprisoned in their own egotistical self-love. Nevertheless, despite this self-imposed exile, they still possess the identity and the heritage of their divine origin, as well as their longing for the paradise they lost.

Orthodox thought recognizes that opposing forces operate within human history, not only in general but also in the history of each human being. One can see this in the natural world as well, where on the one hand an extraordinary harmony bears witness to divine agency and, on the other hand, there exists a parasitic force that gives rise to every possible form of disruption and disharmony.

This atmosphere of gloom was transcended when a decisive event occurred within human history, once again at the initiative of the trinitarian God: through a supreme act of love "the Word became flesh and dwelt among us, full of grace and truth" (Jn 1:14). The incarnation of the Son offered humanity a new way for the human person to advance toward "communion" with the trinitarian God, and also with other human beings, who are images of God. Preaching this message has been the decisive contribution of the Christian gospel.

Fundamental Rights

In the Orthodox view, any elaboration of the principles of dignity, equality and freedom must be based on the theological fundamentals roughly outlined above.

Human dignity is not some vague kind of civic pride but arises from the certainty that each human being is indeed a sacred person, the creation of a personal God. Human dignity has nothing to do with egotistical arrogance but is associated with an awareness of human greatness and its limitations. Dignity is marked by discretion, consideration, and respect for others. Moreover, this concept of dignity is not merely theoretical but has been experienced by thousands of people: the ranks of the Church's saints, who have served as models to guide the faithful and as a source of blessing for all humanity.[7]

Freedom is one of Christianity's most central ideas. As Berdyaev aptly summarizes, "The idea of freedom is one of the leading ideas of Christianity. Without it the creation of the world, the Fall, and Redemption are incomprehensible, and the phenomenon of faith remains inexplicable. Without freedom there can be no theodicy and the whole world-process becomes nonsense."[8] This message of freedom recurs in the New Testament in a variety of contexts (Mt 17:26; Jn 8:32, 36; 2 Cor 3:17; Gal 5:1-13). The Greek Fathers of the Church repeatedly expound the truth that a free God created free human beings, who are therefore responsible for their actions.[9] Taking responsibility is linked to human dignity.

There has certainly been no lack of Christians who, in the course of time, have sought to restrict this freedom, allegedly in the interests of maintaining social order. In the end, however, the Christian conscience has always rejected them.

It is within this context that certainty arises regarding human equality. A well-known pronouncement in the New Testament states, "Here there cannot be Greek and Jew . . . barbarian, Scythian, slave, free man, but Christ is all, and in all" (Col 3:11). There is also the conviction that through the incarnation of the Son and Word of God, and through our salvation in Christ, the entire human race has been elevated.

---

[7]K.E. Tsiropoulos, "A Theological Overview of Basic Human Rights" in *Human Rights* (in Greek) (Athens, 1977), 154-60; and *Human Dignity* (in Greek) (Athens, 1967).

[8]Nicholas Berdyaev, *Freedom and the Spirit* (Russian title *Dukh i realnost*, 1927), 9th ed. (London, 1948), 119.

[9]According to St Gregory the Theologian, this freedom is not the same as license, but is limited by the divine commandments: "From the beginning the Creator allowed human beings their freedom and a free will; they were bound only by the law of his commandment" (*Orations* 14.25 ["On Caring for the Poor"], PG 35:892A); and "Freedom and wealth were the mere observance of his commandment" (ibid., 892AB). Gregory of Nyssa elucidates: "Freedom means being one's own master and ruling oneself; this is the gift that God granted to us from the beginning" (*On the Soul and Resurrection*, PG 46:101CD); and "the most excellent and precious of all goods" to be given as a gift by God was "the gift implied in being his own master, and having a free will" (*The Great Catechism* 5, PG 45:24C [trans. NPF, 2d ser., vol. 5]). Abuse of this gift led the human race to the fall. See also A. Marinos, *Religious Freedom* (in Greek) (Athens, 1972).

These truths are immediately discernible in the Church's liturgical practice. In Orthodox Christian worship all people, regardless of social status, class, race, or nationality, stand as equals before God, and in his presence everyone has the same value.

These views, which were groundbreaking ideas in the course of world history, have a central place in the teaching of the Fathers, who persistently speak about human equality: about *homotimia* (that all people have equal value) and *isotimia* (that all are entitled to equal privileges).[10] Equality, in their view, lies at the very essence of human nature, and they are unconditional when they call any departure from equality a form of injustice.[11]

There is another human right that has never been included in any rights charter, but which is constantly singled out in Christian thought: the right to love and to be loved. This is seen as the basic defining characteristic of a human being, because human beings are complete only when they love and are loved. God himself, who loves humanity to a degree that the human mind can only struggle to fathom, gave us this right in a most awe-inspiring fashion. Everything that has been said above is expressed in all its organic and dynamic fulness in the Christian pronouncement of God's love for humanity and humanity's love for God and for all the creatures that he created "in his image." This is the light that illuminates our concern for human dignity and equality; this is the source from which we draw the strength and inspiration that is needed to make human dignity and equality a reality.

With this love, which could be called a sixth sense, the faithful Christian uncovers the deeper reality in things and sees each and every human being as he or she really is: a creation of God, an image of God, a child of God, our sister or our brother. The freedom found in Christian love is a tremendously powerful force. It is not restricted by what other people believe, nor can any obstacle inhibit its initiative.

---

[10]Cf. Basil the Great, *On the Holy Spirit* 20, PG 32:160C-161D.

[11]For related patristic views, see below in chapter 6: "The Dynamic of Universal and Continuous Change." Previous centuries have adopted the church fathers' ideas concerning dignity, equality, and freedom.

The knowledge that millions of people do not accept the theological premises held by Christians does not lessen the importance that these premises have for the Christian conscience as the basis of our respect for human rights.[12] The fact that others hold views different from our own in no way prevents us from respecting their freedom to believe as they wish, nor does it raise the slightest doubt in our minds that they fully possess the equality and rights that are inherent in human existence, because human existence, for us at least, has been indelibly imprinted with the image of God.

HUMAN RIGHTS IN THE HISTORY OF THE ORTHODOX CHURCH

We can distinguish four distinct periods in the history of our Church with regard to the subject at hand.

The First Three Centuries of Christianity

The first period covers the first three centuries of Christianity, when the Church, far from being in a position to determine the relationship between citizen and state, was itself being persecuted. Immersed in the eschatological perspective of the gospel's message, the Christians of this period were unanimous in their insistence upon the value of every human being and upon humanity's inalienable right to equality, freedom, dignity, and brotherhood. Moreover,

---

[12]Agnostics, for example, refuse to discuss any views of this kind; followers of the Buddhist tradition operate within a completely different system of thought, which makes no reference to God or to sin and which is totally optimistic regarding the ability of human beings to achieve "enlightenment" through their own powers. Certain schools of Hinduism, by amending the Brahman-Atman equation within their own conceptual system, would readily accept the transcendental principle of a sacred spark in human existence that eventually returns to the absolute. In certain religious forms found among peoples living in a state of nature (in Africa, Oceania, etc.) it is possible to detect some vague hints of similar ideas, but in general neither immediate agreement nor emphatic denial emerges. As far as Islam and Judaism are concerned, although they share the belief that Adam was created by God and that all human beings have their origin in the first human pair, they reject every idea concerning the Trinity, God the Father, and the redeeming work of Christ. See A. Yannoulatos, *Islam* (Athens, 1976), 135-37.

the early Christians condemned any violation of these rights, as can be seen in their thought, their way of life, and their martyrdom. No specific social doctrine, however, was promoted. The Church had not come into being as a social or political revolt, but in order to announce the kingdom of God.

The Byzantine Period

The second phase, from the fourth to the fifteenth centuries, is the era when Christianity became the official state religion. The previously mentioned principles continued to be preached publicly during this period by the great teachers of the Church, who insisted upon the value, freedom, and equality of all human beings. Although these leaders of the Church did not wield any political power, they strove to mold the conscience of the faithful in accordance with Christian principles.[13]

In Byzantium, as in the Roman empire before it, legislative power was vested in the emperors. The Church never became a state authority, nor did its leaders ever obtain state power. The clergy and the monks preserved the doctrines of the gospel intact and diligently cultivated the scripture's teaching about humanity, revealing particular sensitivity in their respect for every human person.

The Byzantine emperors had the task of organizing and unifying a vast empire that included a variety of nationalities and an array of religious traditions. Faced with the constant danger of fragmentation, the emperors tried to ensure unity and peace by imposing on the entire state the religion they believed to be superior. The phrase "whoever would follow me," which is a basic, founding principle of Christianity, was very often forgotten or ignored. Byzantine rulers did not always respect religious freedom. There were certainly great Fathers of the Church, such as St Gregory of Nazianzus and others, who protested, but the state's general policy was to root out idolatry by force. Religious tolerance was shown only toward the Jewish religion, whose followers were granted a number of prerogatives.

---

[13]For relevant texts, see below in chapter 6, "The Dynamic of Universal and Continuous Change."

To be sure, the denial of religious freedom—which was accompanied by the seizure of movable and unmovable property—is not one of the most savory chapters in Byzantine history. As is usually the case in history, principles that were admirable in theory were not put into practice. Even today, states that profess to defend human rights do not hesitate to violate them in the name of expediency and other priorities. Most importantly, however, let us not forget that every historical period must be assessed within its own specific cultural context. Judged on the basis of the barbaric customs of its time, Byzantium unquestionably raised the level of human life.

The Period of Turkish Domination

In the third period, which began with the fall of Byzantium in 1453 and lasted until the middle of the nineteenth century, the Orthodox Christians of Asia Minor and the Balkan peninsula found themselves under the oppression of a non-Christian state. During this period the Church not only acted as an advocate of human rights for the subjugated peoples but also defended and consoled them when those rights were cruelly violated. For despite the special privileges that Mehmet the Conqueror had granted the subjugated Christian population in 1454, Ottoman religious fanaticism would periodically erupt, resulting in the constant violation of Christians' basic human rights: cruel disregard for individuals, confiscation of property, social humiliation, unjust taxation, and the mass abduction and forced Islamization of healthy Christian children by janissaries. There was no end to the storms of persecution coming down upon the Orthodox. Indeed, under Selim the First (1512-1520) the forced Islamization of all Christians was undertaken. During these tragic years the clergy constantly supported the people by defending their rights and attempting to organize the Christian community on a basis of equality, dignity, and brotherhood.

The Past Two Centuries

The fourth period began in the nineteenth century with the formation of independent states by Orthodox populations in the Balkans.

Orthodox peoples showed a spontaneous respect for most human rights, demonstrating that their long years of hardship had not led them in the opposite direction, toward intolerance. Rigas Velestinlis (1757-1798), one of the pioneers of the Greek revolution, persistently refers in his *Revolutionary Manifesto* to people's "natural rights," which "no one on earth has leave to take from them" (article 1) and which belong not only to Greeks but to all human beings without exception.[14] His basic position is that "all people have the right to be free and not slaves of another" (article 2). Rigas particularly insists upon religious freedom. In his *Proclamation of Revolution* he writes: "I am speaking about all Christians and Turks, without any religious distinction (for they are all creatures of God and children of Adam)."[15] In *The Rights of Man* he stresses that "all people, Christians and Turks, are by nature equal" (article 3) and proclaims the "freedom of every kind of religion, Christianity, Islam, Judaism, and all the others" (article 7). The other articles contain detailed discussions about freedom of opinion, freedom of the press, and freedom of assembly. Despite conflicts with the ecclesiastical circles of his day, Rigas is nevertheless operating within the Orthodox tradition.

All Greek constitutions drafted since the Greek War of Independence in 1821 have contained provisions that emphasize human rights and declare faith in the principles of equality and freedom; moreover, these were all ratified by an overwhelmingly Orthodox people.[16] The history of these constitutions attests to the fact that the

---

[14]Rigas' *Revolutionary Manifesto* includes his *Proclamation of Revolution, The Rights of Man*, his major work *A New Political Constitution*, and finally his *Thourios* (war hymn). In his *Proclamation* he calls these rights "sacred and pure, since they were given to the people by God," and this is followed by the "public declaration of the precious rights of man" in thirty-five articles. "These natural rights," article 2 explains, "are first, our right to be equal and not inferior to anyone else; second, our right to be free and not the slave of another; third, our right to live in safety, without anyone being able to deprive us of our lives unjustly or capriciously; and fourth, our right to our possessions, without anyone being able to take them from us, since they belong to us and to our heirs." L.I. Vranousis, *Rigas Velestinlis (1757-1798)* (in Greek), 2d ed. (Athens, 1963), 116-17 and 153-58. [1999 Addendum: See also G. Spandonis, *Rigas Velestinlis: The Revolutionary and His Hymns* (in Greek) (Athens, 1995), which includes the full text of "The Rights of Man" (225-32); P.M. Kitromilidis, *Rigas Velestinlis, Theory and Practice* (in Greek) (Athens, 1998); and *Rigas Velestinlis Selected Works* (in Greek) (Athens, 1998).]

[15]L.I. Vranousis, *Rigas Velestinlis*, 153.

[16]See: A.I. Svolos and G.K. Vlachos, *The Greek Constitution* (in Greek), 2 vols.

liberal sentiments of the Orthodox were not corrupted by their harsh experience of persecution and oppression.

Other free states established by Balkan peoples in the nineteenth century immediately adopted human rights and the provisions of international human rights declarations.

After the victory of communist regimes in most of the Balkan peninsula, apart from Greece, the Orthodox Church faced difficulties with which we are now all too familiar. While "freedom of religion" usually remained on the books, in practice it was repeatedly contested.[17]

In general, over the last six centuries of Balkan history, faith in the right to equality, dignity, and freedom has been kept alive by the Orthodox Church in the hearts of the oppressed people. Moreover, at critical moments in the lives of these peoples, their religious leaders have stood in the front lines of their struggle to achieve human rights.

Turning to our own era, the Orthodox Church has actively participated in the work of the World Council of Churches since its inception and has wholeheartedly endorsed the statements and decisions of this interfaith organization regarding a variety of human rights, particularly with regard to religious freedom. Orthodox representatives at the WCC convention in Amsterdam in 1948 joined in proclaiming that "the right to religious freedom is a consequence of the fact that humanity was created free by God; as a result, the granting of religious freedom cannot be dependent on any government whatsoever." The following year, in Chichester, England, Orthodox members of the WCC's Central Committee co-signed a declaration on religious freedom that stressed, among other things, that "religious freedom is the prerequisite for and the guardian of all other freedoms."[18] With similar unanimity the Orthodox Church has

(Athens, 1954); P. Vegleris, *The Treaty on Human Rights and the Constitution* (in Greek) (Athens, 1977); and A. Manesis, *Individual Freedoms: University Lectures in Constitutional Law* (in Greek) (Thessaloniki, 1979).

[17]Albania offers us the unique example of a country whose constitution, in force from 1967 to 1990, abolished the right to express any kind of religious conviction whatsoever.

[18]*Religious Freedom: Main Statements by the WCC 1948-75* (Geneva, 1976).

endorsed other related statements and declarations made by the
WCC on human rights issues.

The current social and political ferment and efforts in pursuit of
human rights offer the Orthodox new reasons to delve more deeply
into biblical sources and to reassess their "witness." The Church is
called upon to play the role of critic in the modern world, and it is
only right, therefore, that this process should always begin with a
critical reevaluation of the Church itself.[19]

In its support of human rights, the Orthodox Church draws not
only on its doctrines but on its profound experience of faith and its
liturgical life. These enable the Church to inspire its members, helping them strive toward inward reevaluation and repentance, so that
in their lives they can become bearers of justice, peace, and love.
Faith can have a profound influence on peoples' consciousness and
on their willingness to comply with the basic principles of freedom,
equality, dignity, brotherhood, and all the other human rights that
derive from these ideals.

THE ORTHODOX VIEW OF FUNDAMENTAL HUMAN RIGHTS

Although many who concern themselves with human rights would
like to avoid religious issues, when we ultimately ask ourselves
about the meaning of human existence we are forced to take a "metaphysical" stand. Even those who deny that the question itself exists
must, in the final analysis, take some such position, even if only a
negative one.

[19][1999 Addendum: On confronting the issue of human rights in the Christian
world more generally, see note 22 below. The 1986 declaration on justice and human
rights by the Third Pre-Council Pan-Orthodox Conference eloquently summarizes the
common Orthodox view, stating among other things that "Orthodox Christians experience divine condescension every day and fight against every form of fanaticism and bigotry that divides human beings and peoples. Since we continuously declare the
incarnation of God and the deification of humanity, we defend human rights for every
human being and every people. Since we live with the divine gift of freedom through
Christ's work of redemption, we are able to reveal to the fullest the universal value that
freedom has for every human being and every people." *Episkepsis* 17 (1986), issue
369/15.12.1986.]

The Significance of the Concepts "Person" and "Human Personality"

Like most human rights declarations, the Universal Declaration refers to the "worth of the human person" (preamble) and to the "free and full development" of the "personality" (article 29). The idea that political institutions and other social structures that express the life of the individual should recognize the concept of the human personality as one of their fundamental, founding principles is something that has only gradually formed in peoples' minds, through a long and complex process. With the declaration of the French Revolution in 1789 the bourgeois class sought to define every aspect of social life on the basis of their radical individualism. This did not result, however, in the long-awaited liberation of the individual; on the contrary, the state's responsibility for policing society was expanded to a nightmarish degree, and popular claims and demands were met with repression. This form of radical individualism paved the way for philosophical liberalism, and this led in turn to pure formalism, which separated law from ethics and society from the state. The moral principle of autonomy ultimately ignored the more profound aspects of human life and the intrinsic problems of human existence.

The ideology of liberal individualism utilized the concept of the personality, but mainly in order to limit the activity of the state and to prevent it from intervening in the economic, social, or cultural spheres. The individual, it was argued, is free to do whatever is not prohibited by law, and the state is obligated to execute only what has been explicitly delegated to it by law.[20]

As the framework of modern society continues to become increasingly pluralistic, the twentieth century searches for a new principle on which to establish and expand the state, the law, and the economy. As a result, modern society tends more and more to see human beings as individual, autonomous entities, as "personalities." Humanism originally associated the concept of autonomy with moral and intellectual freedom. Socioeconomic liberalism used the same argument as a basis for restricting the activity and intervention

[20]See G. Vlachos' analysis in *The Sociology of Human Rights* (in Greek) (Athens, 1976).

of the state. Events, however, have demonstrated that socioeconomic liberalism was neither interested in actual human needs nor in a position to understand them.

The class wars of the nineteenth century and the social and political events of the twentieth gravitated even further in the direction of universal human freedom, not as a logical idea but as a moral demand. Thus, as a result of the numerous crises that humanity faced in the twentieth century, the idea of the personality has once again emerged as a pivotal principle, one that enables all other principles— political, economic, ethical, and legal—to evolve in harmony.

Humanity in the twentieth century has been harassed and tyrannized by two different forms of social organization: by the capitalist mentality of the West, which has fostered agnostic individualism, and by various types of totalitarian regimes that have transformed people into masses of nameless individuals, whether through overt dictatorships or dictatorships that have hidden behind various slogans and naïve messianic ideologies.

Western European humanism, in its efforts to develop a theory about humanity, has sidestepped and replaced Christian concepts and linked the notion of personhood with an autonomous ethics or with a purely humanistic philosophy. However, the very meaning and experience of personhood grew out of and was framed by Christian theological thought, particularly by the Greek Fathers. This notion of the person has always been a key concept in any Orthodox attempt to understand the problems of human existence and society; in fact, it is a concept that one directly associates with Orthodox theology,[21] which interprets the words "in our image, after our likeness" (Gn 1:26) as a reference to human beings as persons, not as individuals.[22]

---

[21]For the concept of the person in Orthodox thought see I. Zizioulas, "From Mask to Person," in *Festschrift in Honor of the Metropolitan Elder of Chalcedon Meliton* (in Greek) (Thessaloniki, 1967).

[22]This anthropology of course differs radically in its view of humanity from other religious systems. Man according to the teaching of Buddhism is *anatta* (no self)—continuously changing combinations of mental and material states, such as feeling and understanding—not as selves. While many religious and philosophical systems limit themselves to human accomplishments, Christianity proclaims God's intervention in history, a process that continues in the life of the world and in the life of every individual through the Holy Spirit.

Development and Fulfillment of Personhood

The very notion of society clearly implies that each person's rights are inseparably connected to the rights of every other person. Rights and obligations are interdependent; moreover, individual rights must be brought into harmony with social and political rights. Respecting human dignity requires more than just passive recognition of the rights of others, particularly in an era of social pluralism. It requires our active participation at critical moments in the lives of our fellow human beings; it means giving them our wholehearted support and assistance as they change and develop as human beings.

Here lies the decisive importance of the Christian understanding of *agape*, Christian love. It is this alone that can transform society from a heap of individual grains of sand, each isolated from and indifferent to the next, into an organic whole composed of cells, each contributing to the growth of all the others. Every person has a "right" to be loved by the other people in society; God himself, in his love, has given us this right. In order to be truly free, every person must love, for it is in love that freedom is fulfilled. In the Orthodox doctrine of the Holy Trinity, personhood and society become harmoniously linked: the person is fully incorporated into society, yet the integrity of personhood is fully preserved.

In an era such as our own, when the worship of human rights has almost reached the point of idolatry, Christian thought and the Christian experience of life insist upon the human right to freely sacrifice even one's "rights" for the sake of love. This is not imposed on anyone, but is freely chosen. Love is an active choice that radiates beyond the narrow framework of legal constructs; unlike Mosaic law or any other form of human law, love grants freedom. "Love is the fulfilling of the law" (Rom 13:10).

Personal Conscience and Integrity

The various human rights declarations in existence are assuredly of great importance for the organization of society, and the regulatory role of the state has crucial significance. Nevertheless, in our complex society there are a great many clever and cynical ways to circumvent or violate human rights. There is never any lack of opportunity for people to take advantage of others, and no inventory of human rights can protect anyone against this. Rights declarations are incapable of inducing anyone to implement their contents voluntarily. The hypocritical manner in which the question of human rights has been handled internationally is the most cynical irony of our century.

Moreover, the question of protecting human rights is not limited to the level of the state and its organs, but extends to the behavior of every type of group in society that encroaches upon the rights of others. The whole world knows that there are private interests that work together with state agencies to abolish the human rights of people in other countries.

The problem is how to transform existing declarations from intellectual and legal constructs into living realities. A law can only define transgression, revealing the nature of sin; it cannot eliminate it.

The root of evil is still human selfishness, which always finds ways to violate the law in order to serve its own egotistical ends. This explains the enormous significance of personal conscience and integrity, if there is going to be respect for the rights of others. In order to use our logic and exercise our will properly, we must continually cleanse our hearts. In this regard, one's religious faith and the cultivation of a genuine and healthy religious conscience have an unquestionably important role to play. By developing this sense of personal responsibility, every one of us can become a fortress of resistance against the violation of human rights, both around us and within our own hearts. Materialist theories based on philosophical naturalism stand in contrast to this approach: on the one hand, their theoretical premises lead with logical necessity to the conclusion that human beings are not equal, since inequality reigns in the animal and plant kingdoms; psychologically, on the other hand, they encourage our egotistical and selfish impulses, completely eliminating any restraints imposed by the will.

Toward Inner Freedom

In Orthodox tradition, the pursuit of freedom is directed toward a different, higher plane: it is directed, above all, at achieving inner peace, which is a necessary condition for the fully developed human personality. This quest for freedom is a central feature of Orthodox Christian thought and life, and it explains the emphasis in Orthodoxy on self-control, on the ascetic life, on limiting one's needs, on fasting, and so forth.

In order for people to become transformed into true persons and not end up as fragmented personalities, they must be protected from their own selfishness, from the threat that their own egos represent. Christian thought stresses that our rights are in danger of being violated not only through the tyranny of others but also in the ways that we tyrannize ourselves when we allow ourselves to be driven by uncontrolled impulses. Christian thought thus sheds light on the existential abyss of self-destruction that threatens humankind.

In contrast to the notion that "my rights" are unconditional, one can still hear the emancipating call of the Christian precept: in order to find yourself you must sacrifice yourself (cf. Mt 16:24). The mindset expressed in these words is diametrically opposed to one that sees "my rights" as being absolute, for it advocates a free and sometimes existential choice to allow oneself to be raised on a cross. The power and means for promoting worldwide equality and brotherhood lie not in waging crusades but in freely accepting the cross.

The person that Orthodox tradition holds up as a model for our lives and as an exemplar of the consummate human personality is not the comfortable bourgeois with his carefully protected individual rights, leading a prim and proper life of social respectability, but rather the saint, the martyr, the ascetic: the human being who is free of any desire for money, property, fame, or recognition and who experiences the joy and fulness of inner freedom. This does not mean that people who live "according to the Spirit" and "in Christ" ignore their physical body, concerned only with some incorporeal element in their existence. On the contrary, they take part in the social life around them and strive, under the guidance of the Spirit, to free themselves from every form of selfishness. Naturally, this kind of approach toward life cannot be imposed or established by law. It is an expression of personal freedom, an outpouring of love for the crucified and resurrected Lord; it arises from the certainty that what makes a human being "like" God is the freedom that is to be found in love.

This inner freedom has the power to assert itself even under unfavorable conditions and in environments that lack any trace of respect for human rights—in prisons, in concentration camps, and under hostile and oppressive regimes in general—because no external power can restrain it or destroy it.

It is not my aim here to disparage what has been written at various times in praise of human rights. My goal is simply to describe what Orthodoxy considers to be "binding, needful, right, and proper"—*deon,* in Greek—for the human race. This Orthodox *deon* is something that lies beyond the compass of human rights, both in its scope and in its power.

The Greek word for "rights"—*dikaiomata*—has been in constant use in Orthodox worship ever since the first generation of Christians. It appears repeatedly in the Psalms and by way of the Psalms entered church hymnology as a reference to God's ordinances, laws, and statutes. Psalm 119 is a good example: "The earth, O Lord, is full of thy steadfast love; teach me thy statutes!" (verse 64); "O that my ways may be steadfast in keeping with thy statutes" (verse 5); and "Blessed be thou, O Lord; teach me thy statutes" (verse 12). From this perspective, Orthodox thinking views human *dikaiomata* in conjunction with God's *dikaiomata*: with the justice, the truth, and the love of God, who has laid down institutions, obligations, and principles that provide humanity with the most fertile ground for the fruition of human rights.

The Rights of Future Generations

Self-limitation and an ascetic way of life are also related to an awareness of humanity's place within a much wider, organic whole—the world of nature and the animal kingdom—and to the recognition that thoughtlessly wasting our natural resources exclusively on ourselves cannot be justified.

When we speak about human rights we usually only consider the rights of people who live in the same era as ourselves. However, the knowledge that history continues and that other generations will follow us should make us more sensitive to their rights as well: their right to enjoy nature and health and to survive in a decent fashion within the universe. Many of our overwhelming problems, such as environmental pollution, pollution of the seas, contaminated food supplies, and the squandering of energy sources, among others, are issues that concern the human rights of future generations.

The Supreme Right of All Human Beings
To Become What They Were Created For

Finally, a basic idea and conviction of Orthodox Christians is the unshakeable certainty that we have the right to become that for which we were created. Our most important right is our right to realize our deepest nature and become "children of God" through grace. If the various other benefits that life can provide ignore this right, which is basic to our existence, they can disorient us and ultimately make us indifferent to what is most essential: to the sacred proclamation of Christian faith, which unceasingly draws our attention to the fact that human beings have the right and the obligation to use the powers they have received through the grace of God in order to conquer their own sinful nature, to conquer death, and to advance toward "deification."

— • —

Orthodox Christian thought enables us to delve more deeply into the meaning of human rights and to do what is necessary to prevent human rights declarations from remaining dry, legal documents. It also helps us broaden the scope of human rights to encompass other essential issues as well, such as the right to pursue one's own true nature and purpose in life.

Christians never abandon their critical stance toward historical developments. They are happy when they see humanity's various accomplishments, but they never stop pursuing something more substantial. They know that "no human rights declaration will ever be complete or definitive. Such declarations always go hand in hand with the ethical conscience and culture of a specific moment in history."[23] It is for this reason that Christians must be vigilant, striving to make the legal and political structure of their society ever more comprehensive through constant reform and reassessment.

As to the Christian churches, if they want to make their own distinctive contribution to the cause of human rights, they should not limit themselves to fine analyses and admonitions, but should become in reality what they were meant to be: centers of moral and spiritual inspiration, where personalities can be molded; laboratories of selfless love; a place where the kingdom of God reveals itself on earth; a place where the level of human life is elevated from a collection of individuals, who merely coexist biologically, to a "communion of persons," which takes as its model the supreme reality: the Holy Trinity, whose praises the churches ceaselessly extol.

Orthodoxy nurtures a willingness to accept people as they are, with deep respect for their freedom and without requiring them to adopt Christian views. This makes it easier to communicate with others, including those who belong to other religions or hold other ideologies. It also instills deep respect for human rights and an eagerness to work with others to attain universal acceptance for human rights and to defend them.

POSTSCRIPT: HUMAN RIGHTS AND RELIGIONS

A commemorative conference was organized by UNESCO in 1979 to consider "The Position of Human Rights in Religious and Political Traditions Around the World." This conference, which took place in Bangkok on December 3-7, discussed the following issues: (1) views on human rights within the major currents of religious thought—Hinduism, Buddhism, Judaism, Orthodoxy, Roman Catholicism, Protestantism, Shinto, and Islam; and (2) plans for a declaration to prevent all forms of bigotry, oppression, and discrimination based on religious faith, as resolved by the United Nations Commission on Human Rights on March 14, 1979. The Declaration on the Elimination of All

[23]*Human Rights* (in Greek) (Athens: Euthyni, 1977).

Forms of Intolerance and of Discrimination Based on Religion or Beliefs was officially issued on November 25, 1981.

There was agreement at the conference on the following point: the Declaration on Human Rights and other related efforts of the United Nations constitute an important step toward the recognition of the value and dignity of human beings. The problem of human rights, regardless of the meaning or interpretation it receives from any particular religious community, is a serious issue for nearly all the religions of the world. Respect for human rights and the general recognition of a human being's sacredness facilitate cooperation between religious communities and international organizations involved with the issue of human rights.

Although motivated by different criteria, the spokesmen for the various religions were able to agree on a number of basic positions such as the fact that every human being is unique. In addition to individual and social rights, human beings are always in a relationship with and have access to a different dimension of reality, which can be called transcendental, sacred, or divine.

The reference to individual rights implies a responsibility to acknowledge the rights and freedom of others. Naturally, each religion confronts this issue with different fundamental principles in mind, using different standards. For most religious traditions there does not exist an unbridgeable gap between the transcendental or vertical dimension and the horizontal—that is, the social and historical—dimension. Admittedly, however, many religions fail to place proper emphasis on economic and political factors in human life.

Confronting the problem of evil is an essential element in any understanding of human rights. Although most religions assure us that their role regarding this problem is not fulfilled simply by promoting the United Nations declaration and that they consider the assumptions on which the 1948 declaration is based to be foreign or even unacceptable to their own traditions, in the end they acknowledge that this declaration provides every religion with an opportunity to examine itself and, at the same time, to open itself up to cooperation with the rest of the world in order to reduce the weight of oppression suffered by humanity today. They recognize the

challenge, as well as the fact that they bear the responsibility for an
enormous task. They also concede that they can and should become
a driving force in the effort to make human rights a reality.[24]

[24][1999 Addendum: The Roman Catholic and Protestant papers presented at the
Bangkok conference were published in *Christianisme et Droits de l'homme*, ed. E. Hirsh
(Paris, 1984) and include M. Schooyans, "Le catholicisme et les Droits de l'Homme," 13-
41; M. Lienhard, "Le protestantisme et les droits de l'homme," 43-67; Pope John XXIII,
"Pacem in terris" (selections), 69-78; and J.M. Aubert, "Les droits de l'homme interpel-
lent les église," 81-111.

During the last twenty years many books and articles have been published on the subject of human rights and religious traditions. See U. Schenner, "Les droits de l'homme à
l'intérieur des Eglise protestantes," *Revue d'histoire et de philosophie religieuse* 58 (1978):
379-97; E. Weingartner, *Human Rights on the Ecumenical Agenda*, CCIA Background Information 3 (Geneva, 1983); and *L'Eglise et les droits de l'homme*, Commission Pontificale
"Justitia e Pax" 11:17, 3d ed. (Cité du Vatican, 1983). Cf. G. Filibeck, *Les droits de l'homme
dans l'enseignement de l'Eglise: de Jean XXIII à Jean-Paul II*, Recueil de texts du Magistère
de l'Eglise catholique de Mater et Magistra à Centessimus Annus (1961-1991) (Vatican,
1992); L.S. Swidler, ed., *Religious Liberty and Human Rights in Nations and Religions*
(Philadelphia, 1986); *Forms of Solidarity: Human Rights* (Geneva, 1988); N. Koshy, *Religious Freedom in a Changing World* (Geneva, 1992); E. Roukounas, *The International
Defense of Human Rights* (in Greek) (Athens, 1995); K. Delikostantes, *Human Rights: Western Ideology or Universal Ethic?* (in Greek) (Thessaloniki, 1995); J.D. Van der Vyver and
J. Witte, Jr., eds., *Religious Human Rights in Global Perspectives*, 2 vols., in the series Reli-
gious Perspectives (The Hague, Boston, and London, 1996), which includes a selected
bibliography; and K. Bey, ed., *Religious Freedom: Theory and Practice in Greek Society and
Legal Order* (in Greek) (Athens, 1997). See also N.S. Iwe, *The History and Contents of
Human Rights* (New York, Berne, and Frankfurt, 1986); P. de Senarclens, "Les droits de
l'homme ont-ils un avenir?" in *Festschrift in Honor of Ph. Vegleres* (in Greek and French,
French title *Mélange en l'honneur de Ph. Vegleris*) (Athens, 1988), 363-83; K.N. Kakouri,
"The Universality of Human Rights—The Right to Be Different: Some Observations" (in
Greek), *To Syntagma* 1 (1994): 5-20; C.S. Nino, *The Ethics of Human Rights* (Oxford,
1994), reprinted as "The Relativist Challenge and Related Matters" in *Human Rights Quar-
terly* 19 (1997), 461-507; T. Stahnke and J.P. Martin, eds., *Religion and Human Rights Basic
Documents*, Center for the Study of Human Rights (New York, 1998); S. Agourides, *Human
Rights in the Western World: A Historical and Social Survey* (in Greek) (Athens, 1998); and
B. van der Heijden and Bahia Tahzib-hie, *Reflections on the Universal Declaration of Human
Rights: A Fiftieth Anniversary Anthology* (The Hague, Boston, and London, 1998).

Books and articles by various international organizations as well as studies on
human rights have been multiplying at a great rate. See *Yearbook of the European Convention on Human Rights* (Council of Europe, published since 1955); and *Human Rights: A
Compilation of International Instruments of the United Nations*, United Nations Publication
Sales, no. E.88 XIV, 1 (Geneva and New York, 1988). For recent bibliography see *Docu-
mentation Sources on Human Rights* (Strasbourg, May 1998).

The Office of the United Nations in Geneva (Centre for Human Rights) also publishes the series *Human Rights Fact Sheet*, a pamphlet intended for the general public.
Each issue deals with a selected topic of special interest on the issue of human rights; the
twenty-fifth issue was published in May 1996.]

~ 3 ~

Culture and Gospel

SOME THEOLOGICAL OBSERVATIONS BASED ON
ORTHODOX TRADITION AND EXPERIENCE*

The phenomenon of culture has revealed astonishing diversity throughout the centuries and, as with all enterprising human achievements, is difficult to define. The message of the gospel, for its part, has been expressed in a variety of altered versions, due to the diversity of actual forms that Christianity has taken. It is useful, therefore, before examining the relationship between culture and gospel and the influences that each has had upon the other, to examine the range of meaning inherent in each of these two terms.

CLARIFYING THE TERMS "CULTURE" AND "GOSPEL"

The Term "Culture"

In general, culture is a human victory over the darker aspects of humanity and society, a transcending of humanity's merely biological existence. It is a conscious act of the human race to define and regulate its life and its physical surroundings, or, according to

*This chapter was one of the main papers presented at "Culture and Gospel," a theological conference convened in Riano, Italy, by the Department of World Mission and Evangelism in June 1984. It was published in *International Review of Mission* 74 (1985): 185-98, under the title "Culture and Gospel: Some Observations from the Orthodox Tradition and Experience." Since that time, this subject has become one of the central issues addressed by the World Council of Church's Commission on World Mission and Evangelism.

79

another, more concise formulation, culture is "to varying degrees and in different ways, the concrete realization of human potential" (M. Weber). In spite of the great variety among human cultures, certain stable elements, which we may call "crosscultural constants," have been observed. These can be summarized schematically as follows: (1) the creation of a communication system or code, i.e., a language; (2) the development of a rudimentary technology and economy that solves the basic problems of human survival, the need for food and shelter; (3) some regulation of the basic human social unit, the male-female relationship, to ensure the propagation of the species; (4) a form of social organization, such as the clan, the tribe, or the nation, which defines social relationships; (5) the establishment of social rules that determine what is right and wrong; (6) forms of art that express the beliefs and concerns of the individual and society; and (7) an experience of the "sacred"—i.e., of that which lies beyond daily life—through some form of religious belief.[1]

More concisely, culture provides a series of responses and solutions to the fundamental categories of existence and is in turn reshaped by those solutions. It defines a means of survival (economic structures), good and evil (ethics), truth (philosophy and science), justice (law), and beauty (the arts).

In the past, Europeans made a distinction between "civilized" and "savage" peoples, perpetuating the ancient antithesis between Greek and barbarian. Modern anthropological research has demonstrated, however, that culture is universal to all human beings. All societies have some type of culture, even if only in embryonic form. The ethnological record documents more than three hundred

---

[1]According to another view, religion, language, and culture are three different and independent human phenomena, and language and religion should not be seen as lying within the sphere of culture. See A. Hilkman, "Geschichtesphilosophie, Kulturwissenschaft, Soziologie," *Saeculum* 12:4 (1961): 405-20. That language and religion have a special structure is clear, but they do not cease to be closely interdependent with other expressions of culture. For more on culture, see N.I. Louvari, "Culture" (in Greek), MEE 20:459-60; R. Benedict, *Patterns of Culture* (London, 1935); A. Papaderos, "Culture" (in Greek), ThEE 10:507-14; K. Spetsieres, *The Philosophy of Society and Culture* (in Greek) (Athens, 1946); D. Zakythenos, *Introduction to the History of Culture* (in Greek) (Athens, 1952); G. Simmel, *Philosophic Culture* (New York, 1957); T.S. Eliot, *Notes towards the Definition of Culture* (London, 1962); I. Theodorakopoulos, *Lectures in the Philosophy of History and Culture* (in Greek) (Athens, 1963); and R. Williams, *Culture* (London, 1981).

cultural groups among so-called "primitive" peoples, tribes that live in a natural state. Just as there are languages that have no form of writing, there are also cultures without technological achievements. Various criteria have been used at different times to distinguish more developed cultures. Spengler, for example, placed the number of higher cultures at eight,[2] while Toynbee divided the most important human cultures into twenty-one groupings.[3]

A distinction has often been made between civilization and culture, the former being used to describe the technological, material side of culture and the latter to refer to its intellectual or spiritual dimension. This division was particularly common in the west and is associated with an era that insisted, under the influence of idealism, on distinguishing mind from matter. In the Orthodox view, however, the material and spiritual aspects of humanity are indissolubly united, each influencing the other. On this issue, therefore, we prefer to think of matter and spirit as two sides of the creative human genius.

This principle of unity becomes even more apparent when we recognize that culture is a whole, a totality, which is often self-governing and autonomous, not merely the sum of its individual components. Culture is a kind of organism with its own logical *entelechy*—an inherent, self-regulating and self-directing purpose—that operates within the realm of human responsibility and freedom.[4]

The Christian Gospel

According to the Christian faith, a decisive moment occurred within this realm of culture and human creativity—a realm that functions on

[2]O. Spengler, *Der Untergang des Abendlandes*, 2 vols. (Munich, 1918-22).

[3]A.J. Toynbee: *A Study of History*, 12 vols. (London, 1951-61); and *The World and the West* (London, 1953).

[4][1999 addendum. On culture, see also J. Chay, ed., *Culture and International Relations* (New York, 1990); M. Featherstone, ed., *Global Culture, Nationalism, Globalization and Modernity* (London, 1990); M. Marrithers, *Why Humans Have Cultures: Explaining Anthropology and Social Diversity* (Oxford and New York, 1992); R. Williams, *Culture and Society* (London, 1993); A. Milner, *Contemporary Cultural Theory, An Introduction* (London, 1994); H. Bhabha, *The Location of Culture* (London, 1994); and P. Goodal, *High Culture, Popular Culture: The Long Debate* (St. Leonards, Australia, 1995).]

the basis of certain values and guidelines—when God himself entered the historical process hypostatically, as a person: when "the Word became flesh and dwelt among us" (Jn 1:14). A new *logos*—a new reason or rationale—was thus established for human existence, with a new, vital focus for cultural creativity; a new entelechy was introduced, one that guides the human element in creation, and the rest of creation along with it, toward a new *telos*—a new purpose or end.

The thing that was decisively new here was not an idea, a principle, or a truth preached by some wise man, such as Gautama Buddha, or by some prophet who had received a revelation, such as Muhammad, but the person of Jesus Christ, at once both God and man, whose existence united the divine and the human in a unique and unprecedented way and who himself became hypostatically united with the human element in creation—that is, with all of humanity. This person, who binds history to eternity, was crucified "for us human beings, and for our salvation," was resurrected from the dead, ascended into heaven, and will return again as judge of all the world. He did not merely set humanity on the right path, nor was the cure he offered us based on a principle he had discovered; rather, the thing that he bore witness to was that he himself was "the way and the truth," "the resurrection and the life" (Jn 11:25-26). This Christ, "the same yesterday and today and for ever" (Heb 13:8), remains continuously united with our human nature, leading us toward deification.[5] This is the heart of the gospel.

"The gospel of Christ" changed the chromosomes, one might say, of human nature; it established a new, secret code of evolution for humanity: from human being to *theanthropos* (a being that is both God and human); from reason and the development of logic to humanity's union with the Word and communion with the Logos of Divine Love. At the same time, the gospel also determined the way that all of nature, whose very existence is bound up with humanity,

[5]A. Theodorou, *The Teaching of the Greek Church Fathers on the Deification of Humanity, Down to John of Damascus* (in Greek) (Athens, 1956); G.I. Mantzarides, *The Teaching of Gregory Palamas on the Deification of Humanity* (in Greek) (Thessaloniki, 1963); P.N. Trembelas, *The Dogmatics of the Orthodox Catholic Church* (in Greek) (Athens, 1959-61); and I. Karmires, *Dogmatic and Doctrinal Documents of the Orthodox Catholic Church* (in Greek), 2 vols. (Athens, 1960-68).

will be transformed. For those who do not believe in this revelation, it is a position that remains "a stumbling block" and a "folly." However, for "those who are called," whatever their cultural background may be, the crucified and resurrected Lord is "the power of God and the wisdom of God" (1 Cor 1:24).

"The gospel of the glory of God" is not received merely through the intellect or through a system of ideas, but by opening all the receptive capacities of the human person. The most appropriate time and place for this to occur, therefore, is during worship, when in our offering of praise we invoke the Holy Spirit in order that all visible things might become changed and ultimately united with the living Christ; that all of life might be brought into harmony with the Spirit; and that the entire universe might be transformed through the radiance of the divine energies of the All-Holy Trinity.

The gospel should not be equated with any actual form of "Christianity" articulated either in bygone eras or by contemporary Christian communities and groups. Human failings and infidelities are in no position to corrupt its power or its substance. The gospel—as has been understood in the Church for twenty centuries—remains the standard for and the verdict on every form of Christianity that has ever come into being. Every revival in the Christian community has had its origin in a rediscovery of the heart of the gospel and in the resolution to live it in all its purity and plenitude. Those who genuinely articulate the gospel are not simply intellectuals versed in the books of holy scripture; they are people who comprehend and experience the mystery of the gospel, constantly being transformed in the flame of the Holy Spirit's presence and radiating divine glory and love in their deeds and their existence.

Culture and Religious Experience

A Theological Approach

The idea that culture is a human accomplishment while the gospel represents God's intervention in the world, although offering us a welcome sense of clarity—and in spite of the fact that it does illuminate an important truth—rather oversimplifies things, as do all such formulations that attempt to be extremely unambiguous and definitive. Equally inadequate, in my opinion, is the assertion that culture is a creation of the lower world while the gospel comes to us from on high. Understood as an act and achievement of human beings that were created in God's image, culture does not lie outside the scope of God's divine energies and is not completely removed from the power of the Holy Spirit, who has full command over all things, "the visible together with the invisible."

The exercise of human creativity upon the natural world is a gift, a commandment, and an ability given by the Creator himself to Adam and Eve, his first created. It is a consequence of their "divine image" and of their instinctive impulse to become "in the image of God."[6] In the Orthodox view, the "image" was neither destroyed nor incapacitated with the fall of the first human beings. Humanity has therefore retained its ability to receive indications of God's will and to receive the energies of the Holy Spirit. At the very root of culture we find a gift and a commandment of God (Gen 2:15). God gave humanity the right and the ability to rule creation (Gen 1:28-30). The first chapters of holy scripture present us with the various ways in which God has guided the human race along the path of culture. Despite human disobedience, God has never withdrawn from the world into some unapproachable heaven,[7] but continues to have a relationship and a dialogue with human beings and to enter into "agreements" with them. God took the first step in putting humanity on a rehabilitative course. He took the initiative in establishing a number of covenants: with Adam and Eve, the representatives of the entire human race; with Noah and the human community that was saved from the flood; with Abraham, the founder of a people from whom the Messiah

[6]On "in God's image" see P. Bratsiotes: "Genesis 1:26 in Orthodox Theology" (in Greek), *Orthodoxia* 27 (1952): 359-72; and *Human Beings in the New Testament* (in Greek) (Athens, 1955). See also N. Bratsiotes, *Humanity as a Divine Creation,* volume 1 of *The Anthropology of the Old Testament* (in Greek) (Athens, 1967).

[7]The notion that God withdrew from the world into some unapproachable heaven is one that occurs in many African religions: E. Dammann, *Die Religionen Afrikas* (Stuttgart, 1963); J.S. Mbiti, *African Religions and Philosophy* (London, 1969; reprint 1970); and A. Yannoulatos, *Ruhanga the Creator: A Contribution to Research on African Beliefs concerning God and Humanity* (in Greek) (Athens, 1975).

would be born; and with Moses, the leader and lawgiver of Israel, to whom a special role was assigned in God's plan for deliverance. Cultures later developed on the basis of these "agreements."

The theological position that one takes regarding other cultures is closely related to the way in which one understands human religious beliefs and practices that lie outside this biblical framework. Independently of whether the word "culture" derives etymologically from the root "cult," thus indicating that culture originates in worship, the historical fact remains that experience of the holy, worship of the divine, and reaching out toward the metaphysical are all interwoven with culture. It is worth noting that all twenty-one of the cultures Toynbee designated as "major" evolved on the premise of the sacred—i.e., direct knowledge and experience of the divine. A sound understanding of nonbiblical religious beliefs and practices is therefore an important tool for arriving at a correct position on other cultural forms whose creation has been directly associated with such beliefs and practices.

The attitude of the Protestant world toward non-Christian religions has swung like a pendulum in recent centuries between antithetical views: from an extremely negative position (e.g., the dialectical theology of Barth and his followers) to the extremely positive position of the science of religion school (Otto, Heiler, and Benz), which relativized Christianity.[8] Their various theories have shifted back and forth in this way between two extreme views, either hyper-rejection or hyper-acceptance of non-Christian religions. In Orthodox thought, which is based on twenty centuries of continuous coexistence with people of other religious beliefs within various cultural regions and across various cultural boundaries, and which has maintained the tradition of the undivided Church of the first ten centuries, the dominant tendency is to attempt to reach equilibrium and understanding and to remain in harmony with our tradition of catholicity and universality. It is worth noting that the generations of Christians in the era when the New Testament canon was being established had a more conciliatory approach toward others. The

---

[8]See below in chapter 5, "A Theological Approach to Understanding Other Religions."

views of Justin Martyr (d. 165) regarding the *spermatikos logos* are well known,[9] as is the opinion of Clement of Alexandria (d. 215) that Greek philosophy is "a preparation, paving the way for him who is perfected in Christ"[10] and that the Greeks had received "certain scintillations of the divine word."[11] The universal character of divine revelation to all nations and people and the idea that they all have innate religious feelings is particularly stressed by Eusebius of Caesarea (d. 339). This great church historian accepts that "religion was naturally inherent in them,"[12] and he considers all people in all epochs who were dear to God and "enjoyed the testimony of righteousness" to have been "Christians in fact."[13]

The basic thread that runs through the beliefs of the early Church, as well as later Orthodox thought, is that human beings were created "in the image of God" and that they have never lost this divine "citizenship." Their creativity in the realm of culture is connected to their "desire . . . to seek God."[14] People's longing to create order in their lives and to surpass what they are expresses a God-given impulse and entelechy. The achievements of the human spirit do not lie outside God's plan, his help, or his love. The human intellect is "godlike" and "divine."[15]

The systematic study of human cultures reveals a dramatic duality: the activity of demonic forces exists side by side with a longing for the holy. It also reveals a kind of double process of development: an upward course and a degenerative process.[16]

In the east in general, the Church's attitude developed on the basis of Peter's certainty that "in every nation any one who fears him

[9]Speaking about the Greek philosophers, Justin wrote: "For each man spoke well in proportion to the share he had of the spermatic word, seeing what was related to it. . . . Whatever things were rightly said among all men, are the property of us Christians." *The Second Apology* 13, PG 6:465 (trans. ANF, vol. 1).

[10]Clement of Alexandria, *Stromata* 1.5, PG 8:728A (trans. ANF, vol. 2).

[11]Clement of Alexandria, *Exhortation to the Heathen* 7, PG 8:184A (trans. ANF, vol. 2).

[12]Eusebius of Caesarea, *Praeparatio Evangelica* 2.6, PG 21:140B.

[13]Eusebius of Caesarea, *The History of the Church* 1.4, PG 20:77C (trans. NPF, 2d ser., vol. 1).

[14]Gregory of Nazianzus, *Orations* 28.15 ("Second Theological Oration"), PG 36:45.

[15]Ibid., 17, PG 36:48.

[16]N. Arseniev, *Revelation of Life Eternal: An Introduction to the Christian Message* (New York, 1965), 38-39.

[God] and does what is right is acceptable to him" (Acts 10:35) and on Paul's declaration in Athens that "In him we live and move and have our being" (Acts 17:28). Human affairs operate within the sphere of influence of the "sun of righteousness." Christian experience, optimism, and hope are based on and sustained by the fact that the glory of God extends throughout the entire world. However unapproachable, transcendent, and unknown the essence of God may be, in the same measure the uncreated energies of God's essence—the glory of God—are diffused throughout heaven and earth and to every form of life and existence.[17]

The Importance of Culture for the Spread of the Gospel

Christianity's message was originally framed in the context of a specific world, the Semitic world. The incarnation of the Word of God did not become reality in a vacuum, but in a particular place, at a particular time, and among a particular people. Every form of Docetism—the belief that Christ only seemed to have a human body and suffer and die on the cross—was relentlessly opposed by the Church. The dogma of the incarnation is therefore essential and fundamental to any inquiry or proper overview regarding the matter presently under discussion.

While the kingdom of God was first proclaimed in a Semitic environment and in the Aramaic language, by the time we reach the end of the first generation of Christians the boundaries of this original cultural context had been decisively transcended. The Church's early development took place in the Greco-Roman as well as the Semitic world, and the gospel was disseminated and ultimately set down in written form in Greek, a language quite different from the Aramaic in which it had originally been preached. Even in this first phase we already see that cultures are adopted but do not become authoritative.

The flame of Pentecost abolishes linguistic, ethnic, and cultural borders. Culture is on the one hand accepted but at the same time transcended. While the gospel emphasizes its eternal and divine

---

[17]See chapter 2, note 5 above, and also below in chapter 5, "A Theological Approach to Understanding Other Religions."

character, it has no difficulty in being incarnated in time and again in the specific cultural body of each epoch. The coexistence of various cultures within the ancient Church—Greco-Roman, Syrian, and Egyptian—was a source of considerable creativity. In modern times, the difficulty of accepting the mystery that the gospel is both divine and human has been a source of temptation. Some have thus attempted to eliminate every aspect of the gospel that harkens back to the influence of Greek culture, supposedly in order to find Christianity's Semitic soul (Harnack). Others have become attached to the letter of the written gospel with such dedication and servility that they have lost the life-giving spirit that operates within the mystical body of the living Church which established the gospel. Both of these views ignore the doctrine of the incarnation and its corollaries. Discourse about the Word and about the mystery of communion with him took on the cultural flesh of the world.

The fact that the Messiah, the savior of the world, came at a particular turning point in history, that he was linked to the Jewish milieu in particular, and that the first Church evolved within a particular environment that had been shaped by Greek culture—certainly none of these things lay outside God's divine providence. The Greek world, which based itself upon and cultivated human reason as a universal and supreme value and which, as K. Tsatsos points out, had pursued the course of this trajectory for centuries, had already discerned the existence of a supreme idea, one that transcends reason.[18] Greek reason had thus arrived, through its own powers, at the frontiers of the realm of reason, not only recognizing the significance of the ineffable but increasingly inclined to concede to it the highest position on the scale of values and to confess to the limits of reason in its presence.

Greek reason had already begun to seek something beyond itself, the very thing that it could not obtain knowledge of through its own powers: the nature and essence of the ineffable. These were precisely

[18]K. Tsatsos, "The Zenith of the Greek Spirit" (in Greek), in *Klassikos Ellenismos B* (Classical Hellenism II), IEE 2B (1972), 244-47. More generally, see "The Culture of the Classical Period" (in Greek), ibid., 242-570; and V. Kyrkos, "The Universality of Greek Culture and Its Encounter with Christianity" (in Greek), in *Ellenismos kai Rome* (Hellenism and Rome), IEE 6 (1976), 392-95.

the things it recognized and came to know through its acceptance of the gospel. Additionally, it discovered the faith and hope that lie beyond human logic. In the synthesis that was to follow, the Greek world used every cultural means of expression at its disposal to serve and preach the truth of the ineffable, which had been revealed by the crucified and resurrected Christ.[19]

From the very beginning we see a similar acceptance of local culture in other places in the east where local churches became consolidated, such as Armenia, Egypt, and Ethiopia. Different cultures were accepted from the start, so that they could afterward be baptized and become transformed. In the first stage, the local language, which is the chief means through which a culture expresses itself, became completely acceptable as a vehicle for expressing and spreading the gospel. It was subsequently used in worship, to help people both acquire knowledge of the gospel and also experience it. The language thus became transformed, acquiring new capabilities and new vigor. Biblical and liturgical texts were translated into various languages, and this contributed to the creation of genuine local communities of worshippers. More than forty versions of the liturgy took shape and were in use during the first centuries in the east, and various customs and ways of life were adopted by the Church.

This was the policy and tradition adhered to by the most representative Byzantine missionaries. When Cyril (827-869) and Methodius (815-885) were attacked by the Latin clergy for allegedly introducing new practices—they insisted on using the Slavonic language to preach the gospel among the Slavic peoples—Cyril is reported to have said: "Aren't you ashamed to accept only three languages and to say that the other languages are deaf and dumb? . . . We know that there are many peoples that read books and praise God in their own languages, the Armenians, the Persians, the Abasgi, the Iberians, the Sogdians, the Goths, the Avars, the Turks, the Khazars, the Arabs, the Egyptians, and others."[20] Their struggle

---

[19]I. Zizioulas, "Hellenism and Christianity: The Meeting of Two Worlds" (in Greek), in *Ellenismos kai Rome* (Hellenism and Rome), IEE 6 (1976), 519-59.

[20]A. Yannoulatos, "Byzantium: The Work of Spreading the Gospel" (in Greek), ThEE 4 (1964), col. 44; and *Methodius and Cyril: Signposts of Journey* (in Greek) (Athens, 1966).

to establish the use of the Slavic language was of fundamental importance for the future of both the Slavic world and the Christian world
in general. Few events have had such importance in the history of
the Church. Western Christendom was to lag behind for a considerable length of time before adopting this policy: the Protestants finally
did so seven centuries later, during the Reformation, and it took the
Roman Catholics eleven centuries, until the Second Vatican Council
of our own day.

When the Byzantines spread the gospel they took a direct interest in also passing on the cultural creations and structures that they
had developed up to that time through the gospel's inspiration. They
offered the best they had in the way of art, painting, music, and architecture. They sent their best artists and helped build exceptionally
beautiful churches as symbols of God's glory. They cultivated artistic
sensibilities—that sense of beauty which transforms the world.

They also took an interest in the social and political aspects of life
and in education, offering all the expertise they had gained in their
endeavor to assimilate the gospel, and they helped each people
develop its own creative genius. They basically offered newly
enlightened peoples all the prerequisites needed to evolve into genuine nations, to discover themselves and mold themselves, and to
develop their special talents, their particular personalities, and their
own cultures.[21]

The Byzantine concept of unity in the Christian world was not
based, as in the west, on the creation of a decision-making and
administrative center that sought to impose uniformity. Unity is not
impaired by the existence of a variety of outlooks, languages, customs, or political states. They did not seek to reduce everyone to a
homogeneous mass, but to promote the individual characteristics
and idiosyncrasies of each society.

Russian missionaries faithfully followed the Byzantine tradition
in their own missionary efforts, applying with originality and

[21]See: F. Dvornik, Les Slaves, Byzance et Rome au IXe siècle (Paris, 1929); K.S.
Latourette, A History of the Expansion of Christianity (The Thousand Years of Uncertainty)
(London, 1938); M. Spinka, A History of Christianity in the Balkans (Chicago, 1933);
and G. Konidares, "Byzantium: The Ecumenical Spirit" (in Greek), ThEE 4 (1964), cols.
58-84.

boldness the methods they had inherited from Christian Byzantium: the translation of liturgical books into native languages, with methodical attention to linguistic and theological details; the education of a native clergy; an emphasis on the importance of the beauty of churches as visible symbols of God's glory on earth; the study of local culture (e.g., in Alaska, China, and Japan); and the adoption of local traditions.[22] Orthodoxy continues these efforts today in Asia and in Africa, studying existing cultural data, investigating African symbolism, searching for each tribe's positive cultural elements, translating liturgical texts, and celebrating divine worship in local dialects. This is not a new strategy but simply faithfulness to a twenty-century-old tradition of the Eastern Orthodox Church.

In order for the gospel to be lived in all its universality—in every place and at every time—all peoples in all regions of the world need to reexamine it carefully, experience it in the context of their own cultures, and give it expression with their own voice and their own soul. Every nation is called upon to use its own particular tone and phrasing in the effort to know the gospel. It is incumbent upon every local church to contribute the positive values of its own particular culture and to further develop them, consistent with its own national, linguistic, and tribal character. Furthermore, in order to purify itself, every local church should critically examine all those cultural elements that are antithetical to the dignity and the destiny of the human race, as revealed to us in the gospel. Simultaneously, and without destroying its local identity, every church should further develop its catholicity by experiencing tradition, unity, and communion in an organic way with the "one, holy, catholic and apostolic Church," the Church of the past, the present, and the future.

[22]See A. Yannoulatos, "Orthodoxy in Alaska" (in Greek), *Porevthentes* 3 (1963): 14-22, 44-47; "Orthodoxy in China" (in Greek), ThEE 7 (1965), cols. 566-81; *The Dawn of Orthodoxy in Japan* (in Greek) (Athens, 1971); and "Les Missions des Eglise d'Orient," *Encyclopaedia Universalis* 2 (Paris, 1972), 99-102.

The Strength That Culture Receives from the Gospel

When the Church encounters a culture, it proceeds to initiate three processes: first, it accepts those elements that are in keeping with the message of the gospel; second, it rejects other aspects that are irreconcilable with the gospel; and third, it transfuses new blood and a new spirit into the culture, fertilizing whatever is positive.

A New Dynamic in Greek Culture

With the baptism of the Greek world in the early centuries of Christianity, an internal process of regeneration began that gave new vitality, momentum, and brilliance to a culture already in decline. The platonic form of "the Good" was given new breadth and depth. Greek thought had created a synthesis between reason and the sensible world, and the latter was now elevated to the level of the ineffable.[23]

The philosophical thought of the church fathers offered new solutions and responses to the old unanswered questions of human existence.[24] Byzantine art discovered new forms of expression. It did not limit itself to merely imitating or copying the material world; it became a means of contact with the transcendental, which it attempted to represent. The gospel defined new legal principles, on

[23]See C.H. Dodd, *The Bible and the Greeks* (London, 1935); H. Rahner, *Griechische Mythen in christlicher Deutung* (Zurich, 1957); J. Pépin, *Mythe et Allégorie. Les origins grecques et les contestations judéo-chrétiennes* (Paris, 1958); W. Jaeger, *Early Christianity and Greek Paideia* (Cambridge, MA, 1962); A. Wifstrand, *L'Eglise ancienne et la culture grecque* (German translation *Die alte Kirche und die griechische Bildung*) (Paris, 1962); J.B. Skemp, *The Greeks and the Gospel* (London, 1964); H. Chadwick, *Early Christian Thought and the Classical Tradition* (Oxford, 1966); and M. Siotes, *Greek Thought and Christian Faith* (in Greek) (Athens, 1971). See also notes 17 and 18 above.

[24]See S. Runciman, *Byzantine Civilization* (London, 1933); B. Tatakis, *La philosophie Byzantine* (Paris, 1949); H.W. Haussing, *Kulturgeschichte von Byzanz* (Stuttgart, 1959); H.A. Wolfson, *The Philosophy of the Church Fathers* (Cambridge, MA, 1970); G. Podskalsky, *Theologie und Philosophie in Byzanz*, Byzantinisches Archiv 15 (Munich, 1977); E. Ahrweiler-Glykatze, "Hellenism and Byzantium" (in Greek), in *Byzantinos Ellenismos, Protobyzantinoi Chronoi (324-642)* (Byzantine Hellenism, The Early Byzantine Years), IEE 7 (1980), 6-29; N.A. Matsoukas, *The History of Byzantine Philosophy* (in Greek) (Thessaloniki, 1981; expanded ed. 1994).

whose basis human relationships could now be organized in a way that achieved harmony between old, irreconcilable oppositions, such as authority and freedom, the individual and society, and realism and idealism. It was this synthesis of Greek and Christian principles that gave birth to the Western civilizations of today.[25]

There were several new elements in particular that gave Greek culture a new direction:

⌐ The gospel's emphasis on the unique value of the human person, as expressed in its teaching that the soul's worth is beyond measure.

⌐ The emphasis on freedom and on human responsibility.

⌐ The proclamation of brotherhood and equality for all, without exception.

⌐ The revelation of the supreme law of selfless and sacrificial love, which, by achieving harmony between human diversity and freedom, placed human relationships on a completely new basis.

⌐ Faith in the logically impossible, which gave people the incentive to overcome things that appeared inevitable, thus stimulating the pursuit and advancement of every form of truth that lies behind the appearance of things, including scientific truth.

⌐ The challenge and call constantly to advance in the spiritual life, to expand every human ability, and to keep moving forward "from glory to glory."

The gospel does not concern itself with secondary phenomena but proceeds directly to the source, seeking to change what is most profound in the human person by bringing it back to life. It is this internal regeneration that sets everything else in motion. The gospel changed the basic premises of life. It placed enormous faith in the human being; it revealed humanity's origin ("in the image of God"), its future (deification), and its untapped potential. All of this imparted a creative spirit to art, provided new ideas and prophetic insight in thought and science, and strengthened the will to elevate social and political life.

[25]See P. Kanellopoulos, *Christianity and Our Era, From History to Eternity* (in Greek) (Athens, 1953); and *The History of the European Spirit* (in Greek), 4 parts (Athens, 1966-74).

The synthesis of Greek tradition and Christianity that took place in Byzantine culture did not lead to stagnation. On the contrary, living the gospel in every aspect of culture continues to produce saintly figures in every generation: people who prophetically judge culture's various tangible manifestations and point out dangerous deviations; individuals of exceptional integrity, who make their lives a "testimony to the truth." The gospel has thus maintained, without interruption, its critical, rehabilitative, and restorative role, as well as its transformational activity and power. It penetrates every facet of life. The entire reality of human life must be reforged in the fire of Pentecost. No area of human life lies outside its divine activity. Both the world of the spirit and the material world are called upon to enter into this process of transformation together.

The Fundamental Principles of Transformation: "Gospel Norms"

In defining the dynamic cultural policy that Orthodoxy developed in societies where it was adopted, we would venture to say that it is based on the principle of eucharistic transformation, in which there are a number of spiritual "constants": Incarnation, Transfiguration, Crucifixion, Resurrection, and Pentecost.

The divine eucharist articulates life. Everywhere that the Orthodox Christian faith has spread, from large metropolitan cathedrals to distant monasteries and tiny churches, millions of faithful worshippers gather round the mystic table of the divine eucharist and try to purify their thoughts, ideas, attitudes, and intentions; then, after drawing new strength for love, hope, peace, faith, joy, truth, honorable and gracious conduct, they try to disseminate these in the daily reality of their lives.

The Church's rhythm of worship coordinates our entire life. Like an enormous heart, it beats unceasingly, cleansing the blood of society, passing it through the lungs of evangelical truth where it is restored, and sending it to the most distant arteries of this polymorphous organism called society. The gospel is transfused into the human person not simply in the form of teachings or sermons, but as an event that changes a person's very existence. It awakens

people, transforms them, and sanctifies them in the Holy Spirit. All
the rest of life's manifestations are consequences and effects of the
human person's transformation in Christ.

The Orthodox Church has never accepted any kind of idealistic
separation between a sphere of spiritual or religious ideas and a
material realm located outside the reach of divine activity. The incarnation of the Word has been experienced in all its dimensions and
with all its consequences. Repudiating every tendency toward idealistic division between the material and the spiritual, Orthodox theology insists on the unity of human nature, on the fact that divine
activity transforms all of existence, both spiritual and material. The
Crucifixion and the Resurrection tower in Orthodox consciousness
not as two distinct phases but as a single event that revealed the glory
of God. Without denying the fact that it was the sacrifice on the cross
that reconciled humanity and God, Orthodox thought insists on proclaiming that the mystery of God's love culminates when this tragedy
is ultimately transformed into the final victory over death and the
offer of a radically new life. This emphasis on the Resurrection is the
crucial element in the Christian ethos of the east; it pervades every
thought and action, intensifies faith in miracles, and deepens the certainty that every impasse in human life will ultimately be overcome.
It fills the soul with optimism about the future of humankind. It
transfuses immense hope and strength into our efforts to be transformed in the paschal light.

Ever since the time of Pentecost, when the Holy Spirit flowed into
the world, humanity has been called upon to share in continuous
transformation under the influence of the Spirit, who then draws the
rest of the world into this process along with humanity, since
humanity was the reason for the world's creation. "Reaching out
toward what lies ahead"[26] is both the portion that falls to humanity
and also its vocation. The faithful can never be content with the way
things are at any point along the way. The unceasing critique that
each of us makes of ourselves as people, as well as of our accomplishments—that is, of our culture—is basic to the way that Christianity
functions. Through repentance we enter a dynamic process whose

[26]Gregory of Nanzianzus, *Orations* 19.7 ("On Julian"), PG 35:1052A.

goal is unceasing renewal. This is something that clearly distinguishes Christian culture from other cultures that try to justify the existing world and social order merely on the basis of laws that they believe they have discovered themselves.

Through the power of the gospel, culture realizes all human potential and thus becomes the process through which the entire world is transformed. This vision of continuous expansion is intensified by our anticipation of the ultimate end. Humanity and the world are in a dynamic process of evolution in which they are active participants. The end is the victory of the love of free persons: the harmony and peace of a life lived with the Holy Trinity as our model. This eschatological vision offers incomparable inner strength to human endeavors. The things that lie beyond do not cast us into a hypnotic trance, but become our source of strength in the present.

Incarnation, Transfiguration, Crucifixion, Resurrection, Pentecost, and eschatological expectations: these are not merely tenets of church doctrine but constitute fundamental principles of thought and action that determine the ethos and mold the conscious and the subconscious mind of the faithful, who in turn become agents of culture.

We do not want to give the impression that in the Orthodox world things operate in an ideal fashion. Throughout history there have been many improprieties and deviations. What is important, however, is the fact that the models we hold to be correct have remained alive, as fundamental principles. Basing ourselves on these, new solutions to new sets of givens can be sought and achieved. Mistakes were made and continue to be made whenever we are ignorant of or ignore the fundamentals of the gospel, or when we do not avail ourselves of the powers offered to us by the Spirit. These are mistakes or deviations, not refutations of the basic axioms of our faith. The spiritual "constants" of the gospel have remained absolutely functional throughout all the ages and in all societies, from the simplest to the most developed, from the agricultural societies of the past to the electronic societies of the future.

In summarizing this brief theological look at culture and the gospel from an Orthodox perspective, let me emphasize that the gospel adopts and transforms: it becomes incarnated under new conditions and regenerates culture in the Holy Spirit, giving it new ontological meaning.

A culture that is creative does not identify itself only with one region or one people. It does not become a closed circle. It is constantly open to all groups of people. It does not seek uniformity but a polyphonic unity of minds and hearts. The acceptance of cultural diversity has always been a characteristic of Orthodox Christendom. Every people has been able to express itself freely and create through the experience of "evangelical constants" and at the same time to maintain its own personality and its own intrinsic temperament. Continuous regeneration and self-transcendence is the dynamic of the Christian gospel.

We are talking here about a process of uninterrupted expansion in which one's gaze is firmly fixed on humanity's ultimate destiny. Imprisonment in any of the cultural forms of this world is inexcusable; there is no justification for the closed circle of chauvinism.

The individuality of local churches, each with its own special cultural character, does not prevent different peoples from being of one mind and one heart; it presents no obstacle to the deep sense of unity that is anchored around the mystical center of the divine liturgy. The sacrament of the divine eucharist unites all into "one" in Christ, mystically proclaiming the ultimate recapitulation of everything in him, the final victory of Love, and the communion of free persons in praise of God.

~ • ~

The following brief remarks concern the relationship that Christianity has had with two dynamic, contiguous cultures.

Of particular interest is the relationship that the culture that was created on the basis of the gospel has had with two other worlds, the Islamic and the communist worlds.

It is significant that both of these cultures became consolidated in geographical regions where Orthodox communities had previously developed and, above all, that they adopted and exploited important cultural elements that had been cultivated by the Orthodox Church. One might even venture to express the view that these worlds are the product of a heretical and fragmentary form of Christianity.

When we compare, as is usually done, the first Christian period (first to fourth centuries) with the first Islamic period (seventh to eleventh centuries), considerable differences can be observed. However, when we examine early Islam alongside the simultaneously flourishing Byzantine culture (seventh to eleventh centuries), we can see important similarities and influences. The impact of Byzantine culture, Greek philosophy, scientific scholarship, and the various arts on developing Islamic culture took many forms and resulted from the attraction and brilliance of the former combined with the latter's ability to digest and assimilate.[27]

Christianity preceded communism in the region where the latter held sway for decades, and in spite of the fact that communist ideology rejected Christianity's basic principles, it also adopted important elements from Christianity: its emphasis on human equality, the importance of the material element in human life, faith in the paradoxical, the anticipation of a new society, and a profound hope in the coming of a more equitable and beautiful world.

The originality and distinctiveness of both Islam and communism are due first and foremost to the fact that they reforged many basic principles of Christianity, adding the element of coercion, often violent, through the forced conscription of followers into their ranks. They sought in this way to revise the "scandalous" stand on personal freedom that is so consistently taken in the gospel, with its emphasis on "whoever would." Of course, this same temptation has also influenced Christian circles, as most vividly depicted in Dostoevsky's portrayal of the Grand Inquisitor in *The Brothers Karamazov*.[28]

[27]A. Yannoulatos, *Islam: An Overview* (in Greek) (Athens, 1976; 4th ed. 1985).
[28]F. Dostoevsky, *The Brothers Karamazov*, trans. Richard Pevear and Larissa Volokhonsky (New York, 1991).

The Orthodox Church has been able to resist and endure this pressure by making the best use of precisely those "evangelical constants" to which we previously referred: by encouraging people to live the mystery of the cross and the hope of resurrection, inspiring them with the memory and the ethos of the martyrs. From the fifteenth to the eighteenth century, the years when the churches of Eastern Europe and the near east suffered great hardship under the Ottoman yoke, the Church managed to keep the cultural identity and vigorous spirit of Orthodox peoples alive by preaching and living the gospel. It was thus able to help their culture survive and later to help them obtain their freedom. Something similar also took place in Russia in the sixteenth century, when the Tatars imposed their power. The memory of the Orthodox Church's contribution helps the people of these countries to stand before the gospel of Christ with deep gratitude and reverence.

As happened in the past with Islam, and also quite often in our own day with communism, the mentality of the Crusades—i.e., of violence, hostility, and adversarial methods—has also found its supporters in Christian milieus in the west. What the Crusades accomplished, however, was the very opposite of what they had hoped to achieve, for in the end they maimed and mortally wounded not Islam, but one of the most vital and flourishing cultures, the Byzantine culture, and they reinforced fear and suspicion between Christians and Muslims for centuries to come.

In countries that were dominated by the Islamic or the communist/Marxist worldview, the gospel continued to provide culture with its light and Christians continued to give testimony to their faith, mainly through their quiet presence and resistance.

When the faithful assembled to worship as a community, the gospel was received with longing and praise of God, and worshippers became familiar with its power through the sacrament of the Divine Eucharist.

By transforming life into a liturgy, the faithful experienced inner peace, hope, and the joy of the Resurrection in their daily reality. The phrase "Christ has risen!" summarized their certainty and their resistance to various external constraints. The encouraging words of the Russian ascetic St Seraphim of Sarov were particularly beloved: "Acquire inner peace and thousands of souls around you will find salvation."

When necessary, the message of peace in the gospel of Christ was validated by silent or public martyrdom. In the last five centuries millions of martyrs have been received into the bosom of the Orthodox Church.

The exceptional beauty of the things that Orthodox culture produced has been a major pole of attraction. Byzantine icons, churches, music, and literature, which were all created through the inspiration of the gospel and are triumphs of Christian culture, have not merely been accepted as part of the soul of each people, but have in turn been transformed once again into bearers of the gospel. The deep faith that created these great works and that is stored up within them has once again been "sent up from within" and projected outward.

Through their creative thought and their critical stance, Christians have conveyed their certainty that humanity is called upon to transcend itself and that it is capable of doing so. They have stressed the immeasurable importance of the human person and personal freedom. This critical attitude continues to be expressed, wherever feasible, through dialogue. In such dialogue Christians acknowledge that communism, through its emphasis on the material, has played a part in freeing modern humanity from a tendency toward excessive idealism and has revealed the significance of economic factors in the formation of society and cultural structures.

At the same time, Christians disagree with efforts to interpret everything from an economic perspective, as secondary phenomena of economic structures, and they also disagree with efforts to impose dogmatic paradigms that have been termed a priori "scientific." The latter has been used as a pretext to impose a dictatorship in thought, one that has led to a dangerous state of stagnation in scholarly inquiry and human creativity. The Christian critique further points out that dialectical materialism, lacking a human criterion on which to base its scale of values, has imprisoned itself in the notion of matter and in its own conceptual constructions. Nothing has been transcended; rather, these paradigms, which were created by human beings, have merely become sacrosanct. By denying the importance of the human person and personal freedom, one-party ideology has left little room for the creation of real culture. Imposing a culture of uniformity and monotony always threatens to lead humanity to an appalling state of impoverishment.

As a result of these contradictions, both in the realm of ideas and in the "dialogue of life," there is growing hope that something new lies on the horizon for older forms of culture and for a more genuine experience of the gospel. By way of humanity's digressions and misadventures, God's loving plan for the transformation of the human race and all creation is steadily evolving.

~ 4 ~

Dialogue with Islam

FROM AN ORTHODOX POINT OF VIEW*

The Eastern Orthodox Church has had contact with Islam since the latter first arose, and the dialogue between them has taken various forms. The Islamic religion emerged in a region very close to the geographical area where Orthodoxy was already flourishing, and Islam later conquered vast portions of the territory in which Orthodox Christianity had originally developed: Palestine, Egypt, Syria, and Asia Minor.

Orthodoxy's encounter with Islam not only took the form of military conflict and confrontation, but evolved into a quiet coexistence that lasted for centuries. This relationship was often articulated on an intellectual level in the form of theological dialogues, in which an effort was made to clarify the differences between these two forms of religious experience and to define their positions.

HISTORICAL OVERVIEW

The Three Phases of Byzantine-Islamic Dialogue

Muhammad died on July 8, 632—on the thirteenth day of *Rabi ʿal Awwal* in the eleventh year of the era of the *hijrah*—and in the

*This paper was originally presented in German at an international symposium on "Islamic-Christian Dialogue" organized by the Pro Oriente Foundation in Vienna on October 16, 1986, and was later published in the proceedings of that conference under the title "Der Dialog mit dem Islam aus orthodoxer Sicht": XLVI Ökumenisches Symposion, 16 October 1986 in Wien, R. Kirchschläger, A. Stiernemann (Hersg.), Ein Laboratorium für die Einheit, *Pro Oriente*, XIII, Tyrolia Verlag (Innsbruck and Wien, 1991), 210-22. It has previously appeared in English translation under the title "Byzantine and Contemporary Greek Orthodox Approaches to Islam," *Journal of Ecumenical Studies* 33:4 (1996): 512-28.

decades that followed his death Islamic military expansion developed with lightning speed. Hardly a century after Muhammad's death, the "House of Islam," the Muslim state, extended from the Pyrenees to the Himalayas and the plains of China.[1]

Recognizing the aggressive force of this new religion, Christian Byzantium mobilized every means of defense that it had as a social and political entity. It was in this context that a large number of theological treatises appeared, written in the form of dialogues or "discussions" between representatives of Islam and Christianity. Some of these treatises appear to be summaries of actual conversations or dialogues that took place between Christians and Muslims.

Since the Byzantines lived in such proximity to the cradle of the Muslim world, they had the opportunity to become acquainted with Islam through Islamic sources. This was something that only occurred much later in the case of the Christian west, which was separated by a far greater distance from Islam, not only geographically but also socially and politically. As early as the ninth century, shortly before the time of Patriarch Photius, Nicetas the Byzantine had already written a critical analysis of the entire Qur'an in Greek that included many extracts in translation. The first Latin translation of the Qur'an was completed much later, in the middle of the twelfth century.

The Byzantines' theoretical approach toward Islam passed through several stages. In the first phase, which extended from the middle of the eighth until the middle of the ninth century, their attitude was mainly derisive and disparaging. St John of Damascus (d. 750 or 784), who was among the first Christians to give the subject his attention, did not consider the newly arrived Muslim teaching to be a matter of any significance. From a theological point of view, he saw Islam as a religious fabrication suitable only for primitive peoples, and when he presented a sample of tenets from Islamic teaching, he described them as "worthy of laughter."[2] It is usually pointed out that the Damascene considered Islam a "Christian heresy"; in "Against Heresies," a section of his major work *The Source*

---

[1]A. Yannoulatos, *Islam: An Overview* (in Greek), 4th ed. (Athens, 1985), 221-22.
[2]John of Damascus, *The Source of Knowledge*, PG 94:765A, 772D.

of Knowledge, he characterizes the Ishmaelites or Hagarenes or Saracens as the "one hundred and first" heresy.[3] However, in John's terminology the word "heresy" has a wider meaning and includes schools of Greek philosophy as well as other religious forms.

The new religion received more methodical treatment by Theodore, the Bishop of Harran (or Roman Carrhae) in Mesopotamia, who was also known as Abu Qurrah (d. 820 or 825). His *Against the Jewish and Saracen Heresies,*[4] a work written in dialogue form, can be considered the first serious attempt to understand and confront Islam. Theodore refutes the Muslim critique of Christianity, explaining Christian doctrine with a number of well-chosen examples and pointing out that its truth is evident from the fact that Christianity has successfully made its presence felt, in spite of all its outward weaknesses.

This first period of literary confrontation between Christians of the east and Islam was centered in Syria, where the seat of the caliphate was located. The works of the two theologians referred to above reflect actual experiences based on direct personal dialogue with Muslims. Both of these theologians lived among a Muslim population and knew the Qur'an in the original.

In the second phase, from the middle of the ninth to the middle of the fourteenth century, the center of anti-Islamic literature moved to the capital of the Byzantine state. The impressive success and spread of Islam was becoming a nightmare for the Byzantines. They realized that this religion, in spite of or perhaps precisely because of its logical and ethical peculiarities, was a major threat to the empire. They therefore adopted a more hostile policy. Many works on this subject became widely popular during this period, such as those of Samona Gazes,[5] Euthemios Zigavenos,[6] Nicetas Choniates,[7] Bartholomaios of Edessa,[8] and others. The most representative of these works is *A Refutation of the Book Forged by the Arab Muhammad* by

[3]Ibid. PG 94:764-73.
[4]PG 97:1462-1609.
[5]*Dialexis with Ahmed the Saracen,* PG 120:821-32.
[6]*Dogmatic Panoply,* paragraph 28, PG 133:1332-60.
[7]*Treasury of Orthodoxy,* paragraph 20, PG 140:105A-121.
[8]*Censure of the Haragene,* PG 104:1384A-1448A.

Nicetas of Byzantium,[9] a conventional polemic, in which the author attempts to prove that Islam is an incoherent religion.[10]

The third phase of Byzantium's confrontation with Islam, a period that lasted from the middle of the fourteenth to the middle of the fifteenth century, was distinguished by its gentleness and objectivity. The leading protagonists in these debates and dialogues were eminent Byzantine figures, such as St Gregory Palamas (d. 1359)[11] and the the monk Joseph Vryennios (d. 1425),[12] and emperors, such as John VI Cantacuzenus (d. 1383)[13] and Manuel II Palaeologus (d. 1425).[14] The Byzantines showed greater interest in and desire for dialogue with the Muslims in the final century of Byzantium. The Emperor John Cantacuzenus characteristically notes:

The Muslims prevent any of their own from engaging in dialogue with Christians, in order, it seems, to keep them from ever learning the truth clearly through such an exchange of views. The Christians, however, confident that their faith is pure and that the dogmas they hold are right and true, do not

[9]PG 105:669-805.

[10]For more on this period, see C. Güterbock, *Der Islam im Lichte der byzantinischen Polemik* (Berlin, 1912); W. Eichner, "Die Nachrichten über den Islam bei den Byzantinern," *Der Islam* 23 (1936): 133-62, 197-244; E.D. Sdraka, *The Polemic of Byzantine Theologians against Islam* (in Greek) (Thessaloniki, 1961); J. Meyendorff, "Byzantine Views of Islam," *Dumbarton Oaks Papers* 18 (1964): 115-32; A.T. Khoury, *Les théologiens byzantins et l'Islam, Textes et auteurs (VIIIe-XIIIe s.)*, 2e triage (Louvain et Paris, 1969); and A.T. Khoury, *Der theologische Streit der Byzantiner mit dem Islam* (Paderborn, 1969).

[11]"To the Atheist Chionai, A Conversation Recorded by the Physician Taronites, Who Was Present and Witnessed the Event," *Soter* 15 (1892): 240-46; "Letter Sent to the Church from Asia, Where Its Author Was Being Held Captive," *Neos Hellenomnemon* 16 (1922): 7-21; and "Letter to David the Disypatos, a Monk," *Deltion tes Istorikes kai Ethnologikes Etaireias* (Bulletin of the Historical and Ethnological Society) 3 (1899): 229-34.

[12]"Conversation with an Ishmaelite," *Epeteres tes Etaireias Byzantinon Spoudon* (Yearbook of the Society for Byzantine Studies) 35 (1966), 158-95.

[13]The anti-Islamic work of John Cantacuzenus (PG 154:372-692) is basically divided into two parts. The first, *Against the Muhammedans,* consists of four apologies, and the second, *Against Muhammad,* of four discourses. At numerous points the author appears to have relied on *Confutatio Alcorani* (PG 154:1037-1152), a work by Florentine Dominican monk Ricoldo da Monte Croce (d. 1320), which had been translated by Demetrius Kydones.

[14]*Dialogue with a Persian of the Rank of Mouterizes in Ancyra, Galatia,* PG 156:125-174.

in any way hinder their own; on the contrary, every Christian has full permission and authority to converse with anyone who wishes or desires to do so.[15]

The basic theoretical aspects of the Byzantine dialogue between Islam and Christianity can be summarized as follows.

In the beginning, the Byzantines saw Islam as a variant and a resurgence of Arianism. The Muslim critique of Christianity mainly targeted the divinity of Jesus Christ and the doctrine of the Holy Trinity; secondarily, it criticized certain forms of Christian worship and the inconsistencies of Christians regarding their own faith.

The Christian critique of Islam took the person of Islam's founder as its first target, casting doubt on his status as a prophet. Their main arguments were that his coming had not been foretold by the prophets, that he had no evidence to offer in support of his revelation, that he had performed no miracles, that he had not foretold the future, and that in ethical terms his life had not been as lofty as would befit a prophet. Most Byzantines thought that Muhammad had been in the service of the Antichrist and that he was a forerunner of the final days. Some did not even hesitate to identify him as the Antichrist himself. These severe characterizations were later abandoned, at least in official texts. In any case, a favorite arena in which the Byzantines preferred to engage the Muslims in their theoretical battle was in comparing the teachings and the lives of the two religions' founders, Jesus and Muhammad.

Christian writers also aimed their sights at the Qur'an. By comparing it with Holy Scripture, they pointed to scandalous distortions, misinterpretations, and inconsistencies; moreover, they demonstrated particular fervor in their battle against the Muslim belief that the Qur'an was the uncreated word of God. Through their historical analysis of the Qur'an and its teachings, they reached the conclusion that Islam's holy book represented a regression in theological and ethical teaching. They also had extremely sharp criticism for the family law introduced by Islam—its laws regarding marriage and sexual behavior—for its views concerning "holy war" and slavery,

[15]John Cantacuzenus, *Against the Muhammadans*, PG 154:380BC.

and finally for its materialistic conception of the afterlife, which included descriptions of gastronomic and sexual satisfaction.

Both in their attacks on Islamic views and in their defense of Christianity against the Muslim critique, the Byzantines based themselves on philosophical thought and on evidence from holy scripture. Whether or not their arguments are always convincing, these Byzantine treatises demonstrate that these two religions share a common conceptual ground, which makes dialogue possible. This kind of common theological language does not always exist in Christianity's dialogue with other religions, one example being the religions of India.

The Initiators of Serious Christian-Islamic Dialogue

The Byzantines can be considered the forerunners and initiators of Christian-Islamic dialogue, which in our day is encouraged on an international scale. This can be more clearly seen by pointing to three typical examples.

The atmosphere in which Christian-Islamic dialogue was conducted acquires particular seriousness and eloquence in the brief surviving texts by St Gregory Palamas, who was a monk on Mount Athos and later became archbishop of Thessaloniki. In these dialogues,[16] which appear to be summaries of actual conversations, he was clear and consistent regarding Christian positions, but at the same time gentle and patient when it came to the reactions of the Muslims. His goal was to persuade his interlocutors; he therefore based his arguments on points that the two religions held in common. For example, he begins with a definition of God that Muslims accept and with testimony from the Qur'an regarding Christ as the Word (*logos*) of God.

> God is one; he has always existed and remains eternal, without beginning, without change, without end, immutable, undivided, unconfused, and boundless [he avoids referring to God as the Father] . . . This God, the only God without

[16]See note 10.

beginning, is not irrational . . . nor is he without wisdom; therefore, the *logos* of God is also the wisdom of God.[17]

Nor does *logos* [word, speech, reason] ever exist without spirit, something which you Turks also admit; for by saying that Christ is the *logos* of God, you are also saying that he is the spirit of God, in the sense that he is never separated from the holy spirit . . . Since God never was and never will be either without spirit or without reason.[18]

Finally, alluding to the three hypostases of God, he uses the image of the sun:

Just as the brilliance that radiates from the sun was born of the sun, so too the rays of the sun proceed from the sun.[19]

The argumentation used here by Gregory Palamas is adroit and dialectically subtle. He does not shy away from critical issues or try to maintain a superficial impression of harmony. When questioned on his views about Muhammad, he responds politely but unambiguously: "If you do not believe the teacher's words, you cannot love the teacher; this is why we do not love Muhammad."[20] Palamas sees Muhammad in the same way his Byzantine predecessors did: Muhammad is not attested to by the prophets and performed no miracles, and so is not creditable.[21] In response to the usual Muslim arguments that Islam's successes and victories prove its superiority, Gregory Palamas reminds them that "[Muhammad was involved in] . . . war and the sword and bloodshed and plunder; none of these things is of God, who is first and foremost good."[22]

[17]"To the Atheist Chionai," 241.
[18]Ibid., 241-42.
[19]Ibid., 242.
[20]Ibid., 245.
[21]"We find no testimony in the prophets regarding Muhammad, nor has anyone offered evidence of anything unusual that he did or anything worthy of our faith; therefore we do not believe in him or in the book he wrote." "Letter to David the Disypatos," 232.
[22]Ibid., 233.

Throughout the dialogue St Gregory makes a particular effort not to offend the religious sensibilities of his interlocutors. Although agreement is not reached, an atmosphere of respect and mutual esteem is maintained. "In the end the Turkish leaders rose and with reverence bid the Archbishop of Thessaloniki farewell and departed."[23] Whenever he perceived that his interlocutors found themselves in a difficult position, he would hasten, with grace and affability, to diffuse the electric atmosphere with his tactful humor: "I made them cheerful again by smiling gently at the Imam and then replied: 'If we agreed on these matters, we would be of the same faith.'"[24] A friendly atmosphere was thus preserved, even though agreement was not achieved, and one Muslim hopefully expressed his expectation that "there will come a day when we will agree with one another."[25]

Another eminent Byzantine figure who dealt with burning issues in the Christian-Islamic dialogue in a graceful and low-keyed manner was the Emperor Manuel II Palaeologus. The work that he left behind is clearly an account of a "dialogue"[26] that took place in 1390 and 1391, when Manuel was staying at the Turkish court in Brusa and there had the opportunity to exchange views with educated Muslims on theological issues. The first twenty-six dialogues are critiques of various Islamic views, and the later dialogues deal with theological proofs of basic Christian doctrines and ethical teachings. Manuel's work avoids the derogatory expressions and disparaging adjectives that are met with in earlier Byzantine anti-Islamic literature. The atmosphere is pervaded by his desire for true, objective dialogue. The first dialogue begins:

> After dinner I was seated near the fire, where the Muslim elder, as was his custom, also sat. Those with us included some of our own young men, as well as his; for he had two sons, both of some intelligence and wisdom, who fairly often took part in

[23]"To the Atheist Chionai," 246.

[24]"Letter to David the Disypatos a Monk," *Deltion tis Istorikis kai Ethnologikis Etairiai* (Bulletin of the Historical and Ethnological Society) 3 (1899): 233. Cf. "Letter Sent to the Church from Asia," 19.

[25]"Letter to David the Disypatos," 233.

[26]See note 14.

their father's conversations. And the old man said to me: "If you don't think that I will be burdening you, I would like you to listen to me and to give us your thoughts on certain issues that I have had in mind to inquire about. . . ."[27]

The full work demonstrates that Manuel was an accomplished theologian and an articulate speaker, who also had a penetrating mind and a sincere interest in engaging in serious dialogue with the Muslims.

This desire for serious dialogue continued even in the early years following the Turkish conquest of Constantinople. Shortly after the fall of the city, Mehmet the Conqueror, accompanied by his court theologians, visited the newly elected Patriarch Gennadius—this was in 1455 or at the beginning of 1456—desiring to receive accurate information regarding the Christian religion. The patriarch's exposition of Christian teaching impressed the conqueror, but being a military man he was unable to absorb all the philosophical distinctions made by the theologian. He therefore asked the patriarch for a written summary of everything that had been explained during their discussion, and Gennadius wrote *Concerning the Only Road toward Human Salvation*.[28] This work was translated into Ottoman Arabic by a competent Greek translator and was presented to the sultan, who then requested a shorter and simpler version. Gennadius composed a new, condensed text, known as the *Confession of Faith*, in which he omitted many points in his first work, simplified others, and added new explanations.[29]

[27]PG 156:133B.

[28]The full title of this work reveals both its history and the spirit in which it was written: *By Gennadius, a monk and Patriarch of the impoverished Christians, known in the world by his surname Scholarius, concerning the only road toward human salvation and produced at the Sultan's request following the conversations that took place in his presence at the Patriarchate; after which, another, shorter version was also produced, and both were translated into Arabic and thus presented to him.* L. Petit, X. Sidéridès, and M. Jugie, *Oeuvres complètes de Gennade Scholarios* 3 (Paris, 1930), 434-52.

[29]*By that most wise and honored gentleman Gennadius, Patriarch of Constantinople and New Rome, being a confession to the Hagarenes of the true and blameless faith of the Christians; for when he was asked by the Emir Sultan Mehmet, What do you Christians believe? he replied as follows,* in Petit et al., 453-58; and I. Karmires, *Dogmatic and Doctrinal Documents of the Orthodox Catholic Church* (in Greek), 1, 2d ed., enlarged and amended (Athens, 1960), 429-36.

In the work in question an effort is made to adapt Christian views to the level of Turkish religious thought. The responsible representative of Christian teaching here is a theologian and leader of the Church who finds himself before an all-powerful Muslim despot. Accordingly, the author entirely avoids the polemical and derisive language used by writers of the Byzantine period, who launched their attacks from a position of safety against an enemy who was located far away, easily winning laurels from those who shared their beliefs.

Gennadius writes as objectively as possible about the Christian faith, without directly comparing it to the Islamic faith, which—it goes without saying—is continuously on his mind. He elaborates his own religious views systematically but avoids attacking Islam. He attempts to elucidate issues that are known to be theological points of contention between the two religions, such as the Holy Trinity and christological dogma, using language that is easily accepted and understood by his interlocutors. The image of the flame is employed to illustrate the doctrine of the Holy Trinity more graphically: "We believe that Reason [*logos*] and Spirit [*pneuma*] arise from God's nature as light and heat from a flame."[30] Gennadius avoids any offensive allusions to Islam or its prophet, whose name his listener bears. The discussion remains serious, laconic, and objective. In his dialogue with the Muslims, this austere champion of Orthodoxy uses language that is accessible rather than strictly dogmatic and that above all facilitates understanding and thus makes communication easier. This principle, which he applied in an extremely responsible fashion at that crucially historic moment and which along general lines continues to be applied in interfaith dialogue today, is beautifully summarized in a note at the end of his *Confession of Faith*:

> It is important to understand that the lessons we give to the uninitiated about the exceptional beliefs of our faith must be conducted at the beginning in such a way that they will be well received, as is the case in the present work, rather than

[30]Karmires, 433.

in the most accurate way, and they must be expressed as clearly as possible, so that they can easily be transposed from one language to another, just as the things written here were translated well into Arabic.[31]

Some fifteen years later, Gennadius had another opportunity to engage in dialogue with Muslim leaders. In 1470 a Turkish soldier, on orders from his superiors, met Gennadius at the Prodromos monastery, where the theologian had withdrawn from the world, and brought him to a place near Pherae where two pashas were waiting for him, anxious to be informed about the divinity of Jesus Christ, whom the Qur'an also recognizes as the Word and Spirit of God.

The wise patriarch, making good use of the theological and philosophical weapons at his disposal, took as the starting point for his exegesis of Christian views those points that were already accepted by pious Muslims. Gennadius placed particular emphasis on the self-awareness of Jesus Christ, whom the Qur'an recognizes as the Word and Spirit of God. Furthermore, he did not hesitate to use even the prophecies of the Sibyls or pagan "oracles," which he regarded as vehicles for divine messages. With regard to non-Christian religious beliefs, he accepted that there is nothing to stop God from using even the work of demons to further his plans for redemption. He also emphasized that God educates human beings with boundless forbearance.[32]

With these texts, the austere Orthodox theologian and patriarch Gennadius opened a new road in the area of theological dialogue with Islam, clearly responding to the pressure of new historical conditions. He avoided acrimony, made use of Muslim religious beliefs, and attempted, as simply as possible, and without betraying his Orthodox faith, to adapt his account of Christianity to the theological and spiritual level of his interlocutors, treating them with love and respect, regardless of their beliefs.

[31]Ibid., 436.
[32]*Questions and answers concerning the divinity of our Lord Jesus Christ,* in Petit et al., 458-75.

The Period of Silence and Monologue

Unfortunately, the atmosphere that the Byzantines had begun to create during the final hundred years of their empire soon changed.
During the period of Turkish rule that followed, from the middle of
the fifteenth until the middle of the nineteenth century, the dialogue
that had been initiated was interrupted, and we passed into a fourth
phase. For Orthodox Christians in the Balkans, this was a time of
long silence and resistance; for the Muslims, it was a time of monologue from the seat of power.[33]

In this fourth phase the eastern Church suffered hardships.
Despite the periodic tolerance of certain enlightened leaders of the
Ottoman state, Muslim extremism often broke out and various
sociopolitical pressures gave rise to waves of Islamization in Asia
Minor, the Balkans, and Crete.[34] It was at this time that the so-called
crypto-Christians first appeared. These were groups of the Christian
population who, finding themselves unimaginably pressured by
social and political forces, were coerced into formally accepting
Islam, while in their families and personal lives they secretly maintained their Christian beliefs.[35] In only a few exceptional cases,

[33]The Byzantines' interest in developing a critical approach toward Islam as well as
their centuries of experience and thought on this subject and their awareness of the need
for theological guidance were all transported to Russia by Maxim the Greek (1470-
1556). Maxim wrote three treatises on Islam in Russian. These judicious theological
works helped sensitize the Russian people to this issue and in general strengthened their
spiritual resistance to the pressures of Islam. Gregorios Papamichael, *Maxim the Greek:
The First Enlightener of the Russians* (in Greek) (Athens, 1950), 176-86.

[34]On Islamization, see I.K. Vogiatzides, "Historical Studies: Turkification and
Islamization of Greeks in the Middle Ages" (in Greek), *Epistimoniki Epeteris Philosophikis
Scholis Panepistemiou Thessalonikis* (Scholarly Yearbook of the Philosophical School,
University of Thessaloniki) 2 (1932): 95-155; E. Petrovitch, "Islamization" (in Greek),
Seraika Chronika 2 (1957): 160-74; S. Vryonis, *The Decline of Medieval Hellenism in Asia
Minor and the Process of Islamization from the Eleventh through the Fifteenth Century*
(Berkeley, Los Angeles, and London, 1971); A.E. Vakalopoulos, *The History of Modern
Hellenism: Turkish Rule 1453-1669* (in Greek), 2, 2d ed., expanded and revised (Thessa-
loniki, 1976), 51-73; P. Chidiroglou, "Islamization on Crete," *Proceedings of the Fourth
International Conference on Cretan Studies,* (in Greek), Herakleion, 29 August–3 Septem-
ber 1976, vol. 3 (Athens, 1981), 336-50.

[35]On crypto-Christians, see G.K. Lameras, *On the Crypto-Christians of Asia Minor* (in
Greek) (Athens, 1921); A.A. Papadopoulos, "The Crypto-Christians of the Pontus" (in
Greek) *Hemerologion Megales Ellados* (1922), 169-80; N.P. Andriotes, *Crypto-Christian
Literature* (in Greek) (Thessaloniki, 1953); N.E. Meliores, *The Crypto-Christians* (in

however, did this secrecy last for more than a few generations; in the end, their descendants were absorbed into the Islamic majority.

The Orthodox responded to this Ottoman monologue of coercion by maintaining their intense liturgical life, which was centered around the Divine Eucharist and the great celebration of the Passion and the Resurrection; they shared in the mystery of Christ's Cross as a living experience. This was a Good Friday that lasted for centuries, in anticipation of the Resurrection. It was a singular mystical dialogue, in which Orthodox Christians met external pressure with silent forbearance, filled with prayer and praise of God, their gaze fixed on his paradoxical will and, above all, on humanity's eschatological expectations.

The Modern Era

One could say that in our own era we have arrived at a fifth phase—at least where the Orthodox are concerned—in Christian-Islamic dialogue. During the last thirty years, discussions between Christians and Muslims have become more frequent. This dialogue is promoted mainly within scholarly circles, by representatives of the two religions, research foundations and centers, and international church organizations. There have been two extremely important milestones in our era. The first was the Second Vatican Council, which radically changed the attitude and the conduct of the Roman Catholic world in relation to this issue, especially after their declaration regarding the Church's relationships with non-Christian communities.[36] The second was the interfaith dialogue that began on the initiative of the World Council of Churches and which became a permanent institution in the 1970s, with the formation of its Department on Dialogue with Men of Other Faiths and Ideologies, later renamed Dialogue with People of Living Faiths. The Orthodox have

Greek) (Athens, 1962); A.C. Terzopoulos, "The Klostoi or Crypto-Christians of Sourmenoi" (in Greek), *Archeion Pontou* 30 (1970-71): 398-425; E.I. Nikolaides, *The Crypto-Christians of Spathia: From the Early Eighteenth Century to 1912* (in Greek) (Ioanina, 1979); and P. Chidiroglou, *Islamization on Crete* (in Greek) (Athens, 1981).

[36]See W.M. Abbott, ed., *The Documents of Vatican II, with Notes and Comments by Catholic, Protestant and Orthodox Authorities* (New York, 1966), 660-61.

participated with great interest in this WCC department since it was established. I myself had the opportunity to belong to its first working group for many years.

In addition, particular interest in Christian-Islamic dialogue has developed within the interchurch body of the Conference of European Churches.[37] I can affirm from my personal experience that there is a sincere willingness to engage in serious Christian-Islamic dialogue and to involve the active participation of the Orthodox.[38]

THE MODERN PHASE: CONTEXT AND ISSUES

New Conditions and Horizons

The current phase of Christian-Islamic dialogue has developed under new conditions and with new perspectives.

Scholarly research during the last 150 years has increased our understanding of Islam, removing serious misconceptions and making it easier to identify the issues with greater accuracy and appreciate their significance. Nevertheless, a considerable number of issues still await objective investigation.

What has primarily changed, at least on the Christian side, has been attitude and willingness. Many Christians today are reexamining their own views and exhibit a greater understanding and respect for the spiritual treasures that the Muslims have preserved. Furthermore, Islam is now recognized as a dynamic religious force within

[37]Two conferences, both of them in Austria, have been held on this topic, the first in February 1978 in Salzburg, and the second in March 1984 in Pölten. [1999 Addendum: A subsequent conference was held in June 1990 in Leningrad. See A. Yannoulatos, "Dialogue and Mission: An Eastern Orthodox with Special Reference to Islam," *Bul.* 26 (1991): 61-76.]

[38][1999 Addendum: In November 1986, systematic dialogue between the Orthodox and the Muslims began, in cooperation with the Orthodox Center of the Ecumenical Patriarchate (Chambesy, Geneva) and the Royal Academy for research into Islamic culture (Al Albait Foundation, Amman, Jordan). See Metropolitan of Switzerland Damaskinos Papandreou, "The Interfaith Dialogues of the Orthodox Church," in M. Konstantinos and A. Stiernemann, eds., *Christian-Islamic Dialogue as a Mutual Responsibility* (in Greek) (Thessaloniki, 1998), 31-35, and see 35-42 for special reference to Orthodoxy's dialogue with Islam. See also *Episkepsis* 27:532 (1996): 10-21; 28:545 (1997): 4-23; 28:548 (1997): 8-13; and 29:563 (1998): 11-24.]

history. In the past, its negative aspects and the things that made it different from Christianity received the most emphasis. Today its positive elements are stressed, along with the common spiritual ground and common spiritual experience that exist between the two religions.

As the twenty-first century begins, we see Islam as a system of ideas and principles that influences millions of people—people that we are called upon to live with and to cooperate with on this small planet of ours, this unified megalopolis, where human beings are increasingly interdependent upon one another. In order to meet the challenges of our era we often have to avoid confrontational ways of speaking to each other, or against each other; instead, we are obliged to make an effort to examine together the new signs of the times, the thorny new problems of our age.

In this modern era of interfaith dialogue, the Christian side is represented by a variety of churches. As we shall see below, something special has been contributed by the active participation of the Orthodox in this dialogue between Christians and Muslims.

Stalemates and Future Prospects

When the aim of dialogue is to gain a sober and objective understanding of each other's religious views and experiences, it can reveal the great extent to which Islam and Christianity share many fundamental beliefs. Indeed, on several points it can even help us Christians rediscover basic commandments we may have forgotten, such as the intense experience of God's transcendence, obedience to his will, awe in our contact with him, and the injunction to marshal our entire psychosomatic being in prayer.

Nevertheless, we must not view things too romantically. Dialogue presupposes that both sides desire to have such a relationship and to explore it. Until today, however, this attitude has been promoted more in the Christian world. We cannot say the same for the Muslim world, where with few exceptions a similar desire has not presented itself. On the contrary, there are quite a few recent examples of a new rise in fundamentalism, promoted by supporters of "Islamic purity," as well as a rise in intolerance, as seen in Iran, Libya, Turkey, and Algeria. Therefore, rather than speak about a dialogue between Christianity—or even just Christians—and Islam, it is more correct to speak of a dialogue between some Christians and a few Muslims.

Such dialogue may well help us get beyond longstanding mis-comprehensions and misunderstandings, but in the end it will naturally have its limits when we arrive at points where these two religious experiences radically differ. Indeed, such inherently structural differences are to be found in Christianity's crowning doctrines: faith in the mystery of the Holy Trinity and in the mystery of the incarnation of the Word—that is to say, in the divinity of Jesus Christ. As we know, Muslims respect Jesus as a great prophet, but they reject the cross and, above all, its significance for the salvation of all humanity.[39]

Thus, while there is agreement at a rudimentary stage of religious experience, Muslims remain at this rudimentary level, refusing to advance or to accept what constitutes the deeper Christian experience: the experience of communion between God and humanity in Christ through the Holy Spirit. Here dialogue can do no more than smooth over the hard edges and primarily correct the caricatures of such experiences that have been created by fanatical and populist polemic, thus helping to rectify the way each religion has been portrayed and contributing, as much as possible, toward a more faithful description of analogous religious experiences. What will remain in the end will be a clearer differentiation between the two religions, along with the freedom to choose.

Christian-Islamic dialogue is more promising when Christians and Muslims sit down together, with respect for their differences, in order to address the new issues and challenges created by our technocratic era and by the newly emerging international community.

[39]The cross remains a "scandal" and a "folly" to classic Muslim thought, which still reacts negatively to the basic experience that Christians have in worship: a personal experience of communion with Christ in the divine eucharist. In the past, whenever Muslims have converted imposing Christian churches into Islamic places of worship, they have hastened to obliterate three things: the symbol of the cross, the holy communion table, and the iconostasis with the figures of saints who had lived "in Christ." The visitor who enters Hagia Sophia in Constantinople cannot help but notice these alterations; the cross, for example, has become the simple letter "I."

The time that is spent in deep thought, with each side sounding the depths of its most profound religious convictions and experiences in order to explain how one or another critical issue can be approached, is not merely sharing information but constitutes spiritual communication and contact. Examples of such critical issues include secularization, the impersonalization of society, the destruction of the natural environment, human rights, and global justice and peace.

It is generally accepted that this rapprochement process between Christians and Muslims has been aided by their mutual participation in broader interfaith meetings, where the interrelationships between religious ideas can be more deeply explored.[40]

The scope of bilateral dialogue has at the same time been broadened by the fact that we are sharing this common experience and that representatives from a variety of religious beliefs are engaged in this common pursuit. This process also illuminates the common ground that exists between religions that share a monotheistic and prophetic religious experience.

The Special Contribution of the Orthodox

It is obvious that the cultural tradition and legacy of eastern Christians places us much closer to the Muslim world, with which we have coexisted for many centuries. In many senses, despite our deep theological differences and our dramatic clashes in the past, we both move within a common cultural landscape.[41]

[40]The courteousness in this rapprochement process was particularly noticeable to me at the first interfaith meeting in Colombo, Sri Lanka (1974), which was organized by the WCC on the subject "Toward World Community." It was also apparent at the interfaith conference in Bangkok (1980) organized by UNESCO to examine the positions of different religions on proclaiming international rights, as well as at the meeting of the World Conference on Religion and Peace in Nairobi (1984), which considered how religious people throughout the world understand the struggle for world peace and disarmament.

[41]My book on Islam (see note 1), which was written mainly as a textbook for students at the University of Athens, contains an epilogue that concludes with the following observation: "Of all the living religions, Islam is the closest, both spiritually and geographically, to Orthodox Christianity . . . Both religions have a common obligation—one that is laden with possibilities—to acquire a deeper mutual understanding of the spiritual wealth of their two worlds."

An important observation that has emerged from scholarly research is the close connection between eastern Christianity and the beginnings of Islam. An Orthodox Christian who understands Islam's various formulations and views will recognize a fair number of kindred points, albeit in altered form. There clearly exist common layers of religious experience in the Middle East.[42] I will explain, in a general way, what I mean. It is an unquestionable fact that the Qur'an absorbed, adopted, and reshaped a large number of Christian concepts, as they were understood by Muhammad through his indirect contact with eastern Christendom. Muhammad's meeting and relationship with one or more Christian monks from the east is well documented. Study of the basic theological lines of the Qur'an reveals the author's secret dialogue with Judaeo-Christian views, a dialogue that sometimes results in affirmation (belief in God, the angels, the prophets, and in written revelation, as well as respect for the person of Jesus and for the eternal virginity of the *Panaghia*, the All-Holy Virgin Mary) and at other times in staunch rejection (the fatherhood of Allah, the divinity of Jesus Christ, the Crucifixion, the Resurrection, and the teachings concerning the Holy Trinity).

Many Muslims consider Christianity to be an altered and distorted version of Islam, while the Orthodox view Islam as a corrupted form of Christianity, the result of a failure to understand Christianity in all its profundity. Many points in Islamic teaching are the result of a "hurried dialogue," in which Christian views were described and interpreted superficially, without having really been understood.

In the more formal aspect of devotional life, the daily pattern of Islamic prayer clearly reveals the imprint of the eastern monastic form of prayer. Describing monastic prayer in the east, St John Cassian (d. 435) writes:

---

[42]According to one view, Islam began in many respects as the fruit of a deficient form of "dialogue" on Muhammad's part with some of the corrupted Christian views that were circulating at that time. One central area of difference of opinion is the question of how much the Qur'an has adapted the basic Judaic and Christian concepts, as Muhammad has conceived in his own immediate connection with Eastern Christendom. For further discussion of this issue, see A. Yannoulatos (1985), 74-75.

All the eastern cenobitic communities, especially in Egypt, have the following rule for prayer and chanting. When the brothers have gathered for this purpose at the time of assembly, they do not immediately rush to kneel as soon as the chanting is completed, but stand for a little while, before bending their knees, and pray with their hands outstretched. After this they fall to the ground and pray again for a little while, in a kneeling position. Then they all rise at the same time, and with hands outstretched, and with greater intensity, at length they complete their supplications. No one bends his knee or rises from a kneeling position until the one leading them in prayer bends or rises first.[43]

One might find this a description of the basic stages of the Muslim prayer *Rak'ah*.

Moreover, Islam's subsequent development took place in constant dialogue primarily with Christians of the east. (Muslims first became acquainted with Christians of the west on the battlefield during the Crusades.) The *Sufi* movement owes much to the dialogue that existed between Muslims and monks of the eastern Church, who lived in close proximity to each other. Christians of the east also played a considerable role in the development of Muslim philosophy and science; the Persian Christians, for example, translated many Greek philosophical and medical works into Arabic during the period of the Abbasids.[44]

During its first eight centuries, the Islamic world was engaged in a constant, productive, cultural dialogue with its great and venerable neighbor, Orthodox Byzantium. Many aspects of Muslim philology, even the method for interpreting Qur'an as described in the *Tafsir* commentaries, as well as manuscript copying techniques, the art of miniatures, and music and melodic transcription are all evidence of Islam's ability to assimilate and exploit the already developed skills of Byzantium. Even after the Byzantine empire was

---

[43]See *Evergetinos* (in Greek), 6th ed., vol. 2, proposition 11 (Athens, 1978), 166.

[44]R. Walzer, "Greek into Arabic," *Oriental Studies* 1 (Oxford, 1962); B. Spuler, "Hellenistisches Denken in Islam," *Speculum* 5 (1954): 179-93; and A. Yannoulatos (1985), 165-66.

conquered, Muslims not only continued to be inspired by the architecture of Orthodox churches, but literally copied it, particularly Hagia Sophia, Byzantium's most distinctive masterpiece. They essentially adopted this great accomplishment of the Christian east as a source of inspiration, and it has determined the architectural design of Muslim places of worship down to our own era, as can be seen in modern Muslim architecture from the middle east to Malaysia.

Because the Orthodox have coexisted for so long with the Muslim world—one could call it a "living dialogue"—they can offer a significant degree of balance to modern Christian-Islamic dialogue: they can offer the testimony of their own suffering and the price they paid as a result of Muslim persecution, which counterbalances the multitude of blunders made by the west. Many Muslims in Asia and Africa are harshly critical because of what they suffered, as they maintain, at the hands of Christianity—referring to the oppression they endured when colonized by Christian states in the nineteenth and twentieth centuries. As a response to this attack by the Muslims, the Orthodox can offer on the Christian side the singular counterweight of their own experience, reminding us that responsibility does not belong to the entire Christian world, but only to certain "Christian" European states. The Christians of the eastern churches can point to an age-long history of hardship in which they were oppressed and harassed by Muslim states.

At the same time, the Orthodox have a duty to remind their brothers in the west that what the west did in the past deeply wounded relationships between Christians and Muslims and that the first victims of their actions were the churches of the east. Even though it belongs to the past, it must not be forgotten that the Crusades weakened the Christian Byzantine empire, aroused distrust on the part of Muslims, gave rise to Muslim fanaticism, and destroyed the balance and harmony that had been cultivated during the period of the Abbasids. The Crusades also embittered Christians of the east to the point where in the fifteenth century the distressed Orthodox preferred the "crescent" to the "protection" of Rome.

Turning to our own century, since the Second World War many western "Christian" powers have abandoned and betrayed the

Christian populations of Asia Minor, looking on with relative indifference as Orthodox Christians from Constantinople and northern Cyprus were once again uprooted. Finally, many of the missionary activities of western churches have only served to wound and divide the Orthodox churches, rather than bring Muslim populations of the middle east to Christ.

These issues do not all belong only to the past, however. Many local Orthodox churches still live today under Muslim rule, which has difficulty tolerating them. The Orthodox try to survive in these regions by discreetly avoiding rather than seeking dialogue, for dialogue presupposes freedom and a confrontation of ideas on equal terms, not fear of the powerful. The necessary conditions for dialogue do not exist in places where Muslims constitute the overwhelming majority and have complete control of state power.

Returning to the mistakes of the west, it is necessary to add that more care will have to be taken in the future to prevent yet new errors from being made, lest the poor and persecuted Orthodox minorities now living within Muslim majorities are forgotten or even sacrificed for the sake of promoting a favorable climate for Christian-Islamic dialogue. Just as there must be consideration and respect for Muslims living in the west, there must also be true solidarity with Christians who are oppressed within hard-core Islamic environments in Africa and Asia. Modern Christian-Islamic dialogue must take into consideration the present conjuncture of world events, the broader situation worldwide, and increasing global interdependence.

Does Engaging in Dialogue Deny or Affirm Our Faith in the Orthodox Christian Experience?

A considerable amount of discussion and disagreement has arisen in the Orthodox world regarding the danger that interfaith dialogue may represent for Christians. Does dialogue ultimately require us to compromise and weaken our faith? The issue of dialogue is related to the more general problem of understanding the non-Christian religious experience and to understanding the proper attitude to take toward people with other beliefs, whether religious or non-religious.

By way of summary, and drawing upon the wealth of our theological past and on Orthodox spiritual experience, one might note the following crucial points.[45]

Eastern Christianity evolved for the greater part of its existence within a culturally, linguistically, and religiously pluralistic environment, and one can observe a fundamental attitude of respect and tolerance for and understanding of the religious experiences of others. It is a basic theological conviction of Orthodoxy that all human beings are guided by a proclivity toward God, by a desire to seek God, and by the possibility of acquiring first-hand knowledge of God through the intellect (*nous,* in Greek), which St Gregory of Nazianzus described as "godlike" and "divine." Religious experience has—I will dare to use the word—"biological" roots in God's living relationship with the first human beings. Our having been created "in God's image" did not vanish as a result of the fall and has continued to make it possible for us to receive intimations of the divine will and the divine presence.

Regardless of what other people do or do not believe, for Christians there is only one God: "the God who made the world and everything in it" (Acts 17:24); the "one God and father of us all, who is above all and through all and in all" (Eph 4:6); the God who acts unceasingly in the world and in history, revealing his glory. People may have various conceptions about him, but there do not exist other gods. "The earth is the Lord's and the fulness thereof, the world and those who dwell therein" (Ps 24:1). Through all the vicissitudes of human history God has always been present, caring for the human race and concerned about the salvation of the entire world. As a consequence, religious experiences not only represent humanity's constant impetus toward the highest reality, they also reveal the fact that we absorb the divine radiance of God's glory in the world.

In addition to the definitive "New Testament"—the new agreement that God concluded with humanity through his Son—there have been other "covenants," some with broader, others with more specific, content, which continue to maintain their importance and their validity: the first was with Adam and Eve, the representatives

---

[45]See chapter 2, note 5 above.

of the entire human race; the second was with Noah and the new human race that was saved from the flood (Gen 9:8, 13, 16); and the third covenant was entered into with Abraham (Gen 15:18), the progenitor of a people that would play a fundamental role in God's soteriological plans. We could say that the Muslims, who stress their devotion to Abraham, also participate in this covenant through their singular step backward in history. Nevertheless, the final and conclusive covenant through Jesus Christ—the "new Adam"—as representative of all humanity, has the potential to include the whole human race in its entirety. For us, Christ remains "The true light that enlightens every man" and that "was coming into the world" (Jn 1:9). The radiant figure of Christ also shines its light, however faintly, through the Muslim experience, albeit distorted through the lens of a fragmented christology and hidden by the fog of various heretical interpretations.

Orthodox theological thought in particular affords the activity of the Holy Spirit a wider scope, one that exceeds definition, description, or qualification. Together with the "economy of the Word," the Orthodox east looks forward with hope and humble anticipation to the "economy of the Spirit." The basic prayer that begins almost every Orthodox service clearly reveals the awareness of eastern Christians that the Holy Spirit is "everywhere present and fills all things," and that it continues to act for the fulfillment and completion of the salvation of the entire world. "The wind blows where it wills" (Jn 3:8) as an active and cohesive force of God's love. "The Holy Spirit has full command over everything," we persistently chant, "the visible together with the invisible."[46]

Throughout the theology of the eastern Church we encounter the certainty that the Holy Spirit works in ways that transcend human thought and imagination, ways that cannot, as a consequence, be contained within any theological paradigm, description, or speculation. Everything that is noble and truly good is an act of the Holy Spirit, and the fruits of the Spirit are the preeminent building blocks for harmonious coexistence: "love, joy, peace, patience, kindness, goodness, faithfulness, gentleness, self-control" (Gal 5:22). This

[46]*Parakletike,* Sunday *Anavathmoi,* First Plagal Tone.

assurance from the apostle Paul leads us to the conclusion that wherever these fruits are found, evidence of the activity of the Holy Spirit can be discerned. Moreover, there appears to be a great deal of such evidence in the lives of many Muslims.

In the end, our relationships and the dialogue we have with every human being are defined by our obligation to love in a way that includes everything and everyone, for this is the central core of Christianity: "God is love, and he who abides in love abides in God, and God abides in him" (1 Jn 4:16). People who belong to another creed never lose their basic identity, their spiritual citizenship, so to speak. Even if they themselves choose to ignore it, they do not cease to be children of God, created in God's image, and consequently our brothers and our sisters.

A dialogue that takes place within the framework of these principles and with this kind of effort to understand others does not lead to syncretism, nor does it dilute our Christianity. In order for it to be genuine and fruitful, however, it requires true Christian understanding, consistency, and repentance; that is, it requires us to re-experience our faith continuously, through humility and genuine love. This is precisely the "perfect love" that "casts out fear" (1 Jn 4:18)—every form of fear—and that fills us with hope. The power of God's truth opens up unexpected doorways to lead us out of life's impasses. It is our responsibility to share with others the certainties and deep spiritual experiences that God has bestowed on us, and we must do so without boastfulness—simply, peacefully, with gratitude and understanding, always respecting the personality and the freedom of those with whom we speak.

~ 5 ~

A Theological Approach to Understanding Other Religions*

With the rapid development of technology and of closer commercial and cultural ties between different nations, our planet is becoming one enormous polity where diversity in ideas and values predominates.

In addition to Christian principles and modern European ideas, the global scene also presents us with other types of thought with deep roots in various other religions, for the most part Asian. As we proceed toward global community, seeking peace and justice, and as the interdependence between nations and peoples continues to increase, certain old questions about religious consciousness are reemerging with ever-greater intensity. We can no longer ignore the fact that today more than two-thirds of the human race does not share our hope in Christ.[1] Nor can we ignore the fact that other religious ideas have molded the thought, consciousness, and unconscious mind of millions of our fellow human beings, with whom we now live and with whom we will continue to live.

---

*This chapter was originally presented at the Third Conference of Orthodox Theological Schools held at the Holy Cross Theological Seminary in Brookline, Massachusetts, August–September 1987. The bibliography has been extended to 1988. It was published as "Facing People of Other Faiths, From an Orthodox Point of View," *The Greek Orthodox Theological Review* 38 (1993): 131-52, and previous edition on this theme: "Emerging Perspectives of the Relationships of Christians to People of Other Faiths," IRM 77 (1988): 332-46; and "How Christianity Addresses Other Religions" (in Greek), *Greek Educational Encyclopedia* 21 (*Religions*), 423-27.

[1]In 1987 the world's total population was 5,004,622,800. The number of Christians came to 1,646,007,800, or 32.9 percent. D. Barret, "Annual Statistical Table on Global Mission: 1987," *International Bulletin of Missionary Research* 11 (1987): 25.

The present essay will focus on the way in which we Christians can regard and assess other religions—seeing them through the lens of our own theological thought, experience, and spirituality—and at the same time remain faithful to our Christian principles.

The question of how to understand other religions from a Christian point of view is not only of theological interest. It also has various practical implications regarding the Christian attitude toward the spiritual searching of our own era, as well as more general implications for the future of humankind.

A BRIEF HISTORICAL SURVEY

Periods of Confrontation

Before venturing any response to the very serious theological issue before us, it is necessary to remember that this problem does not present itself today for the first time.[2] Christians were already dealing with similar questions during the first six centuries of Christianity, when the Church stood face to face with the religious world of the Greeks and Romans. This occurred at a time when Christianity was still taking shape, both organizationally and theologically, and when the Church was also being persecuted by the Roman empire, a state of affairs that lasted for three centuries. Today we see the problem from an entirely different perspective. Nevertheless, the early Christian period continues to provide important guidelines for modern theological inquiry.

In its encounter with Greco-Roman religious practices, Christianity formed an alliance with Greek philosophy, adopting the latter's rational critique of polytheism and popular religion.[3] The

[2]For a historical sketch and relevant bibliography, see Anastasios Yannoulatos, *Various Christian Approaches to the Other Religions: A Historical Outline* (Athens, 1971).

[3]J. Daniélou, *Message évangélique et culture Hellénistique aux IIe et IIIe siècles* (Tournai, 1961); W. Jaeger, *Das frühe Christentum und die griechische Bildung* (Berlin, 1963); E.R. Dodds, *Pagan and Christian in an Age of Anxiety: Some Aspects of Religious Experience from Marcus Aurelius to Constantine* (London, 1965); H. Chadwick, *Origen contra Celsum* (Cambridge, 1965); and idem, *Early Christian Thought and the Classical Tradition: Studies in Justin, Clement and Origen* (Oxford, 1966).

Alexandrian school in particular, led by Clement and Origen, attempted to demonstrate that there is a close link between Greek religious philosophy and Christian teaching.

With the Edict of Milan, Christianity's external position in relation to the world around it changed, but the conflict that had existed until then continued, both on the theoretical plane and in the area of ethics. The confrontation between ancient religion and Christianity became even more complex, because Christianity was simultaneously engaged in a second struggle against internal heresies. It was within this pluralistic environment and in the context of this intense theoretical confrontation, which took place on many fronts, that patristic theology developed, formulating a number of key theoretical positions that it can offer us today.

In the second period, from the seventh to the fifteenth century, Christianity was a religiously and socially integrated whole. The Church now found itself face to face not merely with preexisting religious convictions and systems, but primarily with a new religion, Islam, which entered the foreground of history with religious vigor, military fervor, and pretensions to world domination. This newly established religion claimed to surpass all the revelations of the Old and New Testaments and to be the culmination and fulfillment of all God's promises.

Islam spread with lightning speed, forcing the Christian world to adopt a more vigorous stance in order to contain this dangerous adversary. As a result, important theological positions that had been taken during the first period with regard to other religions were either set aside or forgotten. The Christians were compelled to defend themselves with determination. They saw Islam as a religious and political system that distorted the truth. Viewing it eschatologically, they felt Islam's emergence to be like the outbreak of the final struggle described in the Book of Revelation. The Christian world—first the east, which received the attack directly, and later the west—mobilized its entire system of defense. Within this charged atmosphere there appeared in Byzantium a series of theological treatises in the form of "dialogues" between Christians and Muslims.[4]

[4]For the attitude of the Byzantines toward Islam, see A. Yannoulatos, *Various*

Byzantium's military defense and counterattack were organized
more systematically at this time, in order to protect all that was holy
and sacred.

Under the influence of monastic orders and the ideals of chivalry,
western Christendom developed a military ideology that culminated
in the Crusades, ultimately striking a profound blow against eastern
Christianity and poisoning Muslim-Christian relations.[5] It was also
during this period, however, that noteworthy voices were raised in
the West, such as those of Abelard, Thomas Aquinas, and Nicholas
of Cusa, expressing an attitude of sympathy with people of other
faiths.

A distinctive and little-studied aspect of this period is the attitude
that the Christians of Persia and India took toward Asian religions.
The Persian Church in particular, usually referred to as the "Nestorian" Church, demonstrated great sensitivity to the religious traditions of China, and its missionary efforts are of great interest.[6]

In the third period, from the sixteenth until the twentieth century, several new historical factors emerge.

Following the upheaval of the Reformation, more and more
church communities and confessions began to appear in the west,

Christian Approaches to the Other Religions, 32-40; E. Fritsch, *Islam und Christentum in
Mittelalter* (Breslau, 1930); W. Eichner, "Die Nachrichten über den Islam bei den Byzan-
tinern," *Der Islam* 23 (1936): 133-162, 197-244; H.G. Beck, *Kirche und theologische Literatur im byzantinischen Reich* (München, 1959); E.D. Sdraka, *The Polemic of Byzantine
Theologians against Islam* (in Greek) (Thessaloniki, 1961); J. Meyendorff, "Byzantine
Views of Islam," *Dumbarton Oaks Papers* 18 (1964): 115-32; and A.-T. Khoury, *Les théolo-
giens byzantins et l'Islam* (Paderborn, 1969). Cf. A.-T. Khoury, *Der theologische Streit der
Byzantiner mit dem Islam* (Paderborn, 1969), esp. 319-29 for a detailed bibliography;
idem, *Polémique Byzantine contre l'Islam* (Münster, 1966; 2d ed. Florence, 1969); and D.
Sahas, *John of Damascus on Islam: The "Heresy of the Ismaelites"* (Leiden, 1972).

[5]C.H. Becker, "Christliche Polemik und islamische Dogmenbildung," *Islamstudien* 1
(Leipzig, 1924): 432-49; E. Fritsch, *Islam und Christentum in Mittelalter;* R.F. Merkel,
"Der Islam im Wandel abendländischen Verstehen," *Studi e materiali di storia delle reli-
gioni* 13 (1937): 68-101; and J.I. Addison, *The Christian Approach to the Moslem* (New
York, 1966), 11-40.

[6]On the encounter between eastern Christians and Asian religion, see J. Stewart,
Nestorian Missionary Enterprise: The Story of a Church on Fire (Madras, 1928); E.L.
Browne, *The Eclipse of Christianity in Asia: From the Time of Muhammad till the Fourteenth
Century* (Cambridge, 1933); J. Foster, *The Church of the T'ang Dynasty* (London, 1939);
and A. Yannoulatos, "Missionary Activities of the Eastern Churches in Central and East-
ern Asia" (in Greek), *Porefthentes* 3 (1961): 26-31.

each placing exaggerated emphasis on one or another particular Christian truth. Each of these groups cultivated its own religious climate and ethos. The theological foundations they adopted in order to confront one another became increasingly narrow. Religious enthusiasm rapidly transformed into fanaticism, and the tendency toward exclusivity soon developed into a "Christian principle." Reading certain phrases used by the first reformers—with the exception of Zwingli—one marvels at their very negative stance toward other religions. In the theological writings in which they formulate their creed, an extremely conservative tendency that disparages other religious systems often dominates.[7]

What most characterizes the Christian West during this period, however, are its great missionary campaigns, which started in the eighteenth and continued through the twentieth century, and the theological ideas that were mustered to support these missionary efforts, both theoretically and economically. Inordinate emphasis was placed on the need to bring salvation to all those who lived "in darkness and the shadow of death," and an excessively bleak image of other cultures as uncivilized "savages" was thus projected.

This missionary drive was unfortunately associated with colonialism, which cultivated an attitude of contempt, whether directly or indirectly, toward the religions and cultural values of other peoples.

On the other hand, closer contact and greater knowledge of other peoples led to a more careful study of their traditional religions. In the end, we acquired new and more objective knowledge, and this helped to promote respect and a greater willingness to understand others. This way of thinking has gradually become obligatory in Christian theological thought in recent decades, and today it dominates the Christian world in the West.[8]

---

[7]See: H. Vossberg, *Luthers Kritik aller Religionen* (Leipzig, 1922); and W. Holsten, *Christentum und nichtchristliche Religion nach der Auffasung Luthers* (Gütersloh, 1932). For Calvin's attitude, see H. Kraemer's analysis in *The Christian Message in a Non-Christian World* (London, 1938; repr. 1958). For a critical analysis, see L. Capéran, *Le problème du salut des infidels*, 2d ed. (Toulouse, 1934), 230-36.

[8]A. Yannoulatos, *Various Christian Approaches*, 51-102, which includes a bibliography.

Principal Christian Views Regarding Other Religions

When we attempt to summarize and classify the various theories that
have been formulated by Christians through the centuries regarding
other religions, we find a wide range of opinions, from completely
negative to excessively positive, and from absolute rejection to total
acceptance.[9]

⏤ Religions are the work of the devil. They do not contain any
truth or anything of value. Nothing in them has any place in the new
reality of the Church, which is the only road toward God. This view
was adopted by quite a few early Christians, such as Tertullian of
Carthage (155-200), who looked upon the gentile gods as "demons"
that competed with the true God.[10]

⏤ A more developed formulation of the previous view, based on
a more complex theological analysis and with greater anthropological sensitivity, asserts that religion is the distorted result of humanity's corrupt nature and that the human race does not have the ability
to know God. In the final analysis, "religion is disbelief." The
Christian revelation, or rather the gospel, is something completely
different. It passes judgment on all religions. This was the basic
theological position of the Calvinist tradition, which culminated
in the stand taken by the "dialectical school" of Protestantism
(K. Barth, H. Kraemer, et al.).[11]

⏤ Humanity is not completely incapable of gazing upon the mystery of God. It has not remained in absolute darkness. By the use of
logic, by considering the order that exists in nature, and through
their loftiest intuitions and experiences of conscience, human beings

[9]The paragraphs that follow are a modified version of the conclusions I reached in
Various Christian Approaches (see note 1 above).

[10]"What Indeed Has Athens to Do with Jerusalem?" (*"Quid Athenis et
Hierosolymis?"*), in Tertullian, *The Prescription against Heretics* 7, PL 20B-21A. However,
when he maintains that the soul is by its very nature Christian (*"O testimonium animae
naturaliter Christianae!" Apologeticus* 17, PL 1:433), he establishes an important anthropological basis for approaching the non-Christian religious experience.

[11]K. Barth, *Die Kirchliche Dogmatik,* 3 (München, 1932), 327ff (English trans.
Church Dogmatics, 14 vols. [Edinburgh, 1962]); H. Kraemer, *Religion and the Christian
Faith* (London, 1956); and idem, *World Cultures and World Religions* (London, 1960).
Kraemer slightly modified his positions in his last book, *Why Christianity of All Religions?*
(London, 1962).

have always recognized something of the existence and perfection of God. This preliminary human instinct and knowledge of God is the first step toward the Christian faith. The Fathers of the ancient Church took this line of reasoning,[12] as did the natural theology developed by Thomas Aquinas[13] and the classic theological thought of the Roman Catholics. With regard to the limitations of this natural human ability for knowledge of God, there is of course a wide variety of views.

⁓ Closely related to the preceding theory is the position that the history of human religion before Christ was a kind of training period, preparing the human race for the Christian religion. Christianity is the fulfillment, the completion, and the perfection of humanity's religious life and as such remains unique.[14] This position became the starting point for two very different views. Some theologians maintained that this ultimate fulfillment in Christianity was arrived at through an evolutionary process. Others argued that a radical, revolutionary change occurred, a discontinuity. In other words, Christianity is not the manifestation of an innately human process, the evolution of our religious consciousness; rather, it arose when a completely foreign element entered human history: the transcendent and living God came into history in order to lead humanity to a new realm of life, one that would otherwise have remained completely closed to human beings.[15]

[12]A. Luneau, "Pour aider au dialogue: Les Pères et les religions non chrétiennes," *Nouvelle Revue Théologique* 99 (1967): 821-41, 914-39 (English summary "The Fathers and the Non-Christian Religions," *Bulletin,* Secretariatus pro non Christianis 3 [1968]: 5-19). See also A. Luneau, *L'histoire du salut chez les Pères de l'Eglise* (Paris, 1967), 120-63; P. Hacker, "The Religions of the Gentiles as Viewed by Fathers of the Church," *Zeitschrift für Missions-und Religionswissenschaft* 54 (1970), 253-58; and Anastasios Yanoulatos, *Various Christian Approaches,* 13-31.

[13]T. Ohm, *Die Stellung der Heiden zu Natur und Übernatur nach dem hl. Thomas* (Münster, 1927); M. Seckler, "Das Heil der Nichtevangelisierten in thomistischer Sicht," *Theologische Quartalschrift* 140 (1960): 38-69; idem, *Das Heil in der Geschichte, Geschichtstheologisches Denken bei Thomas von Aquin* (München, 1964); and E.H. Schillebeeckx, "L'Instinct de la foi selon S. Thomas d'Aquin," *Revue des Sciences Philosophique et Théologiques* 48 (1964): 377-408.

[14]F. König, "Das Christentum und die Weltreligionen," in *Christus und die Religionen der Erde* 3 (Freiburg, 1951), 761-68.

[15]Cf. J. Daniélou, "Le problème théologique des religions non chrétiennes," *Archivi di Filosofia, Metafisica ed esperienza religiosa* (Rome, 1956). Cf. also, by the same author:

⸺ Different religions do not merely represent humanity's search for God; they are themselves based on some revelation. There is not a single ethnic group in any historical period that has remained without some gleam of revelation. The supernatural signs of grace exist in all religions. There is "general" revelation and "specific" revelation. All non-Christian religions are based on "general revelation." The revelatory character of religion is expressed by the idea of sacredness.[16]

⸺ Since it is historical religion, Christianity cannot possess the full truth or full divine revelation. It is a microcosm within the macrocosm of religious history, simply the "first-born" among its brothers. The history of salvation is realized by passing through humanity's entire religious history. There were even some Protestant theologians, such as the Marburg "science of religion" school (F. Heiler, and E. Benz), who went so far as to formulate the view that a synthesis of the world's religions would offer the desired completeness.[17]

The above outline is simply a rough attempt to systematize, in a series of six stages, the varied viewpoints that have been formulated at different times by Christians. The great variety of these views has to do not only with the different emphasis of each denomination or theologian but also with the specific political, cultural, and historical conditions under which the people who formulated these views lived. That we have certain basic advantages today is indisputable. These advantages enable us to acquire a more general overview of

Les saints païens de l'Ancien Testament (Paris, 1956); and Essais sur le mystère de l'histoire (Paris, 1955).

[16]N. Söderblom: Natürliche Theologie und allgemeine Religionsgeschichte (Stockholm and Leipzig, 1913); and Der lebendige Gott im Zeugnis der Religionsgeschichte (München, 1942).

[17]F. Heiler, "Versuche einer Synthese der Religionen und einer neuen Menschheitsreligion," in Die Religionen der Menschheit in Vergangenheit und Gegenwart (Stuttgart, 1962), 877-89; idem, "Das Christentum und die Religionen," repr. from Einheit des Geistes, Jahrbuch der Evangelischen Akademie der Pfalz (1964); E. Benz, "On Understanding Non-Christian Religions," in The History of Religions, Essays in Methodology, ed. M. Eliade and J.M. Kitagawa (Chicago, 1959), 115-31; and idem, "Ideen zu einer Theologie der Religionsgeschichte," Mainzer Akademie der Wissenschaften und der Literatur, Abhandlugen der geistes-und sozialwissenschaftlichen Klasse 5 (Wiesbaden, 1960), 421-96. See also J. Hick and Brian Hebblethwaite, eds., Christianity and Other Religions (Glasgow, 1980); and W.C. Smith, Towards a World Theology (London, 1980).

the problem, one that takes into account old as well as new features of Christian theological inquiry and the history of religion.[18]

Having now arrived at the heart of our subject, namely, the problem of how to understand other religions theologically, we can see that the most striking divergence of views continues to exist in the Protestant world.[19] As a result of the freedom Protestantism characteristically affords for individual theological thought, a variety of positions are held, from the most syncretistic to the most conservative. In the Roman Catholic world, the cohesive structure of the Church always provided a more stable orientation in the past, one that has recently demonstrated increased openness and breadth of thought, particularly since Vatican II.[20]

[18]For more general bibliography through 1960, see E. Benz and M. Nambara, *Das Christentum und die nichtchristlichen Hochreligionen, Begegnung und Auseinandersetzung, eine internationale Bibliographie* (Leiden, 1960). For more recent bibliography, see S. Immanuel David, ed., *Christianity and the Encounter with Other Religions, a Select Bibliography* (Bangalore, 1988). The latter includes 880 works and studies by Roman Catholics and Protestants, but is limited to British publications in the English language, with an emphasis on issues related to India.

[19]Among the many studies, see S. Schweitzer, *Das Christentum und die Weltreligionen* (München, 1925) (English trans. by J. Powers, *Christianity and the Religions of the World*, 6th rev. ed. [London, 1960]); P. Tillich, *Christianity and the Encounter of the World Religions* (New York, 1963); S.C. Neill, *Christian Faith and Other Faiths: The Christian Dialogue with Other Religions* (Oxford, 1970); P. Knitter, *Towards a Protestant Theology of Religions* (Marburg, 1974); A. Race, *Christians and Religious Pluralism: Patterns in the Christian Theology of Religions* (London, 1983); K. Cracknell, *Towards a New Relationship: Christians and People of Other Faiths* (London, 1986); and Choan-Seng Song, "The Power of God's Grace in the World of Religion," *Ecumenical Review* 39 (Geneva, 1987): 44-62.

Dialogue with people of other faiths has become an important subject in the ecumenical movement in recent decades. "Dialogue with People of Living Faiths," a department of the World Council of Churches, regularly publishes the statements of the various conferences it organizes, as well as the bulletin *Current Dialogue*. The more important of these publications include S.J. Samartha, ed., *Living Faiths and the Ecumenical Movement* (Geneva, 1971); *Dialogue Between Men of Living Faiths: Papers presented at a Consultation at Ajaltoun, Lebanon* (Geneva, March 1970); *Living Faiths and Ultimate Goals, a Continuing Dialogue* (Geneva, 1974); and *Towards World Community: The Colombo Papers* (Geneva, 1975). See also S.J. Samartha, *Courage for Dialogue: Ecumenical Issues in Inter-Religious Relationships* (Geneva, 1981). Other publications from the World Council of Churches include: *Guidelines on Dialogue with People of Living Faiths and Ideologies* (Geneva, 1979); *Jewish-Christian Dialogue: Six Years of Christian-Jewish Consultations* (Geneva, 1975); *Christian Presence and Witness in Relation to Muslim Neighbours, A Conference* (Mombasa, Kenya, 1979; 2d ed. 1982); and A. Ariarajah, *The Bible and People of Other Faiths* (Geneva, 1985).

[20]On Vatican II, see *The Documents of Vatican II, with Notes and Comments by*

Christians of the East have often lived in societies characterized by cultural, linguistic, and religious diversity. They have consequently developed an attitude of respect, tolerance, and understanding toward other religious experiences. In the Orthodox world we don't have resolutions that have been passed by an official organ of the Church.[21] The Church of the East has always allowed a great deal of latitude regarding personal freedom and expression, but always within the framework of the living tradition. By tapping into the

                    Catholic, Protestant and Orthodox Authorities, ed. W.M. Abbott, trans. J. Gallager (New York, 1966), especially *Dignitatis Humanae* (675-696), *Ad Gentes* (580-630), *Lumen Gentium* (paragraphs 14-16, pp. 32-35), and *Dei Verbum* (paragraphs 3 and 6, pp. 112 and 114); P. Rossano, "Quid de non Christianis Oecumenicum Concilium Vaticano II docuerit," *Bulletin,* Secretariatus pro non Christianis (Vatican I, 1966): 1-22; idem, "Christianity and the Religions," *Bulletin,* Secretariatus pro non Christianis (Vatican IV, 1969): 97-101; E. Dhanis, M. Dhavamony, J. Goets, et al., *L'Eglise et les Religions*, with a commentary on the position of the Second Vatican Council (Rome, 1966); and Secretariatus pro non Christianis, ed., *Vers la rencontre des Religions, suggestions pour le dialogue* (Vatican, 1967).

                    The many studies by Roman Catholics include: J.A. Cuttat, *La Rencontre des Religions* (Paris, 1953) (English trans. *The Encounter of Religions* [New York, 1960]); K. Rahner, "Das Christentum und die nichtchristlichen Religionen," *Schriften zur Theologie* (Zürich and Köln: Einsiedeln, 1962), 136-158; H.R. Schlette, *Die Religionen als Thema der Theologie* (Freiburg, 1963) (English trans. *Toward a Theology of Religions* [London, 1966]); R. Panikkar, *Religionen und die Religion* (München, 1965); idem, *Salvation in Christ: Concreteness and Universality* (Santa Barbara, California, 1972); idem, *The Intra-Religious Dialogue* (New York, 1978); H. de Lubac, *L'homme devant Dieu* 3 (Paris, 1964); J. Ratzinger, "Der christliche Glaube und die Weltreligionen," in *Gott in der Welt, Festschrift for K. Rahner* (1964), 287-305; R.C. Zaehner, *The Catholic Church and World Religions* (London, 1964); H. Fries, "Das Christentum und die Religionen der Welt," in *Das Christentum und die Weltreligionen* (Würzburg, 1965), 15-37; H. Maurier, *Essai d'une théologie du paganisme* (Paris, 1965); P.F. Knitter, "European Protest and Catholic Approaches to the World Religions: Complements and Contrasts," *Journal of Ecumenical Studies* 12 (1975): 13-28; idem, "Roman Catholic Approaches to Other Religions, Development and Tensions," *International Bulletin for Missionary Research* 8 (1984): 50-54; idem, *No Other Name? A Critical Study of Christian Attitudes Towards the World Religions* (London, 1985); and Secretariatus pro non Christianis, ed., *The Attitude of the Church Towards the Followers of Other Religions* (Citta del Vaticano, 1984).

                    [21]Even books and articles by Orthodox theologians on this subject are few in number. See L. Filippidis, "Greece and Paul," *Festival Volume of the 1900th Anniversary of St Paul's Arrival in Greece* (Athens, 1953); idem, *Religionsgeschichte als Heilsgeschichte in der Weltgeschichte* (Athens, 1953); idem, *The History of the New Testament Era from the Universal Viewpoint of All Religions* (in Greek) (Athens, 1958); idem, *Modern Religious Efforts Toward Worldwide Unity* (in Greek) (Athens, 1966); N. Arseniev, *Revelation of Life Eternal: An Introduction to the Christian Message* (Crestwood, NY, 1965); G. Khodre, "Christianity in a Pluralistic World—The Economy of the Holy Spirit," *The Ecumenical Review*

deepest stratum of Orthodox theology and by drawing on Orthodox spiritual experience, I will attempt to sketch out an Orthodox theological position on the subject at hand. First, however, allow me to make some observations with regard to the study of religion in general.

Findings from the Modern Study of Religion

Avoid generalizations and extreme positions. When we discuss things of which we do not have a very good knowledge, there is always a danger of overgeneralizing and oversimplifying. These result in naïve formulations and extreme positions. The various features that are found in religions are neither all wonderful nor all benighted. In the past, the vagueness of our knowledge about other religions sometimes led to the negative and false impression that they were either not worth discussing or were all demonic. With the fragmentary knowledge we have today, we are in danger of being led to another false impression, this time a "positive" one: namely, that there do not exist very many differences between religions and that they are all quite similar. Or else we may generalize our judgments about one religion, such as our neighbor Islam, and apply them to all other religions.

In the twentieth century, it has been possible to acquire better and more scientific knowledge about religion and to investigate the Christian message more deeply. A very significant effort has been made to decode the sacred symbols of other religions and to discern the substance of their message. Theological thought will have to find creative ways to put all this new data to use.

Double development. Through a careful study of the history of religion one can discern a kind of double evolution, both upward and downward. On the one hand, the search for the absolute represents an upward tendency; on the other hand, there is a tendency toward

23 (Geneva, 1971): 118-28; I.N. Karmires, "The Universality of Salvation in Christ," *Proceedings of the Academy of Athens, 1980* (in Greek), 55 (Athens, 1981), 261-289; and idem, "The Salvation of People of God Outside the Church," *Proceedings of the Academy of Athens, 1981* (in Greek), 56 (Athens, 1982), 391-434.

138 FACING THE WORLD

decline and degeneration in religious expression and forms of worship. The simultaneous existence of these two tendencies is reminiscent, in a way, of the two currents in the Atlantic Ocean that meet and intersect, one cold and one warm. Very often, even in polytheistic religions and religions with many evil spirits, "a sudden *breaking through* of a higher conception takes place, felt as a sudden glimpse of, a sudden contact with a Higher Reality—the Divine Reality . . ."[22] There is a constant dialectical process between human freedom and God's love, and the latter never ceases to manifest itself in the world.

Organic wholes. A religion is an organic whole, a system—not a hodgepodge of unconnected, individual parts. The tendency of some people to isolate certain phenomena and draw parallels with corresponding phenomena in other religions often leads to mistaken conclusions. The hidden danger in such phenomenological attempts is that they identify or even equate religious features that have evolved and operate in very different contexts. Different individual elements react differently when they are in close proximity to each other. Salt, for example, also known as the chemical compound sodium chloride, is necessary for life, but chlorine by itself is poisonous.

Religions are living organisms; their parts exist in relationship to the whole. We cannot detach certain parts of their teaching and equate them with similar expressions found in other religions, hoping to construct simple theories, just as it is impossible to transplant the far-seeing eye of an eagle into a human body.

The primary thing that religions offer. Despite the different ways in which they respond to the great problems of pain, death, and the meaning of human existence and society, the various religions affirm the existence of an experience and capacity that are "otherworldly," meaning they lie somewhere beyond daily life and the sensible world. It is noteworthy that in 1987, 70.2 percent of the world's population—3.5 billion people—accepted some religious belief.[23]

[22]N. Arseniev, *Revelation of Life Eternal: An Introduction to the Christian Message* (Crestwood, NY, 1965), 33.

[23]On the basis of numbers given by D. Barret, "Annual Statistical Table on Global Mission: 1987," *International Bulletin of Missionary Research* 11 (1987): 25.

OUTLINE OF AN ORTHODOX THEOLOGICAL POSITION

The debate in the West on how to evaluate other religions theologically has always centered on christological issues. Western theological thought on this subject is defined mainly by the Augustinian and Calvinist legacies, with secondary influences from Luther and Wesley. In the Orthodox tradition, however, theological problems related to this subject—especially with regard to Christian anthropology, i.e., to that part of Christian teaching that concerns the origin, nature, and destiny of human beings—have always been viewed in the light of our theology of the Holy Trinity.

"One God and father of us all, who is above all and through all and in all"

Within this context, I would like to discuss three key concepts: the universal radiance of God's glory; the common starting point and destiny of all human beings; and the fact that God constantly provides for creation and humanity.

Irrespective of what people have or have not believed at different times, there is one God and one God alone. "I am the Lord, and there is no other, besides me there is no God" (Is 45:5; cf. verses 21 and 22). This one God, the "father of us all, who is above all and through all and in all . . ." (Eph 4:6) created the universe and acts continuously within the world and history. People may have a variety of conceptions about God, but there do not exist other gods.

One of the fundamental truths of the Christian faith stresses that God in his essence is incomprehensible and unapproachable. However, biblical revelation overcomes the impasse of God's incomprehensible nature by assuring us that while his divine essence remains unknown, God nevertheless reveals himself in the world and the universe through the manifestation of his glory. It is God's glory alone that makes itself known through various divine manifestations, that people are in a position to comprehend. This is the dynamic, creative, and transforming energy of the Holy Trinity.

Patristic thought sheds light on this crucial question of God's incomprehensibility and his revelation by distinguishing between

God's essence and his energies.[24] It is not possible to define the transcendent God with any human conception or idea, or through any philosophical definition of substance or essence. What human beings are in a position to grasp is God's glory. The distance between the creation and its creator remains immeasurable. God's glory simultaneously reveals both this inconceivable distance and also God's proximity.

The starting point for Christian life and the foundation of our hope is the fact that God's glory pervades his entire creation. The angelic hymn revealed in Isaiah's prophetic vision praises and triumphantly glorifies this central truth: "Holy, holy, holy is the Lord of hosts; the whole earth is full of his glory" (Is 6:3). This hymn expresses, on the one hand, our wonder and awe before the mystery of God and, on the other, our conviction that God's glory pervades all of heaven and earth and every shape and form of life.

Together with faith in the one God and his supremacy throughout the entire world, Holy Scripture also emphasizes humanity's common origin—the creation of the first couple by God himself "in his image" (Gen 1:27) and "in his likeness" (Gen 1:26; cf. Acts 17:26)—as well as humanity's common aim and purpose. All human beings, regardless of their race, their way of life, or their language, bear within themselves this divine "resemblance": intellect, free will, and love. Since the human race was created from one homogeneous substance, the introduction of sin brought on an infirmity throughout the entire human race. Humanity's nature continues to be unified, both in its greatness and in its fall. All human beings share a common place before the judgment of God, "since all have sinned and fall short of the glory of God" (Rom 3:23).

In the East there is unshakable theological certainty that all people have both "the desire . . . to seek God," as St Gregory the Theologian expresses it, and also the ability to obtain some faint knowledge of God through their reason and mental powers, which St Gregory characterized as "god-like" and "divine."[25] People also have an

---

[24]J. Meyendorff, *St Gregory Palamas and Orthodox Spirituality* (Crestwood, NY, 1971).
[25]Gregory of Nazianzus, *Orations* 28 (The Second Theological Oration), 15 and 17, PG 36:48C.

innate ability to love and to sense, even if imperfectly, that love occupies a "greater" position.

The great tragedy of human disobedience did not inhibit the radiance of God's glory. His glory continues to fill heaven and earth and the entire universe. According to patristic thought, the fall did not destroy "God's image" in humanity. What was damaged, but not completely destroyed, was humanity's God-given ability to sense and comprehend this radiance and its meaning. I will dare here to make use of a metaphor. If a television's receiver has been damaged or is not synchronized, or if the television has no antenna, then we cannot establish a proper connection with the central transmitter. When this happens, the picture and sound are distorted. The pagan world experiences a tragic misfortune, because the images it receives are either distorted, or they are obstructed by erroneous representations and projections arising from a muddle of human thought, desire, and consciousness.

The first chapters of the Old Testament provide us with clear evidence that religious experience is rooted in God's revelation to the first human beings. The universal character of divine revelation to humanity is related to our innate religious sense.

Throughout the human tragedy of the Fall, God has never stopped caring for the whole world that he created. Not only have people sought God; God has also sought them. The Old Testament describes many occasions when God took the initiative to help and guide the human race. According to what is written in the Bible, a number of covenants were entered into between God and humanity, and these still maintain their importance and their validity. The first one was with Adam and Eve, who represent the entire human race. The second was established with Noah and the new human race that was saved from the flood (Gen 8). The Book of Genesis repeatedly emphasizes that this was a covenant "between God and every living creature of all flesh" (Gen 9:16). The third covenant was entered into with Abraham (Gen 12), the founder of a people that would play a primary role in God's plan for redemption. The final, definitive, and eternally "new" covenant or "testament" was completed through Christ, the new Adam. All human beings, however, are in a relationship with God through some previous covenant to which he himself set his own seal.

Since the Old Testament is the sacred book of the Israelites, it describes God's care of and concern for his chosen people. This does not mean, however, that God put an end to his relationship with other peoples. The previous covenants with Adam and Noah have continued and are still valid. The relatively large number of appearances that God made during the long period before the era of Abraham, as recounted in the concise outline provided in the Old Testament, is extremely significant. People's experience of this first revelation of God, which Eusebius refers to as people's "initial piety,"[26] was carefully cherished not only within the Jewish environment but also outside it. Enoch, Melchizedek, and Job were not Israelites, but they knew the true God and communicated with him.

Both the Old and the New Testaments repeatedly refer to the power that God has over the entire universe. The Pentateuch first defines the wider context of God's activities in its opening chapters and then draws our attention to one specific aspect, the history and misfortunes of Israel, which also have universal meaning and dimensions. The Book of Psalms, Israel's primary book of worship, repeatedly refers to God's universality: "The earth is the Lord's and the fullness thereof, the world and those who dwell therein" (24:1); "For God is the king of all the earth" (47:7); "for the world and all that is in it is mine" (50:12); "and his kingdom rules over all" (103:19); "The earth, O Lord, is full of thy steadfast love" (119:64).[27]

The prophets, too, explicitly announce God's plan to gather "all the peoples" together at "the final end," on the last day. "This is the purpose that is purposed concerning the whole earth; and this is the hand that is stretched out over all the nations" (Is 14:26). "I am coming to gather all nations and tongues; and they shall come and shall see my glory" (Is 66:18). And Malachi proclaims: "For from the rising of the sun to its setting my name is great among the nations, and in every place incense is offered to my name, and a pure offering; for

[26]*Praeparatio Evangelica* 1.6, PG 21:48C.
[27]Cf. the following psalms: 22:28; 57:11; 65:5; 67:1, 4; 72:19; 82:8; 83:18; 86:9; 95:3; 96:1, 4-5; 96:1; 98:4; 104:28; 113:4.

my name is great among the nations, says the Lord of hosts" (Mal 1:11). With extraordinary descriptiveness the book of Jonah stresses God's compassion and his abundant mercy toward the gentiles. God takes the initiative to save humanity. It is God who acts first. It is God who sends Moses to free the Israelites. It is God who gives the law at Mount Sinai. It is God who selects prophets to speak to his people.

Based on this view, we can see religious experiences as humanity's deep longing and search for the Supreme Reality and also as rays of light that people have absorbed from God's universal and divine radiance. The glory of God has never ceased to envelop the universe, to radiate everywhere, to light up the world, and to draw everything within the scope of his love.

"And the Word became flesh and dwelt among us"

The issue of how to understand other religions theologically acquires particular importance when examined from the viewpoint of Christianity's central principle, the Incarnation.

In many ways, Christianity presents quite a few outward similarities to other religions. All religions, some more and some less, refer to a transcendent reality: the sacred, the divine. It has been shown that even peoples who are considered "primitive" believe in a Supreme Being, to whom they ascribe a variety of attributes—they call this being wise, powerful, good, etc.[28] Other religions also have sacred books, doctrinal concepts, ethical principles, priesthoods, and monasticism. However, the radically new and different message that Christianity offers to humanity is that God, "the living God," is Love. He doesn't simply have love as one additional attribute among many others, like mercy and goodness: *He Is Love.* Furthermore, God truly became a human being.

The mystery of the trinitarian God was revealed on God's own initiative in a way that cannot be comprehended by any human

[28]J. Mbiti, *African Religions and Philosophy* (London, 1969; repr. 1970); idem, *Concepts of God in Africa* (London, 1970); A. Yannoulatos, *"Lord of Brightness": The God of the Tribes Near Mount Kenya* (in Greek) (Athens, 1971; 3d ed. 1983); and idem, *Ruhanga the Creator: A Contribution to Research on African Beliefs Concerning God and Humanity* (in Greek) (Athens, 1975).

thought, concept, or intuition. This mystery is summed up in the fact that "God so loved the world that he gave his only Son, that whoever believes in him should not perish but have eternal life" (Jn 3:16). This Love assumed human nature through the Incarnation of the Word, the second person of the Holy Trinity: "And the Word became flesh and dwelt among us" (Jn 1:14).

All the phases of Christ's life are new manifestations of God's glory. According to Johannine theology, the Passion and the Crucifixion in particular are the revelation of divine glory. Christ himself refers to the truth of this in his last prayer to the Father, where he organically binds together love, life, and glory (Jn 17:1-26). Through his Passion and then his Resurrection, which immediately follows, Christ enters "into his glory" (Lk 24:26), decisively shattering the power of death and receiving "all authority in heaven and on earth" (Mt 28:18). With his Ascension in glory, the resurrected Christ unites heaven and earth by elevating humanity's nature to the right hand of the Father of glory and thus guides human history to its ultimate destiny.

These events, to which the Christian message persistently refers, are unique and radically different from all other events in human history. They offer a completely new perspective on the way we conceive of God and the human race. The incarnation introduced the world's eschatological focus and *telos*—i.e., Christ himself—into world history, giving new meaning to the past, the present, and the future. Human life acquired a new quality and, I venture to use the phrase, "new chromosomes." Life now evolves within a new dynamic. Through Christ a "new creation" has begun.

In order to examine the subject at hand in a christological context, two key concepts are necessary: the Incarnation of the Word, and Christ as the New Adam. Through the Incarnation of the Word, all of humanity's nature—everything we call "human"—was offered to God. Humanity after Christ is consequently very different from humanity before Christ. Through the Incarnation, the "communion" that had originally existed between humanity and God was restored, becoming "much more secure than the first" had been. Through his deeds and his sacrifice, Christ undid "the works of the devil" (1 Jn 3:8). He broke the demonic snares and webs that the devil had been weaving for centuries in the most central areas of human experience, human existence, and human relationships, especially in the sensitive and critical area of religious beliefs.

This demonic element had even infected the religious conscience of Israel, mainly through ritualism and hypocrisy, but it had insinuated itself much more dangerously into other religions. For this reason, wherever the gospel is preached the Church always has to be selective about adopting any preexisting aspects of a region's various religious conceptions and customs. Some aspects are accepted, others are rejected, and others are transformed and brought into harmony with the message of the gospel.[29]

During the last four centuries of Western Christianity, deep faith in the uniqueness of Jesus Christ has expressed itself on numerous occasions as exclusivity. Several verses in the New Testament—such as "no one comes to the Father, but by me" (Jn 14:6) and "there is salvation in no one else" (Acts 4:12)—were isolated from their context and used to defend a Christology of exclusivity.

Christian thought in the Eastern Church has shown a greater degree of understanding. Justin Martyr (100?-165) continued along the path first opened by the evangelist John in his prologue about the Word. Attempting to make use of the philosophical concepts of his time, Justin spoke about the principle of the "seminal word" (*spermatikos logos*). "For whatever either lawgivers or philosophers uttered well, they elaborated by finding and contemplating some part of the Word."[30] "For all the writers were able to see realities darkly through the sowing of the implanted Word that was in them."[31] Nevertheless, he did not unconditionally adopt whatever logic or philosophy had formulated in the past. "But since they did not know the whole of the Word, which is Christ, they often contradicted themselves."[32] Justin had no difficulty using the name "Christians" for those who had lived "with the Word."[33] He did, however,

---

[29]See above in chapter 3, "Culture and Gospel."

[30]Justin Martyr, *The Second Apology* 10, PG 6:460BC (trans. ANF, vol. 1).

[31]Ibid., 13, PG 6:468A (trans. ANF, vol. 1).

[32]Ibid., 10, PG 6:460C (trans. ANF, vol. 1).

[33]"And those who lived reasonably are Christians, even though they have been thought atheists." Justin Martyr, *The First Apology* 46, PG 6:397C (trans. ANF, vol. 1).

maintain Christ as the criterion by which he judged the values and theories of previous forms of religion. He summarized his brief reference to the "seminal word" with the following basic principle (which, strangely enough, is not usually mentioned by those who quote Justin's position): he stresses the difference between the "seed" (*sperma*, in Greek) and the full realization of the life that is innate within the seed. He also distinguishes between inherent "capacity" on the one hand and "grace" on the other. "For the seed and imitation imparted according to capacity is one thing, and quite another is the thing itself, of which there is the participation and imitation according to the grace which is from Him."[34]

Clement of Alexandria (150-215?) returns to the same line of thought when he speaks about "certain sparks of the divine word," which the Greeks had received. In this way, he points out not only capabilities, but also the limitations that existed.[35]

Basil the Great provides us with a very important key to this issue when he extends the meaning of "seminal word" to include the human capacity "for becoming familiar with the good." "Love for God cannot be taught . . . but within a living constitution, I mean a human being, a certain *spermatikos logos* (seminal principle) has been sown, which has an innate tendency to become familiar with the good."[36]

In Christian discourse today, the first verses of the Gospel according to St John lay down the basic christological foundation for a correct understanding of humanity's loftier religious ideas. "This was the true Light that enlightens every man coming into the world." Some manuscripts place a comma after the word "man," so that the text means, "the true light that enlightens every man, *was coming* into the world"; but in either case, the light enlightens "every man."

Crucial for the present subject is the fact that Christ himself acknowledged the extraordinary power of faith—the extraordinarily

[34]Ibid., *The Second Apology* 13, PG 6:468A (trans. ANF, vol. 1).

[35]"For if, at the most, the Greeks, having received certain scintillations of the divine word. . . ." *Exhortation to the Heathen* 7, PG 8:184A. Clement believes that knowledge of truth in the ancient history of religion comes directly from God; furthermore, he considers this "a preparation, paving the way for him who is perfected in Christ." *The Stromata* 1.5, PG 8:728A (both translations ANF, vol. 3).

[36]Basil the Great, *Regulae Fusius Tractatae* 2.1, PG 31:908BC.

powerful relationship with God—in gentiles that he encountered, such as the Canaanite woman (Mt 15:21-28; cf. Mk 7:24-30) and the Roman centurion (Mt 8:10; cf. Lk 7:5). Furthermore, there is an extended description in the Acts of the Apostles of the devoutness of Cornelius (Acts 10:1-11:16) and his relationship with God, which already existed before he received Peter's visit. The description also informs us that the coming of the Spirit occurred *before* Cornelius' baptism.

At Lystra, the apostle Paul preached that even in previous ages God "did not leave himself without witness, for he did good . . ." (Acts 14:17). And lastly, on the Areopagus (Acts 17:22-31) Paul proclaimed, ". . . he himself gives to all men life and breath and everything. And he made from one [blood] every nation of men . . . that they should seek God, in the hope that they might feel after him and find him" (25-27). Paul even adopted phrases from Aratus (*Phaenomena* 5), in order to stress the truth that "in him we live and move and have our being" (28). These formulations did not result in any kind of syncretistic synthesis, nor did they hide the heart of the Christian message. Paul then went on to preach, calmly and firmly, about the extraordinary new beginning that had opened up within human history and about existence through Jesus Christ and through his Resurrection (30-31).

This message lay completely outside the worldview of the ancient Greeks and was in conflict not only with their popular and exceptionally complicated polytheistic religion, but also with the sophisticated atheism of the Epicurean philosophers and the pantheism of the Stoics. Paul provides us here with a clear example of how to understand and respect ancient religious principles and at the same time transcend them with the power and truth of Christian revelation.

When they discuss Christology, many Western theologians tend to focus their attention on Christ's earthly life, from his birth until the Resurrection—the so-called "historical Jesus." In the East, however, emphasis is placed on the risen Christ, on Christ ascended, on Christ who will come again, on the Lord and *Logos* of the world. The work of the Word before and after his Incarnation, particularly following the Resurrection, constitutes the core of Christian liturgical experience in the East, along with profound eschatological expectations: the belief that "the mystery of his will" is "to unite all things in him, things in heaven and things on earth" (Eph 1:9-10). In this divine process, which has global dimensions that include religious phenomena and experiences, Christ—Love incarnate— remains the final criterion.

Just as the life of Christ, the new Adam, has global consequences, so too, the life of his mystical body, the Church, has worldwide importance and impact. Everything the Church is and everything it does concerns all of humanity, throughout the entire world. As an indication and "icon" of the kingdom, the Church is the axis of cohesion in the entire process of "recapitulation"—the process by which all things become united in Christ. It is on behalf of all people that the Church acts, offers the Divine Eucharist, and praises God. It radiates the glory of the living Lord throughout the entire world.

The Paraclete, "who is everywhere present and fills all things"

New horizons of theological inquiry open up when we consider the subject of other religions from the vantage point of Orthodox pneumatology. Orthodox thought sees the activity of the Holy Spirit very broadly, as something beyond all definitions, descriptions, or boundaries. Together with the "economy of the Word," the Orthodox East looks ahead, full of expectation and humble anticipation, toward the "economy of the Spirit."

At the beginning of creation the Spirit was moving over the chaos, and chaos was formed into the *cosmos*. The Spirit has continued to play this same role throughout history, although we are not able to clearly distinguish how and where, specifically. The Spirit, the giver of life, still blows above the "valley . . . full of bones," as presented in Ezekiel's vision (37:1-14), transforming valleys of the dead into places of life. The participation of the Holy Spirit is central in the mystery of the Savior's Incarnation and in the birth and life of "his mystical body," the Church. At Pentecost, the Holy Spirit reveals and manifests the glory of God in yet another powerful way.

The manifestation of the trinitarian God's presence—everywhere in the world, throughout time, and for all eternity—occurs through the constant activity of the Holy Spirit. The one *"who is everywhere present and fills all things"* continues to act for the salvation of every person and the fulfillment and completion of the entire world. As the Spirit of holiness, it carries the inspiration, love, and power of the trinitarian God to humanity and to the entire universe. As the Spirit of power (the two symbols by which it was perceived at Pentecost were fire and the force of a mighty wind) it vigorously renews the atmosphere in which human beings live and breath, burning up anything decayed—whether it be principles, ideas, organizations, customs, or anything demonic—and offering new energy, so that every single thing within creation can be transformed and renewed.

As the Spirit of truth, it motivates and inspires people to crave and search for the truth, every single aspect of the truth that bears any relation to human life, including scientific truth, of course. Uncovering the truth ultimately leads to the crucial discovery of true knowledge about the mystery of Christ, who is Truth par excellence.

As the Spirit of peace, it soothes our hearts and helps to create a new kind of relationship between human persons, who can then bring understanding and reconciliation to humanity as a whole. As the Spirit of justice, it inspires and fortifies people, so that they will yearn for justice and struggle to attain it.

Nothing can restrict the radiance of the Holy Spirit. Wherever we find love, goodness, peace, and the Spirit's other "fruits" (Gal 5:22), there we discern the signs of its activity. Furthermore, it is clear that quite a few of these things are present in the lives of many people who belong to other religions.

We do need to be very cautious, however, concerning theological ideas that arise in this area; moreover, we need to be theologically sensitive and precise. The terms *ruach* ("spirit" in biblical Hebrew), and *pneuma* or *pneumata* ("spirit" or "spirits" in Greek) are used in Holy Scripture in various senses and with various shades of meaning. In many cases there is doubt whether or not they actually refer to the Holy Spirit. Furthermore, the terms *pneuma* and *pneumata* and the corresponding words in hundreds of other human languages give rise to an unbelievable plethora and diversity of semantic nuances. In our own era, even in Christian environments, this word is used to convey a great variety of meanings. In order to avoid slipping into ambiguous notions or performing theoretical acrobatics, theological study of the Holy Spirit should be carried out with constant reference to our doctrines about Christ and the Holy Trinity.

⸺ • ⸺

Lastly, one more important key to understanding the good intentions and actions of every human person theologically is offered to us in these words of St Maximus the Confessor: "The divine Logos of God the Father is mystically present in each of His commandments . . . Thus, he who receives a divine commandment and carries it out receives the Logos (Word) of God who is in it."[37] Naturally, we must not forget that these lines belong to an ascetic text having to do with the Christian monastic experience. Nevertheless, one could view this position as a theological extension of the kind of biblical thought we encounter in the Epistle to the Romans (2:14-16).[38]

Every human being who is of good will, has good intentions, and keeps the commandments of Christ (genuine love, humility, forgiveness, and unselfish service to others)—even if he or she does not have the privilege of directly knowing the ineffable mystery of Christ—receives, we would venture to say, the Christ-Word that is present in his commandment. Since God is love, any expression of love whatsoever is automatically attuned to his will and his commandments.

In the same passage, St Maximus extends the mystical bond between Christ and his commandments to the Holy Trinity. Since

---

[37]Maximus the Confessor, *Chapters on Theology and on the Incarnate Economy of the Son of God* 2.71, in *The Philokalia*, translated from the Greek by G.E.H. Palmer, Philip Sherrard, and Kallistos Ware, vol. 2 (London, 1981), 154.

[38]"When Gentiles who have not the law do by nature what the law requires, they are a law to themselves, even though they do not have the law. They show that what the law requires is written on their hearts, while their conscience also bears witness and their conflicting thoughts accuse or perhaps excuse them on that day when, according to my gospel, God judges the secrets of men by Christ Jesus."

God the Father is completely united "by nature" with his Word, anyone who accepts the Word through his commandments has also accepted along with him the Father, who is in the Word; furthermore, in accepting the Word one has also accepted the Spirit, which is in the Word. After referring to John 13:20, St Maximus concludes: "In this way, he who receives a commandment and carries it out receives mystically the Holy Trinity."[39]

If we explore this perspective in connection with St Basil's extension of the "seminal word" to the human capacity "for becoming familiar with the good," and if we apply these views to the sphere of social life, perhaps new horizons might open up in our theological understanding of the mystery regarding the lives of people with other religious faiths.

CONCLUDING REMARKS

In conclusion, I would like to emphasize the following.

A degeneration of religious ideas and forms of worship can be observed in humanity's religious experiences, together with the growth of demonic structures and forces that distort human existence. On the other hand, sparks from the light of divine inspiration shine through. Religions open a horizon toward a transcendent reality, toward Something or Someone that exists beyond perceptible phenomena. Religions are born out of humanity's yearning for the "sacred," and they keep the gates of human experience open to the infinite. The divine image, which is humanity's essential characteristic, has never been destroyed. For this reason, every human person has the ability to receive intimations of the divine will and intimations of the universal radiance of the glory of the trinitarian God.

Everyone on earth lives under the influence of the Sun of Justice. One could think of religions as batteries that have been charged by the sun's rays—charged with experiences of life and with various great concepts and ideas. Many people have been helped in the course of their lives by the few glimmers of imperfect light these

[39]*Philokalia*, 2:155.

batteries provide. However, we cannot think of the light from these batteries as being self-powered; it does not have the ability to replace the Sun itself.

The criterion by which Christians evaluate and accept different religious ideas and principles is Jesus Christ, the Word of God and incarnation of the trinitarian God's love. The love that his message carries, together with the breadth and profundity revealed in the gospels, constitutes the indisputable core of our religious experience, as well as its fulfillment. We come to know and experience this love through the activity of the Holy Spirit. Christ's work for the salvation of the entire world is continued through time by the Church, which is his body (Col 1:18).

While the Christian attitude is severely critical of other religions as organic and unified systems, Christians should show a great deal of understanding, respect, and love for people who live in environments where different religions and ideologies dominate. This is because every human person's divine origin is never lost, even if his or her religious conceptions and beliefs are mistaken. Every human being was created "in God's image" and is therefore our sister or our brother.

The rays of divine glory that embrace the entire universe are received by everyone. All human beings benefit from the activities of the Holy Spirit—activities that promote life, love, and truth. The Church, moreover, is the mystery of the kingdom, and as such it acts on behalf of and for the sake of humanity as a whole. Since all people share in humanity's common nature, which was restored with the incarnation of the Word, they also enjoy some of the effects of his grace and his love, both of which become fully activated within the Church, which is his body.

As the world continues to bring us all closer to one another, we Christians have a pressing obligation to engage in dialogue with people of other religious beliefs. In order for such dialogue to be sincere, we must first have respect for the personality and the freedom of those with whom we speak, as well as sincere love and understanding. We must also acknowledge the inspiration that exists in other religious experiences.

Nevertheless, this openness toward dialogue does not mean that we stop bearing witness to our Christianity. Precisely the opposite. Every time we engage in dialogue we also interpret and elucidate the testimony of our Christian faith. We have an obligation to speak with people and to offer the priceless treasure that we possess. We cannot remain silent about the things that God's love has revealed to us and has bestowed on us. These include, above all, our certainty that God is *love* and that all people are called upon to participate in a communion of love with the trinitarian God. If we are to be persuasive, however, what we say must grow out of our lives and our experience.

What the world is seeking from Christians is consistency. The world is asking us to reveal the beauty of the Christian message by conscientiously living its principles, in the light of the Crucifixion and the Resurrection. The world is looking for us to reveal, in the course of our daily reality, the beauty, radiance, glory, and power in a life that has been made new in Christ. The world is calling upon us to radiate the presence of the Holy Spirit. It yearns for a living Christianity that bears witness to the mystery of the All-Holy Trinity's Love. It longs for the virtual transformation of human existence and for a communion with the transcendent power of Love.

～ 6 ～

The Dynamic of Universal and Continuous Change

THE TESTIMONY OF THE THREE HIERARCHS
ON "CHANGE FOR THE BETTER"*

A mong the various religious and philosophical viewpoints that
have influenced the life of humanity, there are the ones that
accept the world as it is, others that attempt to escape it, and some
that want to transform it. The Christian outlook is among the most
fervent of those that belong to the last category.

Christianity has of course seen the development of a variety of
tendencies and forms of spirituality. In its Orthodox ideal, however,
Christianity is still defined by its holistic vision: an approach toward
and account of life that embraces everything, life in its entirety, in all
its dimensions and meanings. This all-encompassing vision was
elaborated with force and originality by the three "ecumenical teachers": Basil the Great (330?-379), Gregory the Theologian (329-390),
and John Chrysostom (354-407).[1] With all their being they lived the

*This address was delivered in the auditorium of the National and Capodistrian Univer-
sity of Athens at their official celebration for the Feast of the Three Hierarchs, January
30, 1982. It was published in the university's volume of "Official Addresses" for the
scholastic year 1981-1982 (Athens, 1983), 341-59, under the title "The Testimony of the
Three Hierarchs on 'Change for the Better,' or The Dynamic of Universal and Continuous Change."

The decision to include an essay on the Three Hierarchs in the present collection
was prompted by the consideration that the writing and lives of these three "teachers to
all the world"—ecumenical teachers, as Orthodox tradition refers to them—provide us
with definitive views regarding the dynamic of continuous "change for the better" in
human existence and society worldwide.

[1]"If the authority of certain Fathers were to be placed in the foreground . . . it would

155

Bible's message that everything is reiterated in Christ, and they reflected on, analyzed, and struggled for an all-encompassing change in human affairs, maintaining the gospel as their ideal. They lived this process of "change for the better" (*kale alloiōsis*, lit. "good transformation"), this transformation of everyone and everything, which Christ initiated in both the external and the interior realms.

On the first Sunday after Easter in 383, Gregory the Theologian delivered a sermon entitled "The Lord's Day" in which the call for a radical renewal of everyone and everything, accomplished through the Resurrection of Christ, is masterfully interwoven with the precept that every Christian is under constant obligation to make a personal effort at renewal. Gregory's basic message culminates with the appeal: "'The old has passed away, behold, the new has come.' . . . Experience this change for the better."[2] It is a comprehensive and multidimensional change that is meant here, a deep and continuous change that was brought about through the Resurrection and that has direct consequences on the personal and the social planes.

Of course, I am not unaware that there are many who do not share our hope and who are not particularly moved by such assertions. A host of different philosophical conceptions has destroyed any unity in the way our tradition is understood, and various theories have overshadowed the vision of the Three Hierarchs. Nevertheless, this does not negate the fact that in the realms of culture, philosophy, and ethics their teaching on "change for the good" is the core of our Christian heritage. Moreover, it is a legacy that at critical moments has provided the Orthodox people with inspiration and strength. For centuries now, the ethos of the Orthodox people has been shaped by a tradition steadfastly rooted in the events of Easter. The premises of Christian faith and Christian life constitute fundamental layers in the subconscious mind of our nation, and those of us who share the certainties of the three hierarchs are under an obligation to make these certainties a part of people's consciousness. In

be in accordance with the tradition of the Eastern Church to prefer the three Bishops whom our liturgical texts call 'the holy pontiffs and oecumenical doctors' . . . From such Masters and Fathers in Christ . . . we shall *authoritatively* learn the Orthodox way to holiness." L. Gillet, *Orthodox Spirituality*, 2d ed. (Crestwood, NY, 1996), ix-x.

[2]Gregory of Nazianzus, *Orations* 44.8 ("The New Sunday"), PG 36:616C.

what follows I will try to articulate five different aspects of the hierarchs' teaching on "change for the good."

MUCH IN HUMAN LIFE NEEDS TO CHANGE

Ideas that in recent centuries have been considered groundbreaking advances in world thought figure as central points in the writings of the three ecumenical teachers, who persistently speak about human equality, referring to *homotimia* (that all people are "of equal value") and to *isotimia* (that all are entitled to "equal privileges"). They find the basis for this equality in the very essence of humanity's nature,[3] and any departure from this equality is understood unconditionally as injustice. "Justice," Gregory writes, "means not seeking to have more, and injustice is any departure from equality."[4]

Although they lived in an age when the distinctions and enormous differences between masters and slaves and between men and women were not only axiomatic but were relentlessly enforced by law, the Three Hierarchs raised their voices to challenge these ideas. The three saints saw such segregation as "contemptible divisions." "Who is a master and who is a slave? A contemptible division," writes Gregory. "There is one Maker for all, one law, and one judgment."[5]

Gregory is unequivocal when he states that a law on marital misconduct that is lenient toward men but strict toward women is "unequal and irregular." "I do not accept this legislation, nor do I approve of the practice. Men were the lawmakers, which is why the legislation is hard on women." After citing various biblical texts that he uses to defend equality, he declares: "There is one Maker for man and woman; both are made of one flesh and in one image, and there is one law, one death, and one resurrection for both of them."[6]

In reply to those who invoke biblical passages in order to support theories of male superiority, Chrysostom emphasizes that a woman

[3]Cf. Basil the Great, *On the Holy Spirit* 20, PG 32:161.
[4]*Ethical Verses* 34.59-60, PG 37:950.
[5]Quoted by John of Damascus in *The Sacred Parallels*, PG 95:1373C.
[6]*Orations* 37.6 ("On the Words of the Gospel, 'When Jesus Had Finished Saying These Sayings . . .'" [Mt 19:1]), PG 36:289BC.

is *homotimos*, "held in equal honor"; that is, he does not hesitate to employ the theological terminology of the Trinity, which describes the Son as *homotimos* in regard to the Father, to whom he is obedient. "Even though a woman is obedient to us, nevertheless she is obedient as a woman, as a free person who is held in equal honor. Similarly, although the Son is obedient to the Father, he is nevertheless obedient as the Son of God and as God."[7]

Writing of the standard antitheses that divide people, such as slavery and freedom or poverty and wealth, Gregory unequivocally calls them "illnesses," and "fabrications of evil," which, "having entered the human race" in later times, "have come bringing with them" all their evil consequences.[8] He constantly refers to the fact that humanity was not originally constituted in this way, since human beings were created sovereign and free. Freedom and wealth are found in the observance of God's commandments; true poverty and slavery are the result of their violation.[9]

The words of the Three Hierarchs could be scalding when they spoke against the greed, wealth, and social injustice that prevailed in their era and that were indeed sanctioned by the morals, laws, and general outlook of the time. To my knowledge, no pronouncements more intended to shock and dismay an audience have ever been formulated on the subject of wealth and human greed than theirs.[10] Basil the Great stipulates the unconditional principle that wealth is inversely proportional to love. "If you exceed what is reasonable in wealth, you fall short to the same degree in love."[11] Extravagance, i.e., "expenditure which exceeds one's need," is

---

[7]*Homilies on First Corinthians* 26.2, PG 61:214-15.

[8]*Orations* 14.25 ("On Caring for the Poor"), PG 35:892A.

[9]"Freedom and wealth were simply the observance of commandments, while true poverty and slavery were the transgression of commandments." Ibid.

[10]"A trafficker in human misfortunes" and "cursed by the community" is what Basil called any person who became rich by taking advantage of hard times. *On "I will pull down my barns . . ."* 3, PG 31:268B. Cf. idem, *To Those Who Amass Wealth* 5, PG 31:293A: "A man who loves money will never be satisfied by getting more. Hell has never said 'enough,' nor has a greedy man ever said 'enough.'"

[11]*To Those Who Amass Wealth* 1, PG 31:281B. Cf. idem, *Ethics*, rule 48, PG 31:768C: "Anyone whose possessions are greater, by whatever amount, than those of someone in need is obligated to use that same amount to help the latter, according to the commandment of the Lord, who has given us everything we have."

considered "misuse."[12] If someone is robbed of his clothing, Basil doesn't hesitate to apply the epithet "clothes robber" not only to the thief who stole the clothes but also to anyone else who is able to provide the victim with new clothes and assistance but fails to do so. He then dispels any doubt about his meaning with the unequivocal charge: "You are guilty of having injured all those people you could have helped."[13] Chrysostom is thinking along similar lines when he characterizes the failure to offer others some of our possessions as an act of "robbery" and "deprivation."[14] It appears that the wealthier circles began to react strongly against these sermons. The archbishop responded with a counterattack. " 'Are you railing against the wealthy again?' they ask me. But you are still oppressing the poor . . . You are not yet done with chewing them up into bits and devouring them, and I am not done with admonishing you . . . Since you mistreat my flock, can you reasonably blame me for pursuing you?"[15]

They are particularly resolute about exposing the hypocrisy of those who attempt to make pious charitable offerings using ill-gotten wealth. Before offering gifts to God, each person must carefully ask himself "whether he has oppressed the poor, whether he has coerced the weak, whether he has defrauded any of his subordinates." Instead of doing good to others, "have mercy on the person you injure."[16]

Chrysostom characterizes the words "mine and yours" as "a heartless phrase that has started countless wars in the world."[17] He persistently inveighed not only against the existence of affluence but against the approving attitude toward becoming rich that existed among rich and poor alike.[18] As we see, the hierarchs' admonitions

[12]Basil the Great, *Regulae Fusius Tractatae* 20.3, PG 31:976A.

[13]Basil the Great, *On "I will pull down my barns . . ."* 7, PG 31:277A.

[14]"Failing to give the poor some of what we possess is the same as robbing them and depriving them of life; for the things we are withholding belong to them, not to us." John Chrysostom, *On Lazarus* 2.6, PG 48:992.

[15]*On the Words in Psalm 49, "Be not afraid when one becomes rich . . ."* 4, PG 55:504.

[16]Basil the Great, *Sermons* 4.7 ("On Charity"), PG 32:1164A, D.

[17]*On the Words of the Apostle "for there must be factions among you . . ."* (1 Cor 11:19), 2, PG 51:255.

[18]"Many of the poor, who lack material wealth, happen nevertheless to have extremely greedy intentions. The fact that they are poor does not save them, for they are condemned by their intentions." Basil the Great, *Homily on the 33rd Psalm* 5, PG 29:361A.

extended to all social classes. "Who is greedy? Anyone who is not content with self-sufficiency."[19] And the money one acquires through honest toil will be attributed to theft, "even though it was lawfully obtained, if you fail to make offerings to God with which the poor can be fed."[20] Basil the Great formulates an extremely interesting principle that could easily be taken for a modern view of social economy. "Wealth that is standing still is useless, but wealth that is in motion, passing from one hand to another, is beneficial to the public and productive."[21]

Injustice was not the sole object of the hierarchs' castigation. They also considered "unsociability"—the failure to offer help and assistance to those in need—to be an offense. "For in that case it is not the plunderer who stands condemned but the person who wants no part of other peoples' problems."[22] It is in generosity that they find true religiosity. Struggling for a just society within the political framework of their time, they strike out against "the piety that costs nothing" and demand that the faithful learn to give eagerly.[23]

They repeatedly return to the subject of the social obligation that weighs heavily on each one of us. People are deemed virtuous when they direct all their energies to the public good. "A good man must do everything with an eye to the public benefit."[24] Everything must be directed toward the benefit of one's neighbor. Their line of thought is summed up in the exhortation: anything extra that you possess constitutes a debt to those who are in need.[25] People are deemed worthy when they work constantly for the benefit of others. "Anyone who withholds any of God's gifts for his own enjoyment and fails to offer help to others is condemned like the servant who 'hid his master's money.'"[26]

[19]Basil the Great, On "I will pull down my barns . . ." 7, PG 31:276A.
[20]Basil the Great, Sermons 4.7 ("On Charity"), PG 32:1164C.
[21]Basil the Great, On "I will pull down my barns . . ." 5, PG 31:272B.
[22]Ibid., 8, PG 31:277C.
[23]"I am aware that many fast, pray, sigh, and make a display of every kind of piety that costs nothing, but don't give even the smallest coin to those in need. What good does the rest of their virtue do them? For the kingdom of Heaven will not receive them." Basil the Great, To Those Who Amass Wealth 3, PG 31:288A.
[24]John Chrysostom, On Blessed Babylas 8, PG 50:545.
[25]Basil the Great, Ethics, rule 48, PG 31:768C.
[26]Basil the Great, Regulae Brevius Tractatae 62, PG 31:1124B. This applies to every-

"Change for the better," both personal and social, becomes reality by means of this constant charity, illuminated by the paschal ideal. In "The Lord's Day," the oration quoted above, which was delivered at the inauguration of the Church of St Mamas, Gregory associates proper social behavior with the Christian theological conscience, ending with the following words: "Give to the one who has no shelter, protection, or food, you who have these things in abundance, far beyond your need. . . . Extend forgiveness, you who have been forgiven. . . . Let your whole life and everything you do in life be renewed."[27]

Life as organized in the monasteries provides the Three Hierarchs with a model or symbol for the ideal society, since it embodies equality, common ownership, and love. "I call that manner of communal life perfect," says Basil the Great, "in which private property does not exist, contradictory opinions have been eliminated, all turmoil, rivalry, and discord have been set well out of the way, and everything is shared in common."[28] It is in an equal society that "change for the good" can become reality, leading us back toward our original state of archetypal, ideal beauty, because "From the beginning God has wanted us to be this way, and it was for this purpose that he created us."[29]

CHANGE IS POSSIBLE

The three ecumenical teachers do not confine themselves merely to describing the fundamental social conditions that must change. They assess the potential for change, are optimistic in their assessment, and personally proceed to make the first innovative efforts.

All three lived at a time when the world was being reshaped. It was an era of deep divisions, social and political turmoil, and daring

one, whether or not he is well off. Having "mercy" amounts to a general theological principle. It is the code word for a whole system of concepts that express eagerness to offer help.

[27]*Orations* 44.7 ("The New Sunday"), PG 36:616A.
[28]*Rules for Ascetic Life* 18.1, PG 31:1381C.
[29]Ibid., 18.2, 1384A.

pursuits; an era that witnessed a general reevaluation and realignment of ideas; an era that bears a strong resemblance to our own. The Hierarchs confronted the issues of their time with true tenacity, courage, and wisdom. With penetrating astuteness they analyzed the contradictory reality of human life, which proceeds within a set of dialectical oppositions: rationality and irrationality, faith and knowledge, downfall and ascent. They were nevertheless convinced of human beings' ability to transcend the tragic aspect of their existence and were filled with optimistic confidence about their future. Every person can have hope for himself, regardless of his social position. He can also have hope for others. Everyone has the ability to "repent," that is, to change the direction of his life and rediscover the "ancient beauty."

Human beings are by their nature changeable and alterable, capable of being transformed. Even for one who has fallen to the lowest point, there is a path upward. The language of Christianity does not suggest stasis or lack of motion, but calls for continuous creative renewal. This call to "make life new" is not only directed toward those who have taken the wrong road in life but is also addressed to those headed in the right direction. If you sin, Gregory stresses, return to the right path; if you are walking along the right path, increase your efforts.[30]

Their optimism springs from the fact that they continuously contemplate the mystery of humanity in relation to the mystery of God. Evil has no substantive existence; it does not exist in itself, as God does, although some dualistic religions would have us think otherwise. Evil lacks substance. It is a departure, the product of an egocentric and self-serving use of freedom on the part of humankind. It is nothing but an epiphenomenon, one that can be shaken off through synergy with the divine. Whatever there is within us that is fundamental and divine is ours "by nature"; behavior "contrary to nature" is the product of a freedom that has become estranged from

---

[30]"The Word [Christ] does not want that you should remain in the same state but that you should be forever in motion, moving freely, an entirely new creation. If you sin, return to the right road; if you are doing well, try harder." *Orations* 44.8 ("The Lord's Day"), PG 36:616D-617A.

the God of Love. "Sin is alienation from God."[31] "Changing one's ways in favor of the good" is possible and necessary. No matter how deep the alienation and fall, human nature never ceases to bear God's image and is therefore in essence good.[32]

Nevertheless, the Fathers' optimism is not based on humanity in and of itself. They do not place such faith in the adequacy of *nous* ("mind" or "intellect"). Their optimism is based on the fact that a new human being, a second Adam, fully assumed human nature, put human freedom back on the path of unselfish love, made "turning back toward the good" a reality, and provided the human race with a new orientation. "Christ's Incarnation was my re-creation," says Gregory.[33] Through the Incarnation of Christ "human nature, which had been divided and broken up into countless bits" was gathered "back into itself and into God."[34] Christ reassembled human nature within itself and within himself; he called human nature back to its previous, unified state of communion and love.[35] The victory has already been won.

With Christ's Resurrection everything was made new again; everything was restored.[36] From that point on, the question posed for every human being has been whether or not to participate in this restoration. In the code language of Christianity, this call to participate is known by the term "repentance," which Gregory defines as "a turn toward better things."[37] Repentance calls on us to make the effort to change by becoming new, through the process initiated by

---

[31]Gregory of Nazianzus, *Ethical Verses* 8.184, PG 37:662.

[32]Gregory of Nazianzus, *Orations* 43.48 ("Funeral Oration for Basil the Great"), PG 36:560A.

[33]*Ethical Verses* 34.189, PG 37:959.

[34]Basil the Great, *Rules for Ascetic Life* 18.3, PG 31:1385A.

[35]Ibid.

[36]"Today is salvation come unto the world, to that which is visible, and to that which is invisible. Christ is risen from the dead, rise ye with Him. Christ is returned again to Himself, return ye. Christ is freed from the tomb, be ye freed from the bond of sin. The gates of hell are opened, and death is destroyed, and the old Adam is put aside, and the New is fulfilled; if any man be in Christ he is a new creature; be ye renewed." Gregory of Nazianzus, *Orations* 45.1 ("Second Oration on Easter"), PG 36:624AB (trans. NPF, 2d ser., vol. 7).

[37]*Ethical Verses* 34.235, PG 37:962.

the events of Easter. "Now let yourselves be new, different in your ways, and entirely altered."[38]

The act of change, however, begins and continuously draws its power from the energies of God, "from whom every human accomplishment proceeds."[39] The three saints connect all their appeals for "repentance" with Christ's assumption of our human nature and his bond with every human person. "While there is time," Gregory writes, "let us attend Christ, look after Christ, feed Christ, clothe Christ, shelter Christ, and honor Christ."[40] The moment when Jesus' clothing was taken from him is seen by Chrysostom to be repeated in the fact that so many people walk the streets of our societies lacking clothing. In their person the hunger and thirst of the crucified Lord is reiterated.[41]

"Change for the better" is not only an individual matter.[42] The act of repentance, of change, of cleansing "God's image" is completed within the life of the Church, which continues the work of the Savior. The people of the Church are not without sin, but they are repenting, continuously repenting.

The enormous significance of this optimism about the potential for ascent and renewal becomes apparent when its glowing light is seen through the fog of other religious systems—systems that see all human endeavor within the confines of an implacable determinism, where the essence of existence is suffering, and an end to this suffering is found only when existence itself is extinguished. Contrary to every pessimistic or individualistic conception of this kind, such as we find promulgated by various philosophical-religious systems

---

[38]*Orations* 44.8 ("The New Sunday"), PG 36:616C.

[39]Ibid., 616D.

[40]*Orations* 14.40 ("On Caring for the Poor"), PG 35:909B.

[41]"I was athirst when hanging on the Cross, I am athirst also through the poor . . . though I am able to support Myself, I come about begging, and stand beside thy door, and stretch out Mine hand, since My wish is to be supported by thee. For I love thee exceedingly, and so desire to eat at thy table. . . ." *Homilies on the Epistle of St Paul to the Romans* 15.6, PG 60:547-48 (trans. NPF, 1st ser., vol. 11).

[42]Caring only for one's own salvation is characterized by Chrysostom as "brutal and inhuman." We all share one common responsibility. "Each of us is responsible for the salvation of his neighbor." John Chrysostom, *To Those Who Share Lodgings with Virgins* 4, PG 47:500.

such as Buddhism, patristic thought directs us toward an active and dynamic acceptance of life and exhorts the faithful to make a continuous effort to improve life by striving together with all the other faithful, with the Church.

This optimism of the Three Hierarchs regarding human life is full of patience, however. They do not think that transformation and change can be realized through violence, as Islam, for example, would later prescribe. "Change for the better" operates within the context of human freedom. The three ecumenical teachers of our Church constantly refer to the freedom of the human person, "the impulse toward being one's own master, which is appropriate for a rational nature."[43] The anthropology of the Three Hierarchs—i.e., their understanding of the origin, nature, and destiny of human beings—remains an anthropology of grace and freedom.

Even before they were ordained, all three saints had been highly acknowledged intellectuals and social reformers, whose work and achievements were extremely significant and multifaceted. On taking up their priestly vocation and shouldering their personal burden in the Church, they advanced to the front lines of social responsibility and sacrifice. They undertook innovative and practical initiatives within society. While still a presbyter at Antioch, John Chrysostom mobilized the manpower and resources needed to ensure the support of three thousand widows and hundreds of others who were either foreign, ill, or imprisoned. He stood alongside the people of Antioch in their anguish when they faced the threat of being collectively punished, after they opposed the emperor by destroying his statues. With the new opportunities that the archbishop's throne offered him, he was able to provide moral and financial support to seven thousand needy people in Constantinople.

When the dominance of Arianism brought dark and hopeless times, Gregory went to Constantinople to wage a determined battle, and he changed the course of events. He later resigned from the patriarchal throne in order to facilitate peace within the ranks of the Orthodox.

---

[43]Basil the Great, *That God is Not the Cause of Evil* 6, PG 31:344B.

The activities of Basil the Great were literally astonishing in their diversity and social impact, particularly his organization of hospitals, orphanages, hospices, schools, and workshops for Vasilia—the new city that later took his name—a project he declined to write about. In order to carry out this work he mobilized large numbers of people based on a definite and systematic social plan that he himself personally supervised, "imitating the ministry of Christ."[44]

The interest of Basil and Chrysostom was not limited only to spreading the message of redemptive change in the regions where they were bishops. They also did whatever they could to organize and assist missionary work beyond their own districts, even in pagan nations outside the empire.[45]

These three saints stood with affection and humility before the powerless, yet bore themselves with nobility, dignity, and courage before the powerful. Basil's opposition to the emperor Valens and the subprefect Modestos is well known, as is Chrysostom's criticism of the Empress Eudoxia's abuses. All three saints were the targets not only of political enemies but also of enemies within the Church. "Avoid one thing," writes Gregory, summarizing the experience of all three, "wicked bishops . . . I hate teachings from people who do not practice the things they preach."[46] With enthusiasm and courage they strove to achieve a change for the better, each one preserving his own distinctive personality.

REAL CHANGE BEGINS AT THE CORE OF HUMAN EXISTENCE

In their struggle for positive change, the Three Hierarchs directed both their intellectual and their practical endeavors toward that crucial point on which the viability of any real change depends: the core of human existence.

[44]Gregory of Nazianzus, *Orations* 43.35 ("Funeral Oration for Basil the Great"), PG 36:544D.

[45]See John Chrysostom, *Correspondence*, PG 52: letter 53 (637); letter 54 (638); letter 55 (639-40); letter 123 (676-77); and letter 126 (685-87).

[46]*Historical Verses* 12.35-40, PG 37:1169A.

The three ecumenical teachers were interested in depth and substance, not superficiality. "He strove not just to seem excellent but to be excellent,"[47] Gregory says of St Basil. Irresolute schemes and vague mental constructs are not sufficient, because egotism and emotion often keep the mind from functioning as it should. Cleansing must begin in the depths of a human being's existence, for that is where corruption first takes hold, once the self has become an object of worship. The fathers therefore insist on inner purity and good intentions. Without individual honesty and genuineness, justice is a mere chimera, "difficult to achieve because some lack the prudence to give everyone an equal share and because others conceal what is just, since they are governed by human passions."[48] A person cannot render justice or work for justice if justice has not been "previously stored up in his soul" or if he "has been corrupted by the desire for wealth or is swayed either by friendship toward some or hatred toward others."[49] The secret of substantive change, the guarantee of change, and the dynamic through which change occurs all lie hidden within the process of restoring and purifying the human person. We must focus on the essence of things, not appearances. "Yesterday you placed value in seeming; today, place greater value in being," Gregory urges.[50]

All three Fathers struggle to awaken our inner consciousness, so that we can focus on ourselves and strengthen the divine spark that exists within us. They exhort us to engage in a continuous effort, so that our lives will be "pure," or, more accurately, so that we will constantly "be purifying" ourselves."[51] This inner effort is a continuous process in which one strives to extend one's spiritual efforts "beyond one's own ability, always reaching with one's soul toward the will of God, his glory being one's goal and desire."[52] Referring to this

---

[47]*Orations* 43.60 ("Funeral Oration for Basil the Great"), PG 36:576A.

[48]Basil the Great, quoted in *The Monk Antonius, Melissa,* 1.11, PG 136:805A. Cf. Basil the Great, *Commentary on the Prophet Isaiah* 114, PG 30:304B: "Justice is useless to unjust men, just as the sun is useless to men with bad eyesight."

[49]Basil the Great, quoted in *The Monk Antonius Melissa,* 1.13, PG 136:805A.

[50]*Orations* 44.9 ("The New Sunday"), PG 36:617A.

[51]Gregory of Nazianzus, *Orations* 16.2 ("On His Father's Silence"), PG 35:936B.

[52]Basil the Great, *Regulae Brevius Tractatae* 211, PG 31:1224A.

internal discipline and vigilance, which safeguards humanity's inner freedom, Gregory advises: "If you depart from rational behavior even in the slightest, try to find yourself again, before you fall completely beyond the pale and are dragged down to death; become new instead of old, and celebrate the re-inauguration of your soul."[53]

Before making their public lives a testimony to the truth, all three ecumenical teachers waged an internal struggle. They went through a period of strenuous ascetic preparation in order to free themselves from the power of the human passions. This later enabled them to live and act with inner freedom: free from the love of material wealth, fame, and physical comfort; free from the love of power, and armed with the power of love.

This ascetic vigilance was not simply an introductory "training" exercise but remained a constant condition of their lives. Throughout their lives they remained simple men, ascetics. As for Basil, "His wealth was having nothing, and he thought the cross, with which he lived, more precious than great riches."[54] This is an asceticism of inner genuineness, which gives priority to how it is practiced, not where.[55] The Fathers brought into harmony things that at first glance seem contradictory, such as monasticism and a socially active life, "in order that the contemplative spirit might not be cut off from society, nor the active life be uninfluenced by the contemplative."[56] They always advised moderation.[57]

[53]*Orations* 44.6 ("The New Sunday"), PG 36:613C.

[54]Gregory of Nazianzus, *Orations* 43.60 ("Funeral Oration for Basil the Great"), PG 36:573C (trans. NPF, 2d ser., vol. 7).

[55]"For a man who remains in his house can still wander abroad in his thoughts, and a man in the marketplace can remain vigilant, as if he were in the desert, paying attention only to himself and to God." Basil the Great, *Rules for Ascetic Life* 5, PG 31:1360C. Cf. "But withdrawal from the world does not mean bodily removal from it, but the severance of the soul from sympathy with the body." Idem, *Letters* 2.2 ("To Gregory"), PG 32:225B [trans. Roy J. Deferrari, Loeb Classical Library, *Basil the Great, The Letters*, vol. 1 (Cambridge, MA, 1926).]

[56]Gregory of Nazianzus, *Orations* 43.62 ("Funeral Oration for Basil the Great"), PG 36:577B (trans. NPF, 2d ser., vol. 7).

[57]"The proper degree of physical abstinence must be determined for each person in relation to his physical strength, so that his effort does not fall below his ability nor extend beyond it. Here, I think, is where care must be taken, lest excessive abstinence destroy the body's endurance, thus preventing it from being able to perform its important tasks." Basil the Great, *Rules for Ascetic Life* 4.1, PG 31:1348B. Also: "The ascetic

Their asceticism is not human centered; it is not a simple exercise for the mind or the will, such as we see practiced in isolation from society by various schools of Indian thought. On the contrary, their asceticism is in constant relationship with God and his people and is carried out within the social life of the faithful, the Church. Personal effort must be combined with tradition and with trust in the grace and guidance of the Holy Spirit, so that one can become conversant with God's energies, on which the entire process of change depends.[58] Throughout their quest, the compass that the Fathers used to find their way did not consist of vague mental intuitions or psychological instincts—it was biblical revelation. "A most important path to the discovery of duty is also the study of the divinely-inspired Scriptures."[59] Ascent toward God was the air they breathed. Their effort was "to establish a stronghold for God within themselves" through prayer.[60] This is asceticism carried out through a life attuned to resurrection. Baptism and the Divine Eucharist, which epitomize the paschal event and are its tangible expressions par excellence, impart the inspiration and the strength we need for positive change.[61]

This experience of life as constant resurrection defines Orthodox spirituality. It was this that the three great hierarchs of the one, holy, catholic and apostolic Church lived and preached. It was this that they enriched with the liturgies that bear their names. Easter once a year and Sunday once a week articulate the year, bringing the great event of Pascha—passage into new life—back to the here and now, rousing a person to make new efforts at renewal, and transmitting the light of the Resurrection into everyday life.

---

should free himself from every form of vanity and truly follow the royal path of moderation, never deviating to the left or the right. He should neither welcome physical comfort nor incapacitate his body with excessive abstinence." Ibid., 4.2, PG 31:1349B.

[58]"But the mind that is tempered with the divinity of the Spirit is at last initiated into the great speculations, and observes the divine beauties, but only to the extent that grace allows and its constitution admits." Basil the Great, *Letters* 233.1 ("To Bishop Amphilochios, who has asked questions"), PG 32:865C (trans. Deferrari, vol. 3, see note 56).

[59]Basil the Great, *Letters* 2.3 ("To Gregory"), PG 32:228B (trans. Deferrari, see note 56).

[60]Ibid., 4, PG 32:229B (trans. Deferrari, see note 56).

[61]Gregory of Nazianzus, *Orations* 45.23 ("Second Oration on Easter"), PG 36:656.

CHANGE EXTENDS TO ALL OF CREATION

When the three ecumenical teachers consider humanity, they do not
see it narrowly, from a purely spiritual or ethical point of view. They
always regard human beings as organically connected to the material
world in which they live. "Change for the better" extends to creation
as a whole.

Understanding humanity's relationship with the material world
is an issue that has acquired particular significance in our time. Some
religions see nature as being animated by divine forces that control
human beings like puppets. Other systems of thought consider a
human being to be a speck, part of an impersonal natural world, an
insignificant dot imprisoned within nature's impersonal laws. Still
others regard nature purely as matter, a mere object useful for serving humanity's needs and desires.

In the Christian view, which the Three Hierarchs set forth with
penetrating insight, humanity and the entire universe are creations
of the infinite and living God, and they were intended to evolve
together in harmony. The human race and the material world have
incomprehensible value and importance. Matter was created by God
himself, not by any other being. It is not a substance that exists par-
allel to or independent of its Creator. Nothing is unworthy of God,
except sin. "If any one of the things that exist in creation were in and
of itself bad, it would not be a creation of God," writes Basil, " 'For
everything created by God,' it is written, 'is good, and nothing is to
be rejected.' "[62] For Chrysostom, anyone who reproaches creation is
"senseless and mad." For creation "is not bad but good, proof of
God's wisdom and power and love for humankind."[63]

At the beginning of human history, nature too became "alienated" from God as a result of humanity's selfish and egotistical use of
its freedom. These clouds of "alienation" continue to contaminate
the way nature functions today. When Christ, the new Adam,

Basil the Great, On Holy Baptism 1, PG 31:424; and Letters 93 ("To Caesaria"), PG
32:484B.

[62]Regulae Brevius Tractatae 92, PG 31:1145C.

[63]To those who make accusations against God for not destroying the devil . . . 3, PG
49:260.

assumed the material stuff of which humanity is made, human freedom became coordinated with a reawakening of sanctification and love, and nature thus began to regain its proper dynamic and purpose.

The three ecumenical teachers persistently return to the point that Christ our Savior assumed a human body. "The Word became flesh"—not spirit or ideas, and not a book, as Islam, for example, would like to see the Qur'an. Jesus Christ transformed the body. He resurrected it, and with it he carried out his ministry. The Christian faith does not preach that the body is a prison from which the spirit and the soul must be liberated.

The teaching of the Three Hierarchs stands in direct contrast to any form of ambiguous idealism or any version of modern, atheistic humanism. It is based on the Incarnation of the Word, which exalted all of humanity's nature, both body and soul.[64] There is no concept in patristic thought of an impenetrable intermediary stratum, the supernatural, that separates nature from God. The basic distinction that begins to take shape in Orthodox theology with Basil the Great is the distinction between God's essence and his energies. From this will later develop the Orthodox line of distinction between the created and the uncreated. The entire universe is the province of God's sanctifying energies and his uncreated grace. The universe was not created to stay as it is; it was created to "become." It is in a state of dynamic motion. It is energy. It does not change through a simple process of evolution. Its end or purpose—its future—exists "within" it. God "proposed . . . a manifest design in His works," Basil notes.[65] Creation moves toward transformation. According to Chrysostom, all creation "is changing its form for the better and will enjoy greater glory."[66]

Far from rejecting the world in any way, patristic thought— which the Three Hierarchs represent in its greatest clarity—calls upon humanity to participate actively, to work for the world, and to extend God's creative energies. According to other religions, such as

[64]"He came forth then, as God, with That which He had assumed; one Person in two natures, flesh and Spirit, of which the latter deified the former." Gregory of Nazianzus, *Orations* 45.9 ("Second Oration on Easter"), PG 36:633D (trans. NPF, 2d ser., vol. 7).

[65]*The Hexaemeron* 3.10, PG 29:76CD (trans. NPF, 2d ser., vol. 8).

[66]*On Anne* 1.2, PG 54:636.

those from India, whatever we comprehend through our senses or the individual ego is all illusion. These religions seek to rally the forces of the human will not for the purpose of transformation but so that the individual can distance himself from this world of deception.

The thinking of the three ecumenical teachers stresses the close relationship between humanity and creation and places particular emphasis not only on the sanctification of our souls but on the sanctification of nature as a whole. The Christian believer stands before every one of God's creations with respect and love in his heart, not thievery. Harmony between humanity and the physical world is restored through a process of love and thanksgiving.

In its liturgical life the Church uses material substances "to stand for creation," and by commemorating and transferring Easter to the here and now, these substances are transformed by divine grace. In the divine eucharist, the foremost expression of the paschal event, the Church offers bread and wine: ". . . and presenting unto thee the holy emblems of the sacred Body and Blood of thy Christ, we pray thee and implore thee, O Holy of Holies . . . that thy Holy Spirit may descend upon us, and upon these Gifts here spread forth before thee, and bless them, and sanctify and manifest them."[67] With this offering, creation as a whole is offered and exalted, and the harmonious relationship between humanity and nature is at the same time proclaimed.

The three "teachers to all the world" reveal the knowledge that the cosmos was created so that it might be transformed in its entirety—together with the human race, which is the heart of the cosmos—into a "eucharist," a loving act of thankfulness toward our loving God.

"CHANGE FOR THE GOOD" CONTINUOUSLY INCREASES HUMANITY'S POTENTIAL FOR ASCENT

The change that has been described above is closely connected, in all its breadth and depth, to a glorious future of unfathomable splendor.

---

[67] *The Divine Liturgy of Saint Basil*, in *Service Book of the Holy Orthodox-Catholic Apostolic Church*, trans. Isabel Florence Hapgood, 6th ed. (Englewood, NJ, 1983).

As believers in Christian revelation, the three Fathers stress that humanity is not defined by its place within the cosmic system but by its relationship to the Creator of all, the *Pantocrator*, our loving God. Humanity's true essence is not fulfilled by living in the simple way that plants and animals live, "according to nature." The fulfillment of humanity's essence reaches "beyond nature," which is where its true nature ultimately lies. This fact determines humanity's inner dynamic, its process of continuous becoming. Having been created in God's image, human beings are innately inclined to become a likeness of God. Herein lies their splendor, "that their one . . . natural and unique task," Gregory writes, "is to be borne upward and become united with God, in order to gaze, in every way and for all time, upon that to which they are akin."[68] It is humanity's *entelechy*—the self-actualizing fulfillment of its distinctive nature— to proceed "upward."

There is clearly a correlation between humanity's nature and what we are called upon to do. Our lot in life and our vocation are "to strive toward what lies before us."[69] Gregory defines a human being as "a living creature, trained here and then moved elsewhere . . . deified by its inclination to God."[70] The three ecumenical Fathers refuse to confine humanity to its outward dimensions or to see humanity as a mere episode in the history of the cosmos. Our goal is "to hold communion with God, and be associated, as far as man's nature can attain, with the purest Light."[71]

Thus, in a most extraordinary fashion, they describe humanity's inconceivable abilities, mapping out an extremely powerful vision of change. They speak of an unending expansion of human abilities, not only in the present but for all eternity. We have here a most glorious prospect of freedom and love, one that has never ceased to scandalize the pragmatic human mind. It is here that the Fathers' confidence and optimism regarding humanity's future reach their highest peak.

[68]*Ethical Verses* 10.63-65, PG 37:685.
[69]Gregory of Nazianzus, *Orations* 19.7 ("On Julian"), PG 35:1052A.
[70]*Orations* 45.7 ("Second Oration on Easter"), PG 36:632B (trans. NPF, 2d ser., vol. 7).
[71]Gregory of Nazianzus, *Orations* 21.2 ("On the Great Athanasius"), PG 35:1084B (trans. NPF, 2d ser., vol. 7).

This deeply profound meaning of human existence is what the three "teachers to all the world" persistently illuminate, attempting to awaken believers to the fact that we stand ready to embark on an evolutionary journey of incredible and indescribable proportions.

The call to embark on this journey is addressed to all human beings without exception, not only to those who are gifted or privileged. All human beings, as bearers of the divine image, are without exception "god-like." We are all "capable," according to Gregory, "of containing God within ourselves,"[72] and we are "all striving toward purification, toward ascent, and toward what lies before us."[73] (The difference between this and various elitist conceptions, such as those of Plato and the Gnostics, is striking.) Nevertheless, despite the fact that all are equally summoned, the upward path toward deification is not the same for everyone.[74]

Transformation and change for the good have in fact already begun to take place. They are the fruit of the Incarnation of the Word, a consequence of the Cross and the Resurrection. They constitute the reality of Easter. No one can boast about them; they are gifts. For this reason, the more that the faithful advance and become aware of this reality, and the more they move toward positive change, the more humble and free they become—the more they become part of the reality of Easter. They understand that they are advancing through the power and grace of God. By calling on "the names of the Son" to guide them, the faithful consciously make their ascent, "that thou mayest become a god," as Gregory writes, "ascending from below, for His sake Who came down from on high for ours."[75]

The process of "turning back" to God and becoming like him begins in this life. Our goal is "always to attain God and to become a possession of God by becoming intimate with Him and ascending toward him."[76] Such transformation does not take place all at once:

[72]*Orations* 30.6 ("Fourth Theological Oration"), PG 36:112B.
[73]Gregory of Nazianzus, *Orations* 19.7 ("On Julian"), PG 35:1052A.
[74]"There is not only one path to virtue, but more even than the number of rooms in the heavenly mansions." Gregory of Nazianzus, *Orations* 32.33 ("On Proper Conduct in Discussions"), PG 36:212B.
[75]*Orations* 30.21 ("Fourth Theological Oration"), PG 36:133A (trans. NPF, 2d ser., vol. 7).
[76]Gregory of Nazianzus, *Letters* 212 ("To Sacerdos"), PG 37:349A.

it involves constant change, an upward evolution from one atonement to the next, one repentance to the next, one virtuous deed to the next, one insight to the next, and one moment of glory to the next. It involves the dynamic motion of constant renewal in the Spirit.[77]

This ascent consists of participating continuously in God's energies. God's essence remains the fixed boundary, the thing that human beings can never achieve. A human being does not participate in "God's essence" but rather ascends and is "deified" in the radiating brilliance of his divine energies. What we call "deification" is participation in God's energies, not in his essence.

The Fathers were not unaware that this is the point where common sense takes umbrage. It is precisely here, however, that the soul, with the inner light of faith, senses that being confined within the boundaries prescribed by worldly wisdom would be "folly." The three ecumenical teachers did not look down on the achievements of human civilization. They assimilated the Greek cultural legacy, transcending its many impasses and dilemmas through their prophetic insight and the revelation of scripture, and they introduced a new synthesis.

They consider the wisdom of the world to be "folly" when it demands that human beings be confined by worldly limits—limits that remain, despite their incalculable breadth, narrow and impotent. It is possible, however, for wisdom to get beyond this "foolish" phase by realizing that human reason is only part of the mystery of the human person; in order to become complete, worldly wisdom must become conversant with the Word.

Naturally, one may not accept the Christian axioms from which all these ideas and hopes arise; nevertheless, it is beyond doubt that they open up a glorious prospect for the future of humankind and broaden the meaning and purpose of our lives to the utmost degree. Generating light and inner power, this ascent toward the God of love and freedom results in an active and responsible attitude toward life that has numerous implications, both personal and social.

[77]A perpetual and never-ending "ascent toward God." "Ascent and deification" have no limits. Gregory of Nazianzus, *Orations* 4.71 ("Against Julian"), PG 35:593B.

⌣ • ⌣

The testimony of the three ecumenical teachers on "change for the better" reveals a dynamic understanding of humanity's abilities and prospects that is incomparably bolder and more splendid than any other vision of humanity. One could call it a religious vision, but it is not that alone. It is also personal and social, as I hope has become apparent in the various parts of the preceding discussion. Religion's contribution lies in its ability to break through the supposed limits of the human mind, to strengthen our will, and to fuel our struggle, through the prospect and hope of overcoming what at first glance seems to be the impossible.

The Three Hierarchs played an important role in bringing about profound and revitalizing social change, and today their ideas on radical reform still remain daring and relevant. They lived outside time, free from the conventions of their age, with an intimate understanding of the past and prophetic insight into the future. They reconciled social involvement with creative solitude, the "divine darkness" of dogma with the clarity of moral standards, and worldly wisdom with its transcendence, harmoniously combining all through acceptance of the cross and the joy of Easter. They had originality and drive. They labored for their own, personal sanctification, yet remained closely linked with humanity as a whole and all of human nature. They encompassed everything within themselves, enveloping all with the light of the resurrection.

They remain highly relevant to the here and now. With the rigor of their thought and the genuineness of their lives, they steadfastly point to the fact that humanity has been called upon to proceed toward radical transformation and change. This is not merely an external or superficial change, but a change in the nature of our very existence, one that can transform all of creation. It is a change that takes place with a profound awareness of the unity in the cosmos. It is a change whose end lies in deification.

The Three Hierarchs do not belong to the past but continue to participate in the life of the Church. They are a contemporary and timeless reality, steadfastly giving voice to the thought of the Church.

Together with all the other saints, they constitute a living limb of the Church. For the saints continue to live and act through the Church's sacramental life, in liturgical time. Their sacramental presence and inspiration ceaselessly contribute, if I may be allowed so bold a comparison, to a biological cleansing of the refuse produced by human frailty and meanness, which accumulates through all our mistakes, inadequacies, and inconsistencies.

Orthodoxy has always lived by and continues to live by the testimony of the Three Hierarchs regarding dynamic and continuous renewal. Orthodoxy experiences this journey toward "change for the better" not as legalistic coercion, full of moralistic rigidity, but as a feast, as the celebration of a resplendent exodus from the "oppressive and gloomy" Egypt of our lives, with Christ, crucified and resurrected, as our guide.

"If you think and act in this way," Gregory the Theologian would say, even today, to each one of us, to our Church, and to people everywhere, "and if you comprehend the reason for these things, heaven and earth and everything else will become new for you."[78]

This light of the Resurrection penetrates the mind, the senses, and the consciousness of the Orthodox. This paean to the Resurrection heightens our sense of commitment. This vision of the Resurrection fills our dreams and our imaginations with the vastness of what we have been called upon to accomplish.

[78]*Orations* 44.9 ("The New Sunday"), PG 36:617A.

~ 7 ~

Globalization and
Religious Experience*

I n the past, the idea that all the people and nations of the world
might one day come together, become better acquainted with each
other, and learn to live together productively was an alluring dream.
In our own century this dream became a conscious objective. Most
recently it seems to be in danger of turning into a definite nightmare.
Nevertheless, no matter how one represents it, this is a process that,
due to a combination of many factors, is accelerating daily and
whose final outcome is still uncertain.

The word "globalization" has acquired a special meaning and is
used to summarize certain developments and trends that have characterized the final quarter of the second millennium. In the area of
economics in particular, this term denotes the process by which the
economies of different countries have become fully integrated into a
worldwide economic system, one that has concentrated production,
trade, and information around the globe in a few geographical centers. The ensuing process of internationalization has led to a greater
degree of mutual dependence among societies around the world.

Many books and articles have been published in recent years on
this subject, and the discussion now in progress is multifaceted.[1] In

*This paper was originally delivered on May 20, 1998, at an official ceremony where the
author was awarded an honorary doctorate, jointly conferred by the Department of Political Science and Public Administration, School of Juridical, Economic and Political Sciences, University of Athens, and by all the departments of the Philosophical School of
the University of Athens.

[1]For example, see S. Gill and D. Law, *The Global Political Economy: Perspectives, Problems and Policies* (Baltimore, 1988); E. Luard, *The Globalization of Politics* (London,
1990); M. Featherstone, ed., *Global Culture, Nationalism, Globalization and Modernity*

what follows, I will limit myself to a number of general characteristics that have defined the new context in which religious life is developing in our era.

FACTS ABOUT GLOBALIZATION AND ITS CONSEQUENCES

Factors that Contribute toward Globalization

The most important contributing factor in the process of globalization has been the rapid development of technology, particularly the revolution in electronics, which has led to far-reaching changes in the areas of production, communication, education, and entertainment. These changes have facilitated the expansion of profit-seeking interests and impersonal, international economic activity, which by its very nature is centralized.

A second factor has been the collapse of the entire world of ideas, aspirations, and social structures that existed in the countries of the former Soviet bloc, together with the disruption of their economies, and the emergence of capitalism as the only alternative solution.

Third, the actions and decisions of large states and international organizations have demonstrated that globalization is no longer an independently developing phenomenon, but has become the political ideology and policy of the economically powerful.

(London, 1990); M. Featherstone, *Undoing Culture: Globalization, Postmodernity and Identity* (London, 1995); R. Robertson, *Globalization: Social Theory and Global Culture* (London, 1992); E.B. Kapstein, *Governing the Global Economy: International Finance and the State* (Cambridge, MA, 1994); M. Shaw, *Global Society and International Relations* (Cambridge, 1994); M. Waters, *Globalization* (London, 1995); D. Held, *Democracy and the Global Order: From the Modern State to Cosmopolitan Governance* (Cambridge, 1995); E. Hobsbawm, *Age of Extremes: The Short Twentieth Century, 1914-1991* (London, 1995); C.W. Kegley, Jr. and E.R. Wittkopf, *The Global Agenda: Issues and Perspectives* (New York, 1995); D.C. Korten, *When Corporations Rule the World* (London, 1995); B. Axford, *The Global System: Economics, Politics and Culture* (Cambridge, 1995); K.C. Abraham, "Globalization: A Gospel and Culture Perspective," *International Review of Mission* 85 (1996): 85-92; J. Adda, *La mondialisation de l'économie*, 2 vols. (Paris, 1996); W. Andreff, *Les multinationals globales* (Paris, 1996); H. Henderson, *Building a Win-Win World: Life Beyond Economic Warfare* (San Francisco, 1996); P. Hirst and G. Thompson, *Globalization in Question* (Cambridge, 1996); H. Mowlana, *Global Communication in Transition: The End of Diversity?* (Thousand Oaks, CA, and London, 1996); M. Patterson, *Global Warming and Global Politics* (London, 1996); S. Amin, *Capitalism in the Age of Globaliza-*

The speed with which these changes have been effected in all major areas of the economy, of technology, and of information systems has often left people feeling dizzy and apprehensive. While early efforts to bring countries together and coordinate them globally seemed beneficial, like welcome rain that would fertilize the whole earth, that rain has now turned into storms and floods, whose sweeping currents threaten every corner of the planet.

A number of institutions, whose activities have had both positive and negative effects to varying degrees, have played the leading role in the process of globalization: first, the several hundreds of multinational corporations with power over the worldwide production and distribution of goods and information; second, organizations such as NAFTA and ASEAN, through which different nations have started working together; third, non-governmental organizations that function on a global level; and fourth, worldwide economic institutions, such as the International Monetary Fund (IMF) and the World Bank, which seek to play a coordinating role.

Our general conceptions about progress and development are based on western models and have evolved primarily within large cities—in the megalopolis. The various information media, particularly satellite television, continuously feed people all over the world with models of modern life that have been manufactured in these centers of power and that have self-serving goals.

tion (London, 1997); J. Baylis and S. Smith, eds., *The Globalization of Politics: An Introduction to International Relations* (New York, 1997); M. Castells, *The Information Age: Economy, Society and Culture* (Oxford and Maldon, 1997); U. Beck, *Was ist Globalisierung? Irrtümer des Globalismus—Antworten auf Globalisierung* (Frankfurt, 1997); Clark, *Globalization and Fragmentation: International Relations in the Twentieth Century* (Oxford and New York, 1997); S. Gill, ed., *Globalization, Democratization and Multilateralism* (Tokyo, 1997); A. Hoogvelt, *Globalization and the Postcolonial World: The New Political Economy of Development* (London, 1997); K. Raiser, "Oikumene and Globalization," *Echoes* 12 (Geneva, 1997): 3-4, and in the same issue see H. Mousson and P. Taran, "Globalization and the Social Clause Debate," and L. Boff, "A New Alliance between Humankind and Nature"; J.M. Rao, *Globalization: A View from the South,* Employment Papers 8 (Geneva, 1997); M. Albrow, *The Global Age: State and Society beyond Modernity* (Stanford, 1997); E.B. Albanes, *Globalization* (in Greek) (Athens, 1998), and see 317-39 for bibliography; Fu-Chen Lo and Yue-Man Yeung, eds., *Globalization and the World of Large Cities* (Tokyo, New York, and Paris, 1998); and D. Haralambes, *Democracy and Globalization* (in Greek) (Athens, 1998), and see 337-78 for bibliography. For further bibliography see notes 2, 3, 6, and 8 below.

A number of analysts have defended the neutrality and positive aspects of this phenomenon, such as American Paul R. Krugmann in his book *Pop Internationalism*.[2] Others, however, like Frenchman E. Todd, dispute the very existence of globalization. "There is no basis for the assumption that an abstract principle called 'globalization,' which acts 'from without' upon all nations, even exists. It is nothing more than a myth, the fabrication of the sense of helplessness of the political and cultural elite."[3]

Radical Changes

It is a fact that the process known as globalization is producing radical changes in people's lives. These include both positive changes—which might easily be overlooked as self-evident—as well as negative ones.

Foremost in the first category are: (a) the rapid progress and development of technology and all the sciences; (b) the rapid distribution of goods and new discoveries; (c) the extreme ease with which people all over the world can now communicate, thus eliminating distances (through sophisticated telephone networks, the Internet, satellite television, and modern means of transportation); (d) the combating of many diseases worldwide; (e) the reduction of illiteracy; (f) the recognition of the place, importance, and role of women and youth; (g) a broader conceptual framework that helps safeguard freedom and basic human rights, at least theoretically; (h) the promotion and reinforcement of democratic principles and structures; and (i) various forms of mutual help and support between nations that make it possible for more and more people to participate in the new world that is taking shape .

In general, globalization has made an astonishing contribution toward humanity's development, by providing individuals and entire peoples with the ability to know about and exploit

[2] P. Krugmann, *Pop Internationalism* (1996). It is revealing that the French translation was given the title "Globalization Is Not Guilty": *Le mondialisation n'est pas coupable. Vertus et limite du libre échange* (Paris, 1998).

[3] E. Todd, *L'illusion économique. Essai sur la stagnation des sociétés développées* (Paris, 1998), 297.

opportunities that were inaccessible and even unimaginable for previous generations.

At the same time, however, the negative consequences of globalization are making themselves known with increasingly greater rapidity:

⟋ The gulf that separates the countries of the world is growing deeper. Wealthy countries are becoming even wealthier, while poor countries are becoming poorer, reeling under the weight of enormous foreign debt. Furthermore, new internal disparities between the privileged and the deprived are appearing in every country. "In the developed countries only 20 percent of the population derives any benefit from free commerce."[4]

⟋ Small, economically strong minorities with tremendous power to influence have formed in every country, and these minorities are concerned for the most part with pursuing their own interests. Individuals and groups that lie just beyond this privileged social nucleus try to adapt their own way of life to that of this small circle.

⟋ At the same time, millions of people are being marginalized and end up living under conditions below the poverty level. Concurrent with this, the ability of local societies to stabilize themselves through their own intellectual and social structures is being disrupted.

⟋ We are seeing new, major shifts of labor power, with new waves of immigrants and economic refugees flooding the prosperous countries. The increase in unemployment is becoming a significant threat, and xenophobia and racism have reached dangerous proportions in many countries.

⟋ The patterns of uninterrupted development and consumption of goods through thoughtless and relentless exploitation of natural resources is leading to ecological catastrophes throughout the planet.

⟋ Crime and corruption have increased uncontrollably on a global scale, availing themselves of the most up-to-date technology. Under the strong influence of this whirlwind, a large part of our

---

[4]Ibid. Although the inhabitants of the Nnorth represent approximately 20 percent of the planet's population, they control more than 80 percent of global income. At the same time, however, there are more than fifty million poor in the European Union. See Ign. Romonet, *Geopolitics of Chaos,* English trans. A. Lyn Secara (New York, 1998), 6.

populations, especially of our youth, is seeking escape through violence, self-abandon, and narcotics. Despite our many declarations
concerning the value of human beings, disregard for human life still
predominates.

An abyss of hypocrisy separates the general pronouncements and
theoretical principles of world organizations from their actual practice in the various regions of the earth. As Christos Yiannaras so eloquently expresses it, we have "the 'free market' and its regulative
demands, which have been made sacred, and the expedient version
of individual rights (which, because it is expedient and has been
made a religion, is easily reconciled with inhuman, 'sacred,' phari-
saical aims)."[5]

⌐ In the political sphere, many of our democratic institutions are
being undermined and their strength, authority, and effectiveness
weakened. The centers of power in each country do not have complete control over economic policy, but must conform to directives
from other international centers and to wider global trends. With the
triumph of the market economy, two possibilities arise. As Gérard J.
Lafay has pointed out, "On the one hand, there is the process of globalization, which is being promoted by business and has also been
made easier by the decreasing costs of transportation and communication. On the other hand, there is the question of the continued
existence of nations that are devoted to their land and that seek to be
organized on a regional basis. . . ."[6]

Moreover, the end of the Cold War has not brought peace to the
world. Almost fifty different wars have begun, and of those about
forty are still in progress. Thus, according to Boutros Boutros-Ghali,
there has been created "a new category of states which are neither
developed nor developing, nor are they in a transition stage, but
belong, rather, to a fourth category: they make wars, either wars
on each other or civil wars, or else they are still in a transition
period following a war that lasted for years." The former secretary
general of the United Nations concludes: "The real problems that

---

[5]Christos Yiannaras, *Culture: The Central Problem of Politics* (in Greek) (Athens,
1997), 27.

[6]G.J. Lafay, *Comprendre la Mondialisation* (Paris, 1997), 7-8.

will beleaguer the planet are problems that can only be solved on a global level."[7] These problems include sea rights, climatic changes, water resources, new chemical and biological weapons, and the movements of millions of immigrants on a global scale.

Globalization is clearly associated with the invasion of a culture whose creators claim that it is the best. The origin of this entire system, its criteria, and the method by which it functions are all based on western capitalism and on the logic of a free economy, whose dynamic is dependent on the uninterrupted flow of profit. Globalization is not merely an economic process. It is the invasion—whether by direct or indirect means—of a system of thought that either ignores or destroys the unique characteristics of individual peoples and nations; that brushes aside or completely dissolves values such as friendship, honesty, and self-restraint; and that puts forward consumerism and the neverending pursuit of profit as a model, under whose influence human relationships are often crushed.

In his recent book *Globalization*, Philippe Moreau Defarges concludes: "Globalization seems to offer humanity two extreme paths. It can give people the feeling that they are enclosed within a prison, the earth. . . . Or it can give birth to an awareness of humanity's unity. . . . Globalization is not the end of humanity or of human history. It is nothing but a by-product of technological progress. It is clearly not by chance that globalization became a reality the moment that humanity suddenly found itself immersed in two infinities: the infinite smallness of the atom and the infinite largeness of the stars."[8]

RELIGION AT THE END OF THE TWENTIETH CENTURY

Striving to approach the infinite is the most characteristic feature of religious experience. This kind of experience—and by extension any religion that expresses it in space and time—is not an epiphenomenon of ethics, logic, the workings of the mind, or society; it is an

[7]D. Dhombres, "The Big Problems Can Only Be Solved on a Global Level," *Le Monde* and *To Vima* (May 10, 1998).
[8]Philippe Moreau Defarges, *La mondialisation* (Paris, 1997), 124-25.

independent occurrence which takes as its primary point of reference something that is peculiarly its own: the sacred, the holy. Religion begins as awe before the sacred and culminates in a personal
encounter—an experiential relationship between a human being
and the holy. It is an encounter in which intellect, emotion, volition,
the conscious and the subconscious all take part. Human beings
have an innate proclivity for and an impulse toward the infinite.
They experience a continuous "expansion" of their existence that
reaches beyond the limits of what can be known through the senses,
toward the beyond and the eternal. Religious experience operates on
this plane. It can be detected in primitive religious manifestations,
such as spirit possession, and reaches states of mystical and spiritual
exaltation, culminating in the transcendence of one's existence; in
ontological transformation "from one degree of glory to another"
(2 Cor 3:18); in a communion of love with God.[9]

The Major Religions Have a Global Perspective

Offering some vision of a global society has always been a typical feature of the major religions.[10] They have all attempted to achieve spiritual and cultural globalization by spreading their faith over an
ever-greater geographical area. This first occurred with Buddhism,
later with Christianity, and most recently with Islam. It is because of
such efforts in the past that these religions have their well-known
spheres of influence today. The various schools of Hinduism, which
stresses the relativity and pluralism of religious truths, were not
driven by this fervor to expand outward. The religions that flour-
ished in China followed their own path: Confucianism was adopted
long ago, after its precepts had been reconciled with the sayings of
Lao-Tzu, to which they were antithetical, and important ideas from
Mahayana Buddhism were also assimilated and further developed.[11]

[9]A. Yannoulatos, "Religion" (in Greek) in *The Religions*, EEE 21 (1992), 172-75.
[10]For the most authoritative articles on religious subjects, see M. Eliade, ed., *The Encyclopaedia of Religion*, 16 vols. (New York, 1987). Among the more recent works, see N. Smart, *The World's Religions: Old Traditions and Modern Transformations* (Melbourne, 1989; reprint 1997); M. Malherbe, *Les religions de l'humanité*, 2d ed. (Paris, 1992); and J. Bower, ed., *The Oxford Dictionary of World Religions* (Oxford, 1997).
[11]For an overview, see A. Yannoulatos, "Buddhism," "Hinduism," and "Islam" (all in

In our own century, the Chinese people—who, it should not be forgotten, comprise one-fifth of the world's population—embraced the theory of Marxism, which was elaborated by Mao Tse-Tung and ingeniously readjusted afterward by his successors.

The basic difference between a religious global vision and modern globalization is that religions have always sought to become universal by propounding their own doctrinal truths and principles of behavior. In one way or another, however, all of them emphasized the need for compassion, mercy, charity, temperance, and justice. Among the monotheistic religions, the fixed point of reference for dealing with other human beings and coping with social problems has always been faith in the living God, the Creator, who guides the universe.

Although religions have helped to bring people and nations closer together, they have nevertheless been the frequent agents of terrible conflicts and unbridgeable divisions, raising various iron curtains across our planet, creating impenetrable cultural boundaries, and inhibiting progress toward harmonious world coexistence. The occasions have not been few when religions, in combination with various political forces, have supported arrogance and aggression on the part of many nations.

The Endurance of Religious Diversity

At various times in history, certain centers of religion have promoted the belief that a global society could be brought into being by imposing one religion on everyone. To this end they rallied all their efforts, employing not only the written word, the spoken word, and philanthropic work, but also turning with equal enthusiasm to violence and war. Naturally, all of this was done in the belief—or under the pretext—that it was for the good of everyone.

Today, no student of religion would assert that such a policy is capable of succeeding. Religious pluralism is an undisputed fact. One of the most recent statistical analyses, made in 1991 and based

Greek) in *The Religions*, EEE 21 (1992). Cf. idem: "Confucius" (in Greek), EEE 5 (1982), 9-10; and "Lao-Tzu" (in Greek), ibid., 177.

on a global population of 5,480,010,000, gives us the following figures: Christians, 33.4 percent (1,833,022,000); Muslims, 17.7 percent (971,328,700); people with no religion, 16 percent (876,232,000); Hindus, 13.4 percent (732,812,000); Buddhists, 5.7 percent (314,939,000); atheists, 4.4 percent (240,310,000); followers of Chinese religious traditions, 3.4 percent (187,107,000); followers of new religions, 2.6 percent (143,415,000); followers of traditional tribal religions, 1.8 percent (96,531,000); and religious communities whose members are less than 0.3 percent of the world's population include Sikhism, Judaism, Shamanism, followers of traditional Confucianism, Bahai, Jainism, and Shinto.[12]

The arrival of large immigrant populations in different countries—especially in the new, large cities that now exist on almost every continent—has at the same time introduced many new religious communities to those regions and societies. Christians are found in 270 of the world's countries, people with no religion are

---

[12]I.S. Markham, ed., *A World Religious Reader* (Oxford, 1996; reprint 1997), 356-57. These estimates are based on data published by the United Nations, *World Population Prospects 1990* (New York, 1991); and D.B. Barrett, *World Christian Encyclopaedia—A Comparative Study of Churches and Religions in the Modern World, AD 1900-2000* (Nairobi, 1982). Projections are based on trends in 1991 as well as on more recent data. For many reasons, statistics on religion should be considered only as rough indications. For example, the number of Christians is based here on the number of people baptized, whereas the number of Muslims is based on the total inhabitants in Islamic countries. The number of agnostics or atheists is correlated with the number of inhabitants in states (such as China) where atheistic ideology predominates. According to another estimate, in 1995 the major religions in the world had the following approximate strengths: 1,470 million Christians, 910 million Muslims, 720 million Hindus, 330 million Buddhists, 220 million animists (followers of tribal religions), and 1,200 million agnostics and atheists. V. Odon, *Les Religions dans le Monde*, (Paris, 1995), 14. On page six of his massive work, cited above, D.C. Barrett carefully analyzes the statistical data and after elaborate calculations predicts that in the year 2000, out of a world population of 6,259,642,000, there will be:

Christians	2,019,921,366	32.3%
Muslims	1,200,653,040	19.2%
No Religion	1,071,888,370	17.1%
Hindus	859,252,260	13.7%
Buddhists	359,092,100	5.7%
Atheists	262,447,550	4.2%
Followers of Chinese Religious Traditions	158,470,664	2.5%
Followers of New Religions	138,263,800	2.2%
Followers of Tribal Religions	100,535,850	1.6%

found in 236 countries, Bahai in 220, Muslims in 184, atheists in 139, Jews in 134, and followers of tribal religions in 104. Each of the remaining religions is found in less than 100 countries. These statistics, even if relative, indisputably attest to the religious diversity that exists today.

During part of the twentieth century, the belief was fostered—mainly due to the successes of communist ideology—that "religious" convergence and uniformity would finally be achieved through the active eradication or complete repudiation of religion. The most extreme example of this scenario was Albania, where atheistic uniformity was imposed by force. Comparable expectations were promoted in countries on the other side—i.e., those that were culturally influenced by capitalism—where the viewpoint spread that religion would simply lose its usefulness. Since the solutions to our problems could be found through science and technology, humanity would need religion less and less. It was thus maintained that religion would either die through its own gradual decline or suffocate to death and that people around the world would finally be able to come together, once religion had come to an end. This prediction, however, has not been borne out.

The twenty-first century has barely begun, but events have shown how superficial and oversimplified these notions were. The nineteenth century ended with Nietzsche's pronouncement that "God is dead . . . and we killed him!" Nonetheless, the twentieth century—and the second millennium along with it—ends with a new and impressive resurgence of religion. More than 70.2 percent of the world's population has adopted some religious faith, and more than half of the human race today continues to believe in God in one form or another. This new dynamic has also acquired an important role in politics: e.g., the Khomeini movement in Iran, Muslim guerrillas in Algeria, Hindu movements in Sri Lanka, and the rise of extremist Protestant currents in the third world.

Since the decline of communist ideology, a special type of Islam has developed in many countries, one that offers people protection, unity, and refuge, promises dignity for the poor, and provides the world's marginalized with the hope that they will finally become worthy of recognition and receive social justice.[13] A new proletariat has thus been forming, one which has armed itself with religious determination, tenacity, and militancy.

At the same time, we are also seeing the development of a powerful vortex of new religious ideas and groupings of various types. There has thus appeared a sudden "inrush of relativism," which seeks to supplant religious absolutes, affirming pluralism and contrasting itself with the absolute precepts and absolute truths that are regarded as authoritarian dogmatism. Priority is given here to experience and intuition, not to knowledge, doctrine, or institutions. The idea of "alternative absolutes" is advocated, with Indian thought as the leading protagonist. Lastly, we are also seeing the disruption of many religious faiths, as well as the creation of a new galaxy of groups in which various types of mysticism and ancient eastern "wisdom" and practices have been brought together.[14] Poor societies of the third world as well as former communist countries are particularly susceptible to these influences, but Europe and North America are not immune to their titillating appeal.

By now it is clear that in the coming century religion will be important for the future of civilization. Several years ago the eminent American professor of strategic studies Samuel P. Huntington, in his book *The Clash of Civilizations,* predicted a conflict between western civilization—as it was created by Roman Catholicism and Protestantism—and the East, in which, in addition to Islam, he also included Orthodox Christianity.[15] Of course, the manner in which this specific author analyzes religious phenomena easily provokes serious objections on the part of a student of religion, just as a

[13]D. Hiro, *Islamic Fundamentalism* (London, 1988); J.L. Esposito and J.O. Voll, *Islam and Democracy* (New York and Oxford, 1996); Z. Anwar, *Islamic Revivalism in Malaysia* (Kuala Lumpur, 1987); R. Wright, *In the Name of God: The Khomeini Decade* (New York, 1989); F. Burgat, *The Islamic Movement in North Africa,* trans. W. Dowell (Austin, TX, 1993); and J.O. Voll, *Islam: Continuity and Change in the Modern World,* 2d ed. (Syracuse, NY, 1994). For the relationship between Islam and capitalism, see the classic work by M. Rodinson, *Islam et capitalisme* (Paris, 1976).

[14]S. Bruce, *Religion in the Modern World: From Cathedrals to Cults* (Oxford and New York, 1966); and F. Fernandez-Armesto, "Religion," in *The Future Now: Predicting the 21st Century,* ed. F. Fernandez-Armesto, F. Heisbourg, et al. (London, 1998), 35-38.

[15]S.P. Huntington, *The Clash of Civilizations: Remaking of World Order* (New York, 1996).

historian would call into question both the way he uses the findings of historical research, as well as the seriousness of many of his assertions.[16]

What seems to lurk behind such predictions of a conflict between civilizations is the arrogant supposition that one's own culture is better, as well as concern about how it will be preserved. What is more, these predictions indirectly convey the message that "we are threatened and must prepare to defend ourselves." This conclusion is based on a priori conceptions regarding an affinity between the Orthodox world and Islam, as well as on the complete failure to recognize the differences between the two religions, both in their theological foundations and in their history and culture.

Religious experience follows its own dynamics, however, and these do not abide by the logical framework on which great powers base their strategies. In the religious quest and on the path of religious experience there is always something imponderable that comes to us from beyond the realm of human prediction. In the religious consciousness of billions of people, there exists another power, providence, and love—that of God—that stands above the course of human events.

Regardless of how radically one may disagree with many of the points in Huntington's historical analysis, his book nevertheless reveals that religion is a constant, that it has maintained its exceptional importance, and that it will acquire even greater importance in the years to come.

[16]These predictions remind me of certain others made in the past by the notable American historian K.S. Latourette: speaking about the future of Islam, he predicted that in the second half of the twentieth century "the course appears to be downwards" (*A History of the Expansion of Christianity* 7 [New York and London, 1945], 493). What followed, however, was precisely the opposite. In the second half of the twentieth century Islam has achieved exceptional successes in Africa and Indonesia, has contributed to the formation of the state of Pakistan, and in general is exhibiting particular vitality. See W. Cantwell Smith, *Islam in Modern History* (Princeton, 1957 and 1996); N. Ahmad, T. Grin, J.-C. Froelich, *L'Afrique islamique (Islamisches Afrika, Africa Islamica)* in *Le monde religieux*, 29e volume de la nouvelle série (Lezay, Deux-Sèvres, 1966); and B. Lewis, *Islam and the West* (Oxford, 1993). For a detailed bibliography on Islamic revivalist movements throughout the world, see Y.Y. Haddad, J.L. Esposito, and J.O. Voll, *The Contemporary Islamic Revival: A Critical Survey and Bibliography* (Westport, CT, 1991), and see also note 13 above.

The Readjusting Relationships between Religions

Within the process of globalization, the relationships that have existed between different religions are also undergoing readjustment.

By the end of the nineteenth century groups of intellectuals from various religious persuasions, in search of common denominators, had already begun to speak about the formation of a new, common religion. In particular, following the Second World War there developed a movement toward cooperation between religions on concrete issues, such as peace—the World Conference on Religion and Peace being one example. As usually happens, however, the solidly conservative core of most religious communities resists such efforts, which therefore remain limited, becoming a trend among certain intellectuals, who often become separated from the organic life of their own religious communities. Since these intellectuals tend to remain on the periphery, what they have to say ceases to be of any interest to the majority of others. In spite of this, however, the discussion regarding a "global religion" has continued.[17]

In the beginning, various attempts at dialogue between representatives of two or more religious communities fostered many hopes that people could be brought closer together. Once a closer acquaintance has been established, however, a sense of disappointment usually follows, because both sides start to recognize the contradictions and differences that exist between them. Nevertheless, the pathway of discussion and dialogue remains important, if for no other reason than to promote mutual understanding.[18]

---

[17]From the longstanding proposal of F. Heiler (*Die Religionen der Menschheit in Vergangenheit und Gegenwart* [Stuttgart: Ph. Reclam. Jun., 1962], 877-89: "Versuche einer Synthese der Religionen und einer neuen menschheitsreligion") to the letter of N. Smart (*The World's Religions* [see note 10], 549-61: "Some Final Reflections on Global Religion").

[18]For a summary of the "dialogues" between Christians and other religions, see S.W. Ariarajah, "Dialogue, Interfaith," in *Dictionary of the Ecumenical Movement,* ed. N. Lossens, J.M. Bonino, J.S. Pobee, T.F. Stransky, G. Wainwright, P. Webb (Geneva, 1991), 281-87. Among the many relevant articles here, see S.I. David, *Christianity and the Encounter with Other Religions: A Select Bibliography* (Bangalore, 1988), which emphasizes contact with India; R.B. Sheard, *Inter-Religious Dialogue in the Catholic Church since Vatican II: An Historical and Theological Study* (Queen Town, Canada, 1987); *Guidelines on Dialogue with People of Living Faiths and Ideologies* (Geneva, 1979); S.J. Samartha, ed.,

A third trend places emphasis on our obligation to respect the freedom and individuality of others, on learning to accept diversity, and on making a conscious effort at peaceful coexistence. In order to overcome isolation and stop people from nurturing hostility, it advises greater cooperation, as far as possible, on mutually agreed-on issues of common interest: social justice, for example, or the peaceful settlement of differences on local and worldwide levels. Every religious community, over the course of the centuries, has developed its own principles, ideas, and practices, and these may prove to be invaluable for our efforts to achieve harmonious coexistence.

On the narrower issue of globalization, it has been anticipated that religious communities will become centers of resistance to the tendency of a particular center of power to impose one culture on everyone else. Religion is offered to many peoples as a stronghold of identity that enables them to preserve their own characteristics. Religions may well evolve into islands of safety, where people take refuge to avoid the evils brought about by globalization. Ultimately, the search for the supreme reality, for truth, and for the transcendence of death remains a profound longing and a right of every human being.

Globalization will probably also contribute to the germination of seeds and encourage tendencies now lying dormant in the depths of different religions. Religious creeds are organic wholes that evolve; they are influenced by, assimilate, and appropriate new ideas. They do not exist in a vacuum, but continually readapt. In the last century, which has placed emphasis on the issues of peace, justice, equality between peoples, freedom, human rights, and love, many writers from different religious backgrounds have not only adopted these causes but have also attempted to put them forward as basic components of their own religions. The historical accuracy of such claims is not so relevant to the issue at hand as is the fact that there exists this desire to converge. Religious consciousness is kneaded and shaped; it renews itself, and adapts to new situations. It is influenced

Living Faiths and the Ecumenical Movement (Geneva, 1971); S.J. Samartha, *Courage for Dialogue: Ecumenical Issues in Inter-Religious Relationships* (Geneva, 1981); and Metropolitan of Switzerland Damaskinos Papandreou, "The Interfaith Dialogues of the Orthodox Church" in *Christian-Islamic Dialogue As a Common Obligation* (in Greek), ed. M. Konstantinos and A. Stiernemann (Thessaloniki, 1998), 31-51.

by ideas, both new and old, along the road toward globalization, but also has the ability to influence its own ultimate form.

THE RESPONSIBILITY AND CONTRIBUTION OF ORTHODOXY

The Power of Religious Experience

We will have to take corrective measures to alleviate the many negative consequences of globalization, and the contribution of sound religious experience in this regard will be crucial and irreplaceable. Religious faith can affect the very depths of human consciousness and the human will; it can reshape people's thought, their ethos, and their character. Powerful segments in society, usually composed of egotistical individuals who wield their power in an arbitrary and arrogant fashion, are capable of leading the world into tragic predicaments. The only thing that is in a position to neutralize this lethal virus of selfishness is genuine religious experience. If we are going to cope with the negative consequences of globalization, we need people at every decision-making level who have sound and fair judgment and a good conscience, people who long for peace in the world and who respect the freedom and individuality of every human person and every nation. The more genuine and pure the religious experience, the more decisively it can make a positive contribution within the global process, awakening a spirit of struggle within organized groups and peoples.

A Global Perspective: The Spiritual Ground of Orthodoxy

Christians in general, and we Orthodox in particular, are neither puzzled nor surprised by the process of globalization. The necessity for maintaining a worldwide perspective in spiritual matters has always been self-evident to us. This global dimension is a basic ingredient of Orthodoxy. The very first chapter of holy scripture (Gen 1:1) states that the heavens, the earth, the human race, and everything else were all created by God; the last chapters of holy scripture (Rev 21-22) are devoted to the vision of a new heaven and a new earth

(Rev 21:1). Through his Incarnation, the Word of God fully assumed the nature of humanity and summoned everyone to his kingdom—everyone, with no exceptions and without making any distinctions regarding race, language, or ethnic background. Ultimately, the universality of the gospel of Jesus Christ transcends even the sphere of the human, extending itself to include all of creation, of which the human race is an organic part.

The teachings of Christianity were first heard in a specific place and time, but from the beginning they had a global and eschatological character that has been steadfastly preserved. In his letters, the apostle Paul particularly stresses universality in connection with the mystery of the Church. His all-inclusive vision reaches its zenith when Paul refers to the will of God, to the "the mystery of his will," which would be realized "in Christ as a plan for the fulness of time, to unite all things in him, things in heaven and things on earth" (Eph 1:9-10).

During the first phase of its spread throughout the world, the Christian message was set down in the Greek language and expressed through Greek culture, one of whose basic characteristics was its universality.[19] It was this universality, above all, that permeated Greek philosophy, science, and art, as well as the Greek language, and that made it possible for individuals and entire peoples to communicate more easily in diverse ways. This universal consciousness was cultivated with new power by the great hierarchs and ecumenical teachers of the fourth century, who achieved a synthesis between the universalistic thought of ancient Greece and Christian faith. Later, in its encounter with the peoples of southeastern Europe, "The Byzantine empire sacrificed the ecumenical character of the Greek language in order to preserve the universality of its culture."[20]

The entire life of Orthodox worship is carried out in the context of this universal vision, the core of which can be found in the Lord's

[19]B. Kyrkos, "The Universality of Greek Culture and Its Encounter with Christianity" (in Greek), IEE 6 (1976), 392-95.

[20]D. Zakythinos, "Byzance et les peoples de l'Europe de Sud-est. La synthèse Byzantine," *Actes du Premier Congrès international des etudes balkaniques et sud-est européennes* 3, "Histoire" (Sofia, 1969), 22.

Prayer: "Thy kingdom come. Thy will be done, on earth as it is in heaven." Not simply in me or in us, but "everywhere on the earth."[21] Before addressing their immediate problems concerning their daily bread, faithful Christians are called upon to place themselves in a worldwide context. The personal and the specific do not hinder them from thinking about the whole world. In every Divine Liturgy, which recapitulates the mystery of salvation, the supplications begin with the words "For the peace of the entire world" and culminate in the offering of the precious gifts, which is done "on behalf of all and for all," "on behalf of the entire world."

All the great Orthodox feast days open global vistas within our souls. This atmosphere of universality is particularly powerful during the periods of Easter and Pentecost. In general, a global vision has been and remains the dynamic perspective of Orthodox teaching and worship.[22]

From an Orthodox point of view, finding the right way to deal with the phenomenon of globalization is not an issue only for priests or certain lay theologians. It is an issue that requires commitment and a responsible approach on the part of all the lay members of the Church, by seriously studying and analyzing the scientific, political, cultural, and economic data and then making proposals. There will need to be constant and creative thought on this issue in all branches of the humanities, political science, and economics.

What Is Asked from Orthodoxy?

The Orthodox Church should certainly not allow itself to be misled by the allure of Rome, rushing to pronounce judgment on every issue that arises, prescribing detailed solutions. This is work for specialists who do research in the political and social sciences.

The great thing that is sought from the Church remains the spiritual rebirth of the human race, salvation in Christ, the giving of

[21]John Chrysostom: "For He did not at all say, 'Thy will be done' in me, or in us, but everywhere on the earth." *Homilies on the Gospel according to St Matthew* 19.5, PG 57:280 (trans. NPF, 1st ser., vol. 10).

[22]Anastasios of Albania, "The Global Vision of Proclaiming the Gospel," *The Greek Orthodox Theological Review* 43 (1998).

meaning to life. In this way, the Church offers what is most important: it cultivates consciousness and shapes the personalities of people who, by leading responsible lives, can strengthen and revitalize
society's immune system. What we need most in the modern era are
people with character, vision, and tenacity; people with love that is
not hypocritical; people who oppose self-centeredness—whether it
be individual, national, or racial. Arrogance, lust for power, and
hypocrisy are not only characteristic of large and powerful states, but
lurk in the souls of us all.

The Church cannot be a member of the club of the rich and powerful. The strength of Orthodoxy has never identified itself with or
relied on the exercise of worldly power. Dostoevsky's famous portrayal of the Grand Inquisitor clearly delineates the great temptation
of worldly power that the West encountered, a temptation that was
not unknown in the East.[23]

The Church should take an unremittingly prophetic and critical
stand against every form of callousness toward human misery. It
does this by sacrificing itself in the performance of its ministry; by
summoning people to constant, conscientious repentance; by constantly participating in efforts to achieve justice and peace; and by
leading a simple, ascetic, and self-restrained existence. The Beatitudes, as Christ formulated them in the Sermon on the Mount,
define the authentic ethos of the Church. The goal of Orthodox
Christian life is still to acquire the Holy Spirit in our lives.

Moreover, this goal has a direct effect on human relationships at
local and global levels, because "the fruit of the Spirit" does not mean
taking some voyage into the extraterrestrial realm, but "love, joy,
peace, patience, kindness, goodness, faithfulness, gentleness, self-
control" (Gal 5:22); it means transcending human aggressiveness
and social conflicts and achieving harmony in relationships among
human beings and between entire peoples.

By encouraging this sense of universality, the Church not only
helps bring people together but also proclaims—both symbolically
and in practice—a worldwide communion of love. The Church

---

[23]F. Dostoevsky, *The Brothers Karamazov*, trans. Richard Pevear and Larissa
Volokhonsky (New York, 1991).

offers us a foretaste of this global society or communion (the Greek word *koinonia* has both meanings) in the form of an eschatological hope, a vision, and a celebration. Let anyone take part who wishes to do so. The Church does not forcibly impose this on anyone, but proclaims it through the lives of the faithful. The kingdom of God "has come and is coming." This "event" has been experienced in the lives of the saints—both well-known saints and those we have never learned about—and it provides prophetic solace regarding the possibilities that the future holds for the human race.

What makes the Church different from any other religious system is that it offers us an actual relationship with the living God through the power and the grace of the eucharistic community. "For God is at work in you, both to will and to work for his good pleasure" (Phil 2:13). The world is not in our hands, but in his. We proceed with a realistic outlook along the path our lives have taken, bearing our cross and looking forward to the Resurrection. "But according to his promise we wait for new heavens and a new earth in which righteousness dwells" (2 Pet 3:13). These words pinpoint the specific distinction that makes Christianity's global vision essentially different from every other form of globalization.

Christ assumed all of humanity's nature and renewed it. Any and all who truly believe in him and conscientiously participate in divine worship return to their daily lives ready to fulfil their obligations in their local surroundings by aspiring to a vision that is global.

Conclusion

Globalization is a process that is now in progress, and there appears to be no power capable of stopping it. It has opened up wonderful possibilities and unforeseen prospects for the human race. Along with these, however, it has also produced a chain of upheavals and realignments. Nevertheless, regardless of its positive or negative repercussions, globalization is taking place, unobstructed by the cries and appeals that may be heard outside the world of finance.

From various corners we hear protests that globalization is moving in directions that do not guarantee the preservation of basic human values, justice, respect for people's identity, and the diversity of human culture, and that the new global order, headed by multinational corporations, is a tool of oppression for new forms of colonialism. Faithful Christians have not been caught unawares by this phenomenon. A universal and global perspective is basic to their faith and to their aspirations. They are convinced that true religious experience has the power to intervene in this process and make a decisive and creative contribution, one that is founded on the eternal principles of respect for every human person, freedom, peace, justice, and mutual support. They believe that religious experience can offer meaning to human life and help people transcend the anguish of death.

This global perspective is in the blood of the Orthodox, blood that is constantly cleansed in the Eucharist by the blood of Christ, the redeemer of the world. Instead of a globalization that transforms nations and people into an indistinguishable, homogenized mass, convenient for the economic objectives of an anonymous oligarchy, the Orthodox religious experience and vision propose a communion of love, a society of love, and call on people to make every effort in that direction. The truly Christian thing is to continue believing when there seems to be no hope, by grounding oneself in the certainty that ultimately there is Another who controls the evolution of the universe—he "who is and who was and who is to come, the Almighty" (Rev 1:8). The truly Christian thing is to live with the certainty that a global communion of love between free persons is an ideal that deserves to be struggled for. The truly Christian thing is to be active and productive at the local level by maintaining a perspective that is global, and to fulfil our own obligations responsibly by orienting ourselves toward the infinite—the God of Love—as the purpose and goal of life.

Instead of an Epilogue

A s the human race pursues its path toward world community, new problems constantly arise and old ones resurface concerning respect for human rights, socioeconomic development, and the peaceful coexistence of different cultures. Several important factors that have emerged within this process are the powerful presence of Islam, the indirect influence of other religions, and the various social realignments that are being created by globalization.

The Orthodox have a duty to take part in the worldwide effort to find appropriate solutions to these problems and—by drawing upon the wealth of their tradition, the living experience and principles of Orthodoxy—to seek solutions that will lead us toward a *koinonia agapes,* a society and communion of love.

1) The Church will continue to preach the mystery of the trinitarian God and divine economy in Christ through the Holy Spirit. It will continue, everywhere and in every epoch, to transform people who are repentant, to lift them up, and to make of them a "new creation." It will continue to be a society of mutual support and a communion of free persons who are loved. It will continue to guide people toward redemption—toward that movement "beyond" that leads to participation in the divine. In other words, it will continue to respond to people's unquenchable longing for *theosis.* All other things—all social and cultural undertakings—result from these and cannot replace or obscure the primarily sacramental and soteriological character of the Orthodox Church.

Down through the centuries, the thing that has made the Church relevant in every era has been and remains its ability to present to the world people who, in their personal lives, experience the mystery of freedom, the mystery of Christ's sacrificing love. Orthodoxy will

continue, in perpetuity, to offer this spiritual rebirth that gives meaning to life, helping people confront dissolution and death with the
inspiration and power of the Resurrection.

2) The intense historical awareness that characterizes the theological thought and ethos of Orthodoxy often gives the mistaken impression that we are an ecclesiastical community concerned only with
the past. Christ, however, is for all ages and all cultures, "the same
yesterday and today and for ever" (Heb 13:8). He transcends time.
As a result, his Church, which is his "mystical body," does not belong
exclusively to any historical period, nor can it be identified with the
character or the context of a single epoch. The Orthodox Church
must remain open to humanity's constant quest, in space and time.
It must also keep its gaze firmly fixed on the one "who is and who
was and who is to come, the Almighty" (Rev 1:8), achieving this
through the inspiration of the Holy Spirit, who turns *time too* into
something new.

When I think about Orthodoxy in the centuries to come, I envision it as being open to development and to the new conditions that
are being created by science, art, and technology. I envision the
Orthodox as being ready to understand and use the new forms of
communication that will take shape. Orthodoxy is not located on the
fringe of history but at the center of social developments and in the
vanguard of progress. At the same time, we have an obligation to
point out the dangers that exist from humanity's excessive interfer-
ence in nature and to struggle in word and deed—as stressed in the
Message of the Primates of the Orthodox Churches on January 6,
2000—to ensure "the freedom and uniqueness of the human person
and the integrity of God's creation."

3) For various historical reasons, Orthodoxy has been associated
with particular national and ethnic groups. We must not forget, however, that God, as St Paul stressed in his speech at Athens, "made
from one [blood] every nation of men . . . that they should seek God"
(Acts 17:26-27). No nation has his exclusive love. Identifying the
nation with the Church does damage to the "One, Holy, Catholic,

and Apostolic Church." It ignores fundamental elements of the Christian creed. The fact that Orthodoxy has been accepted by and incorporated into the life of one or several nations in no way justifies the belief that it is their exclusive property. Respect for and preservation of our identity is natural and necessary, but if we limit Christ to an ethnic or national perspective we can indirectly end up denying him.

Closer cooperation between all the autocephalous Orthodox Churches is essential: they must provide each other with mutual support, but they must also cultivate Orthodoxy's global consciousness. When we are united with Christ in his Church we transcend our personal "I" and our national "we," so that we can join with all human beings and all peoples and nations in understanding and love. Our steadfast vision is a worldwide *koinonia* of love.

Moreover, we must remain open and constructive regarding dialogue with people who have other religious convictions or philosophical positions, "speaking the truth in love" (Eph 4:15). The Orthodox ethos compels us to respect, with complete sincerity, the individuality and freedom of others, regardless of what they believe or even whether they believe. Fanaticism, xenophobia, and the transformation of ecclesiastic belief into some ideological construction are all out of keeping with the free spirit of Orthodoxy. What is needed is sober understanding, a calm and critical approach, consistency, and cooperation with all human beings of good will, so that peace and brotherhood will prevail among all the peoples of the world.

4) In the centuries to come, we Orthodox must actively participate in world events, inspired in our lives and our actions by the comprehensiveness of our Church's "catholicity" and by the global responsibility that this comprehensiveness implies. The entire Church, "the mystical body of Christ," is called upon to offer the full gospel of love throughout the ages with sincere respect for the individuality of every people and culture, with respect for the freedom and dignity of every human person, and with unhypocritical love for the complete human being and for everything that expresses human life.

These issues are discussed in greater depth in other essays, which will be republished in future volumes.

In conclusion, the heart of the Church's message is something that concerns every human being and has global significance. If Orthodoxy is to be equal to its great mission in world events, it must maintain its sacramental, soteriological character intact, it must be open to humanity's constant quest, and it must conscientiously live its awareness of the Resurrection and live up to its global responsibility.

⌐ • ¬

Index